# The Global Conspiracy to Turn Me Homeless

Christos Margelis

# Dedication

I dedicate this book to my beloved mother, Eugenia Margelis, who once told me that she had saved me from being wrongfully imprisoned by the corrupt Montreal police in 2010, when they tried to accuse me of murder as retaliation for my attempt to sue them.

This book is also dedicated to all those who truly believe in freedom and democracy. A case like mine should never happen again. If stories like this remain untold and the perpetrators of such conspiracies are not held accountable, they will continue to harm more and more people.

From the bottom of my heart, I thank you for reading my book.

# Acknowledgment

I would like to sincerely thank former President of Iran, Mahmoud Ahmadinejad, for his stance in 2010. At that time, when the Government of Canada requested that he not grant me asylum, he firmly stood his ground. His response gave me hope that, had I gone to Iran, I could have found refuge and escaped the consequences of being made homeless by corrupt Western governments.

I am also profoundly grateful to Eminent Book Publishers for their professionalism and the tremendous support they provided in publishing my book. My thanks extend as well to all the readers who support me by engaging with my work and recognizing the realities of the governments that rule us and the so-called police who claim to protect us.

# Contents

# Introduction

The person writing this book is me, Christos Margelis. It's a real story that has happened to me and is still happening. It's a police case in Montreal, Canada, where governments from Montreal, Canada, Iceland, Greece, and the United States, along with other Western governments, are involved in this conspiracy.

A case like mine has not happened again, where the police, after wrongdoings they put my life in danger from some drug traffickers. When I went to sue them, they did not let me by blocking the lawyers, telling them not to file a lawsuit. As I tried to sue them, they are now trying to turn me into a homeless person, together with the secret services. The police were involved with a drug trafficking organization, and because I went to sue them, they also tried to kill me and put me in jail for murder, something I had no idea about. With this book, I want the public to be aware of my case and understand what's happening with the police and governments, as well as what they have been doing.

They also gave notice to the Greek authorities, the government, when I went on 25th April 2010 to live. They were applying psychological warfare like they were doing in Canada. They blocked me from the job market so that I don't have any income to turn me into a homeless person of course nowhere near of hiring a lawyer they didn't let me it ended up that my mother came and picked me up from Greece and brought me to Canada the threats and death threats in Greece and Canada that I was receiving from the police (their agents secret services and the police sometimes themselves) were countless. The story I'm writing follows in detail an incredible case that will leave everyone with a big question mark about whether democracy in the West exists or not. Obviously NOT. In Canada, the police and the government are drug traffickers themselves; they work very secretly with the drug traffickers. It's a case that started with the Montreal police. It ended being an international conspiracy where the Canadian government was talking to the following country that I was going to live not to let me work and turn me into a homeless person and of course not let me hire a lawyer all over the world it happened with Greece where they tried to turn me into a homeless person the Greek government put their secret services talking to everybody not to let me get a job.

It was a matter of time before I become a homeless person they also gave notice to the government of the united states in case I try to get asylum there where I tried to get in contact with an immigration lawyer the government under Barack Obama would not let me hire a lawyer like they did in Canada and Greece and after block me from the job market to turn me into a homeless person! The volcanic eruption in Iceland on the 15th April 2010 was planned. It was done on purpose in conspiracy with the government of Canada and the government of Iceland in order that I wouldn't make it to Greece, hire a lawyer there, and refer to the International Criminal Court. On 30th January 2025, I filed my lawsuit against the Montreal police in April 2023. However, the police accused me of filing an abusive case, and the corrupt police and Montreal court subsequently dismissed it. The evidence I have is screaming.

Of course, I knew somewhere they were going to get rid of me, but I couldn't indicate when. Well, now I found out!! Could you believe this? Well, this is what's happening! Read my case and your jaw will drop!

PART 1 OF BOOK (beginning of my case Montreal / 2008-2009)

PART 2 OF BOOK (destruction of my business in Montreal / 2009-2010)

PART 3 OF BOOK (the planned volcano eruption in Iceland 2010)

PART 4 OF BOOK (in Greece, summer 2010, from 26 April 2010 to 14 July 2010)

PART 5 OF BOOK (back to Montreal from Greece after 14th July / 2010-2011)

PART 6 OF BOOK (into the psychiatric clinic 2011-2015)

PART 7 OF BOOK (interference with my credit cards by police, major psychological warfare 2015-2019)

PART 8 OF BOOK (more psychological warfare from the secret services, odious offences, malicious tactics, oppressive acts, still

# Chapter 1

# The Beginning of the Case, Montreal, Canada (2008-2009)

The 26 January 2008 Saturday noon around 1:00 pm and while I was going home in Montreal on Stuart Street about 100m south of Jean Talon I parked my car on the right side of the street I got out of my vehicle start walking a police car following me stops me and the officer asks me if the vehicle is mine I told her, yes it's my car they both get out of there police vehicle and tell me the immigration is looking for me and that I'm under arrest. One other person was carefully watching the scene from the sidewalk (an undercover police officer).

I told Officer Melissa Girard that immigration is trying to find me by the time I become a Canadian citizen. Both officers came close to me, said to me in loud voices that I'm under arrest, to put my hands on the police car, and started searching me all over. Two people would witness the arrest: Mr. Christos and Mrs. Alexandra, both customers of Café Cosmos on Jean Talon Corner. On my arrest, Mrs. Aleksandra was horrified, like I was, and she was holding her head (calling names of historic people from the past, asking for their help)!

I was in shock. They put the handcuffs on my hands and took me towards the police vehicle. The one police officer left the keys to my car in my trunk. I told her to take the keys twice, and then she went to the car and took them. We get in the police car, and the one police officer tells me in a deafening, rude way, "What lawyer do you want? Do you have your own lawyer, or do you want legal aid?"

I would look at her in a panic, trying to understand what was happening. One thing that was for sure was that they had arrested the wrong person. I thought that they thought I was someone else. After thinking more in my panic (first, I told them I had lost my wallet, but it was in Greece), I remembered. However, about 2 years ago, I lost my passport, which came to mind. I told them to hold on a second. Two years ago, I lost my passport, so I visited the passport office in Côte Vertu and obtained a new one. They hesitated for a few seconds. After start asking me again what is my status what lawyer do I want I remembered that the place that I had lost my passport (almost sure) was a car mechanics repair shop and auto parts place at 6484 Boulevard St Laurent Corner, Beaubien and told her that whoever has found it has used it and that I'm not the person you are looking for.

The person who knows about those people (the ones who could have found it and used it) is George Papaspirou, the store's owner. When we reach the police station on Parc Avenue at 7035 near Jean Talon, I get out and go to the station. There was one police officer at the entry. They told me to go to the room on the left, which appeared to have computers and desks. Most probably, they would interview suspects in there. They tell me to sit down on a chair in front of a computer, they open it, and ask me if I was Pavel something (last name of the person that had used my lost passport I told them I have nothing to do, no idea what they are talking about. I don't know Pavel whatsoever. The officer starts talking loudly to me again and tells me what my status is; the other officers were looking (wondering). I ask the officer what the other officer means when she tells me, " What's your status Maybe I thought she was asking if I am married. The officer tells me No, it's not that. What was happening was that the drug trafficking organization, where George Papaspirou and Sterei Craciun, as I mention further in this book, had organized this arrest so that the police would deport me to Romania as an illegal immigrant who tried to enter Canada with a forged passport, and Sterei Craciun, who was from Romania, would send his people to kill me there. The police, when my family would start looking for me, would tell them that they would try to find me, and nobody would ever know what really happened to me.

Sterei Craciun and George Papaspirou wanted to kill me because I knew everything about them, and they feared that I would tell the police one day. They wanted me to participate in the criminal organization, but I didn't, because I didn't want to get involved with illegal stuff. Also, they believed that I had done something that led to the arrest of their partner in crime, Emilio. After I installed a remote starter on his vehicle, he was soon caught in the United States for credit card fraud and other illegal activities. They believed that I told the police, which was, of course, false.

Over here, we see the first piece of evidence that perjurious police officers were involved with the drug trafficking organization, of course, collecting commissions from them. They had also told me the name of the person using my identity (Pavel) and that he is from Romania. The only way to know all this was that the police had arrested him and sent him back to Romania. Within three days of losing my passport, I visited the passport agency and reported it as lost.

A second lawyer I consulted in April 2009 informed me that the person using my passport had never entered the country. They deported him as soon as he came to the airport. When they showed me the computer for a second, I noticed that Pavel was a Romanian citizen. I asked them, "You're looking for someone with my name, but you don't have a picture of the person?"

So finally, they showed me the face on another computer. It was a sketch that looked like me. Basically, it was *my* sketch. While I understood that something was going on, I told them, "No, I don't know that person at all."

So, the police started asking me if my car had been stolen. I told them that I don't remember whose name my car is, my mother's or my name. I felt very dizzy at that point because of the unbelievable stress. I had forgotten whose name my car is, because in the past, I had put the car under my mother's name, as I wanted my mother to drive it. I tried to get a new car, but it finally didn't happen after I transferred it back to my name.

The police officer at the station asked me questions to verify my identity and confirm whether I was the original person or the one using the passport. I told him which hospital I was born in, where we used to live when I was a kid, and what medication I'm taking. So, after a while, he told me, "Okay, he found out I wasn't the person they were looking for."

This was a trick, trying to show that it was an identity issue. The truth was, they wanted to send me to Romania! If they wanted to find out my identity, they had other methods; within 2–3 days, they could uncover everything about me through their secret agents. Then why all this façade? I told them that I don't know how they got the passport. I believed that it had fallen out of my pocket while getting in and out of my car.

That morning, I went to the Greek embassy to obtain the necessary paperwork, which required me to have two identities with me. After that, I went to install a remote starter at Ferrari Autoparts, the car mechanics repair shop at 6484 St. Laurent, Montreal. Some people used to go there, including friends and customers of the store, as well as my own customers. I used to see them there quite often. They had doubts about my Canadian citizenship, and that day, I showed them my passport, which they possibly found a way to steal from my jacket.

The officer asked me the name of the person who asked to see the passport. I told him I had made a check out to him a long time ago, and his name was on it, but I didn't know if it was him; maybe it was someone else just using that name. The next day, I gave it to the police officer. It was Sterei Craciun, and I told her that I hadn't gone to that place for about a year. They weren't behaving well, and I didn't feel comfortable in that place. It seemed very suspicious to me, hearing about drugs and illegal things.

I once saw a person named Emilio. He was a drug trafficker, partner with Sterei Craciun (Gigi), and he used to install devices for copying credit cards. He was caught in the States around 2007 by the police for copying credit cards. It was shown on the CNN TV station. I saw him, and I remember one day Sterei Craciun told me to go and install a device at a gas station that copies credit cards, which, of course, I didn't.

When I went home at night, I noticed my passport was not there. I thought maybe it fell off my jacket when I hung it or when I got out of my car. After one or two days, I went and asked if they had seen my passport. George told me he hadn't found anything. On the third day, I visited the passport office, where I reported losing my passport and applied for a replacement.

A police officer told me, "You see, you didn't go to the police to declare it lost!"

I told her I didn't know that I had to inform the police about that; I thought I had to notify the passport office. The other officer said to me that I had not lost my passport at all; someone had stolen it, and they wanted to harm me, also because the person who was using it looked very much like me. I got furious because I figured out it was a conspiracy against me, so I told them, yeah, it's a bunch of drug traffickers and credit card copiers. Of course, when someone steals passports to bring people into the country illegally, they are also likely involved in other illegal activities. Even I knew that!

I knew they wanted to harm me, but I never imagined it would go that far. I told the officers that I'm self-employed, working under my mother's company, and I install alarm starters for cars. I work with car mechanics in repair shops. I worked for Ferrari Autoparts, located at 6484 St. Laurent, Montreal, from the beginning of 2003, performing both road and electrical work, as well as serving as a car electrician. Those people used to be very friendly and kind, but I knew they didn't have good feelings about me, possibly because I didn't follow them.

At one point, the officer (Melissa Girard) asked me twice if I was going to faint. I told her no. So, the police finally let me go. Nobody apologized, not even a 'sorry,' nothing. They took me to the same place where they arrested me and let me go. When I went home and looked in the mirror, my face was red like a tomato! The officer had also asked me to sue Pavel, the person who had used my passport. I told her no, of course, I don't think it's a good idea to sue drug traffickers!

Late May and for June 2008, I would realize people were behaving and acting suspiciously; the people that used to hang out at Ferrari Autoparts as customers and friends of the place (Sterei Craciun, known as Gigi, that was a person involved in illegal activities, George Papaspirou's friend, and also George Papaspirou, which finally proved out on the 8th July 2008 that he was involved in illicit activities also), too.

Whenever I visited Café Cosmos, located at 880 Jean Talon West, at the corner of Wiseman, Gigi, the boss and operator of the criminal organization, George's partner, would occasionally show up and notice me. He would tell me which night I would go out and which place I would be hanging out. This happened three times. I noticed they were after me. He made it clear that something was going on. About three days before, on May 20, 2008, George Papaspirou came to see me at Café Cosmos in a somewhat hurried manner and suspiciously said, "How are you?" and shook my hand. His hand was shaking a lot. He seemed mad, looked at me briefly, and then left.

Later in mid-June 2008, I noticed one person (maybe a couple of times). He would show up at Café Cosmos just at the time that I was usually there. At the beginning, he would show up and stay outside. A few days later, around the 24th of June 2008, he came inside while I was there. The whole Café Cosmos just froze; they were looking at each other. When he came inside and sat down in the chair next to me, I had just gone to the washroom before he arrived. This allowed me to see where he was going to sit and watch him. And I was not wrong. He sat just beside the chair that I was sitting in, to drink the same type of coffee I was drinking.

Everybody was looking just as if they were frozen (looking with a question mark). The person working that morning, Costas Kouremenos, saw the incident very clearly. I understood what's happening. That person was there to murder me, most probably with a knife. At first, I sat down on another chair a bit further from him, and after leaving my coffee, I left the place in less than 5 minutes.

The police, who were monitoring my emails, noticed that I was searching for a car rental in Greece, as I was about to travel there with a one-way ticket, since I wasn't sure when I would return. So, the police gave notice to George Papaspirou to send someone to kill me before I leave, fearing I may not come back from Greece. So, he stayed there about 20 minutes more, but had changed seats. I didn't know what to do. I went after to see if he was still there.

I looked from the door and left. Right after that, he went outside and stayed for no more than 10 minutes. I saw him from my house, which was a couple of buildings from the café. He was very nervous and then disappeared. I wanted to call the police, but I didn't have a good reason to do so, something to accuse him of, unless he would do something, which would have been too late then.

My first thought was that after my false arrest on 26th January 2008, the police went and busted Ferrari Autoparts in a careless way that implicated me, triggering the drug traffickers to come after me. But that was not the case at all. The police had given notice to Sterei Craciun, known as Gigi, the person running the criminal organization (I have already mentioned him a few times, so far), about the police after I had informed him about them when I gave him the cheque about 2 years ago. This was not voluntary, but happened upon my false arrest on 26th January 2008, and after interrogation by the police.

About two weeks later, on July 2, 2008, I was about to leave for Greece for a while. About 5 days before I left, I visited the police station at 7035 Parc Avenue, Montreal, to report the incident involving that person, which seemed related to my arrest. At that time, I was not aware of what was happening. It never went through my mind that the police were cooperating with the drug traffickers. Later on, I put the puzzle all together. Also, undercover agents showed me what was happening. This occurred around July 2, 2008, at approximately 1:00 p.m.

I went into the police station on 7035 Parc Avenue, close to Jean Talon, and two officers were in at the time. I informed the officer of my name and the details of the police event (my arrest on January 26, 2008), stating that I would be traveling to Greece the following Tuesday, July 8, 2008, should any issues arise. I also asked questions about my case. They checked their computer and assured me it's okay, just take a lot of documents with your identity. I also asked if they had finally arrested Pavel, the person they were looking for. They told me no, that he is still walking around, and if I want to file a lawsuit against him. She also had a paper ready. I told her no; I don't want anything to do with these people.

*(If I were able to sue Pavel for the theft and use of my passport, then why didn't the police arrest him and put him in jail for this act? It was obvious that the police were kidding me. Pavel from Romania never entered the country!)*

Then I told the officer that I had seen someone with characteristics similar to mine, and that he was after me. I saw him the last time at Café Cosmos, 880 Jean Talon West, Montreal. I asked if they could help me, and if I saw him again, I wanted to tell the police so they could come and arrest him and find out who he is and why he is after me. I knew the drug traffickers sent him, but I wanted the police to interview him and put him on a watch list. The police replied that they couldn't take action and couldn't check on someone without a valid reason. This was the second piece of evidence that the police had ties with the drug trafficking organization. In common words, they were harboring them. Afterward, they advised me to contact Mrs. Lambardi, a police officer, if anything were to happen, at phone number 514-280-0133.

I was very sad, still trying to understand what was happening. Of course, I noticed that after my false arrest on 26th January 2008, the police had done something that triggered the drug traffickers after me, but at that time, I wouldn't even have imagined that they were in conspiracy, both of them.

*The police were getting commissions from George Papaspirou and the criminal organization, and they would harbor them, letting them sell drugs mostly to the United States. That's why they told Sterei Craciun and George Papaspirou what I mentioned to them when they arrested me on January 26, 2008. Together, the police and the criminal organization were trying to kill me!*

After George Papaspirou came once to see me at Café Cosmos, and especially after Gigi came three times to see me there, it became clear that something was wrong. I understood that he wanted to do something to me, they tried to kill me. I couldn't believe it. Why was *I* in this situation?

I left the police station, and about 15 minutes later, a police officer called me from a private number on my cell phone. He told me that Mrs. Lambardi would be on vacation for July, returning in August, and then he wished me good luck. Here we clearly see, for the third time, another piece of evidence that the police would not help me against the drug traffickers. They were letting them come after me to kill me, while I had no way to defend myself. I didn't know where to turn for help if the traffickers came to kill me. I was in a panic, still trying to understand what was happening.

During the last five days before I left, I was cautious in my movements. I only went out during the day, and always with someone else. I never went far, always watching where I was going.

On Tuesday morning, July 8, 2008, I went to see a lawyer. She told me that the police were going to arrest those people, that they would be questioned and examined, and that if they were involved in drug trafficking and illegal activities, they would be put in jail. Still, I was terrified.

Later, I went to Ferrari Auto Parts. John Koumparakos drove

me there to see George Papaspirou, who later proved to be a member of the criminal organization. I told George what was happening that I was seeing different people after me, that I had been arrested because someone had used my passport, and that I might have lost it at his store. I advised him that if the police questioned him, he should simply state that he knew nothing.

He then asked me where I worked and where I lived. I only told him "On Wiseman," without giving any more details. He asked me how the stock market was going. I told him it wasn't good at the moment, and he told me to stop playing. Then he left.

I went home with my car around 12:00 p.m. At about 12:30, I left my home to park my car. As I stepped out, I saw a man with a pen and paper in his hand. At first, I thought he didn't know I lived there, but he clearly did. When I drove off and stopped at the traffic light on Wiseman and Jean Talon, I saw him turn around and write down my license plate number.

At that moment, I clearly understood that George Papaspirou was part of the criminal organization. Everything made sense, George wasn't just friends with Gigi (Sterei Craciun), as he pretended; he was a member of the organization!

I parked my car, and a friend took me home, it must have been around 1:00 p.m. By 3:30 p.m., I had to leave for the airport. My friend John Koumparakos drove me there. At the Olympic

Airways checkpoint, a couple approached me and asked if I could take a cage with a bird inside to Greece. I looked at the man, then at the checkpoint agent, then back at him, and said no. He seemed upset and walked away.

George Papaspirou knew I was going to Greece. I had told him I would leave the next day. Most likely, the Montreal police (SPVM) told him the exact time of my departure, because otherwise there was no way he could have known when I was actually leaving.

A week later, while in Greece, I called my brother back home and told him what was happening. I asked him to go to Ferrari Auto Parts at 6484 St-Laurent (corner Beaubien) and tell George Papaspirou to call me on my cell phone. I wanted to confront him, to ask why he was sending people after me, and then tell Gigi to call me as well.

Two days later, George called me from his store. I told him what was happening, but he avoided the subject and started talking about work, remote starters, and other things. I told him that I hoped everything was all right and that I expected his partner, Gigi, to call me too. He agreed. Then I said to him that when I returned to Montreal, I would see him about everything they had been doing. At that point, he realized others (my brother, my mother) knew about the case, and he changed his tune. He insisted that now they were "lawful people" and had no involvement with illegal activities.

I told him, fine, when I came back to Montreal, I would see him. And when I returned in early September (the 5th or 6th, 2008), I did go to see him. I warned him that if I saw any suspicious moves or anything strange, they would all end up in jail.

For a while, things seemed normal. I believed this was the best way to handle the situation without letting it escalate into a major problem.

On the 5th of September 2008, I arrived from Greece. It was around 2:30 p.m. when the plane landed, and we began disembarking. As we entered the airport, all passengers were walking, and two police officers were waiting for me on the right side. They stopped me. They asked, "Christos Margelis?"

I said yes.

The officer said, "You were in Greece, eh?"—implying, "2 months in Greece, eh," with surprise, suggesting that the money must have come from some illegal activities.

I turned around, and she had just insulted me in public. I told her, "Yes, why not? My father's house is there, and I don't pay anything."

She stopped talking and told me to follow them. The whole airport was looking at us.

They told me to go to the immigration area waiting room. I

saw one person there. She took my passport to see it and kept it. She told me to go to the waiting room and stay there. I went, all scared, and waited about 20 minutes. Then someone at the desk told me, "Okay, take your passport, and you can go."

I took my passport and left. When I took my valise and went out, they told me to go through the check area to check the valise. They opened it and put a machine in to look for drugs, as I understood. Of course, they found nothing and let me go.

On Friday, the 19th of September 2008, around 12:00 a.m. at a McDonald's store in Laval on Cure Label corner Notre Dame, a police car, after checking my license plate, and as I was about to get on Notre Dame to go towards the highway going home, put their duty lights on and ordered me to stop. I turned right on Cure Label and stopped there.

In the car with me were two friends of mine, George and Theo Tsoukalas. Both my friends asked me, scared, what was happening and why they stopped us. I told them there was a small case; they were trying to find someone who'd been using my passport since I lost it 2 to 3 years ago.

A police officer approached my car and asked me to hand over my papers. I gave her my papers. They returned to their vehicle.

After 5 minutes, they came and ordered me to get out of my car and give them my keys. I asked the officer, "What's the problem?"

She responded, "Was the car stolen in 2005?"

I wanted to leave, and I didn't want my friends to think there was something suspicious going on. I told her yes, the car was stolen (I didn't remember the year or details). She went back to the car, gave me my papers and keys, and then let me go.

In November 2008, I went to see a lawyer, Anna Colarusso (1 De Castelnau Est Suite 201, Montreal, Quebec H2R 1P1, Canada), and told her about my case. She sent a letter to the police on February 18, 2009, asking for the police report of the arrest on January 26, 2008. On February 24, 2009, we were informed that a police investigation was still ongoing.

The investigation they were talking about basically was that they were trying to find a way to kill me so that the drug traffickers would be happy because I had mentioned them at my false arrest on January 26, 2008, to the police. The police would be pleased too, because then I wouldn't be able to sue them. But they both failed.

Also, a few days earlier, on February 21 at approximately 12:15 a.m., I was heading towards Highway 15 in the Mirabel area, specifically towards exit 31. As I parked my car at a McDonald's, my friend George Tsoukalas and I were on our way to grab a drink when a police car pulled up and asked if the vehicle belonged to me. I answered yes, it's my car.

He started looking at his computer, and by the time another police vehicle arrived, I was standing in front of two police vehicles with their duty lights on. One police vehicle left, and the officer asked me to get in the police car. I went inside, and he was talking on the cell phone for about 10 minutes. After that, he told me, "Okay, we are looking for someone else about one foot taller than you, which isn't you, and you can go now."

I looked at him, one foot taller, maybe a basketball player, it seemed too much. I didn't say anything. I went to McDonald's to eat with my friend.

On Friday, March 20, 2009, at noon, I was with a friend and neighbour, Celestino, when a police car, which had been following us for about 5 minutes, ordered me to stop just 5 minutes before we reached the ski center. I pulled over immediately. The officer came to me, while the other approached the passenger side and asked for my papers. He asked, "Hi, can I have your papers?"

I gave him my papers. The other officer asked for my friend Celestino's identity, so I suggested, "Why not give the police an identity?"

He provided his car license and insurance. They approached the police car and took a look. After 5 minutes, they returned, gave back the papers, and the officer stated that the vehicle had been stolen a long time ago, noting that one digit on the serial number was a mistake. He checked the serial number and said it was okay, then told me I could go.

I told the officer that I know why they would stop me all the time and that they are looking for the wrong person at the wrong place. I thought that they were looking for Pavel, the person who had my stolen passport. He turned around and just left. Ever since, whenever the police saw me on the road and took down my license plate, they would turn on their duty lights and speed off in a panic.

On 8 May 2009 at 12:00 p.m., I observed a person, approximately 20–24 years old, driving a black 1992–94 Honda Accord vehicle, which had been following me. I was parked on Stuard, just south of Jean Talon, on the east side of Stuard, on the south side of the back lane. On the north side of the lane, there was a person around 20 to 24 years old.

As I went to my car, I saw him. He suddenly moved his head up and immediately put his hand on the key to start the car, waiting for me to start first. I started my car, and he began his, keeping his eyes on me carefully so he wouldn't lose me. I saw him in my left mirror. He then put his visor down so I couldn't see his face. I turned and pretended I was going. He then put the visor all up again. Then I pretended I was not going and looked at him again in my mirror.

He then put the visor down again so I couldn't see his face. It was crystal clear what was going on. He was after me to get me trapped somewhere on the road and then come close and shoot me. I knew what he was up to, what he wanted to do. He also knew that I knew. He started to panic. I drove my car back and forth 2 to 3 times, but it wasn't going. He then couldn't stay any longer and went first. I had him now in front of me.

I followed him towards Beaumont. He panicked, didn't know where he should go, and tried to stop at a parking spot on the left side of Stuard just at the corner with Beaumont. I stopped and waited for him. He lowered down to his seat and started going, looking guilty. I wanted to call the police, but the last time I was at the station, they had told me that there wasn't a lot they could do, and, calling me back from a private phone, telling me, "Good luck," we just lost a second obvious killer.

In April 2009, I went to see a lawyer named Sally Butler Grand. I told her my case. She was ready to proceed with my case. I told her I would be in Greece for a while, and after we proceed, we will sue the police. The police, to avoid the lawsuit and the drug traffickers killing me before I leave, both sent the person in a Honda Accord to kill me. Both wanted to kill me. They knew that I would be going to Greece for a while because they were recording all my conversations, even when I was talking with the lawyer. This was the investigation that the police were doing with the answer they gave to my lawyer at that time, Anna Colarusso, trying to kill me to get rid of me.

So, I turned right on Parc Avenue and went towards downtown to think about what I should do. I decided to get a ticket to go to Greece because these people were after me to kill me. I went and got one for the 18th of May 2009.

Around 1:30 p.m., I went to the police station on 7035 Parc Avenue, Montreal. I showed them a card they had given me on 26 January 2008 when they arrested me and told them the scene. The car was black, and the license plate was 078 YYL. I told the police that he was after me, was sent by George Papaspirou and his drug trafficker friends. The police said to me that they have nothing on record on my police report number (on a card the police gave me instead of a police report) of my arrest on 2008 January 26th.

I told him that I was arrested on 26 January 2008 for identity issues. They found out I was not Pavel, the person they were looking for the person who had used my stolen passport, after I had told them they were a bunch of drug traffickers there at Ferrari Autoparts, and that the police had triggered the drug traffickers to come after me to kill me. I informed them about the incident involving my case against George Papaspirou, specifically that he had sent someone on July 8, 2008, to record my license plate number, and I provided an update on the events that had unfolded since then.

The police officer advised me to call him at a private cell phone number and share the information secretly, or to fax it. I also told him that Gigi is the leading drug trafficker, the big guy, the person that operates the drug trafficking organization, and that I saw him coincidentally at the Hudson Bay Apparel Store at the Rockland Shopping Center, Montreal, the first days of April 2009, and that he was caught on the cameras.

All the information was given to him in the police station; there were other people in there, but I was just boiling, I was very mad. I couldn't wait. Those people were undercover agents. They did not want me to tell everything I knew because the police were also involved with the members of the drug trafficking organization.

The officer's name was Guillaume. He also stated that if an answering machine answers, then he stops. I looked at him and left in a panic. I recounted the entire incident to him from the beginning and explained that upon returning from Greece on September 5, 2008, I informed George Papaspirou, the owner of Ferrari Autoparts, that if he were to act suspiciously against me again, I would report it to the police. All he told me was, "Now I'm finished!" (He is finished, George.) Gigi used to be friends with George Papaspirou, and as I found out later, they were partners in crime. I used to see him there at Ferrari Autoparts, George's store.

I finished telling them what was going on around 3:00 p.m. I also told them that some people had called my cell phone and said, "Christos?"

After, they would tell me, "Oh, wrong number."

I gave them the phone numbers. The police officer, Guillaume, gave me a phone number to call him if I need something or if someone is after me, and a fax. I left the police station. They had also asked me if I wanted police protection. I told them that, given these circumstances, I naturally require police protection. I couldn't, though, have a police officer following me everywhere. I just left the station and forgot my license there with some other papers. They called me back to tell me I should go and get them. I went within 15 minutes.

On Sunday, 10 May 2009, around 3:00 p.m., a person called me on my cell phone and said, "Gigi? Oh, wrong number."

I told him, "You are trying to find Gigi on my phone number?"

He hung up. I called him back and told him, "Whom are you telling these stories to?"

He then spoke, "Gigi, Gigi," and hung up again. It was clear they were after me.

I figured out Monday morning that I would call my travel agent and get an earlier ticket for Greece. Things seemed dangerous. I called around 9:10 a.m. and asked if they could get me a ticket for May 14, 2009, if possible. They told me to go there at 10:15 a.m. I prepared and went there. On my way, I saw that the building on Parc Avenue, where we used to live, had caught on fire!

There was a significant conflict between the court and the owner when we lived there. He would often put some people outside, and they would scream and make noise after 11:00 p.m. I would call the police every so often. I had told all this to George Papaspirou. These were the same people who had set the place on fire to blame it on me. It was convenient for them. The police, though, knew everything now.

I went and got a flight for the same day. I prepared my stuff and left. I cancelled my ticket for the 18th May 2009 and got one for the same day, 11th May 2009. When I handed my valise over at the checkpoint to pass through, I noticed someone pulled it aside.

On 18th May 2009, I called my mother from Greece. I instructed her to forward the information I had compiled over the past five months regarding George Papaspirou and Gigi (Steri Craciun) to the police. Around 25 May 2009, she told me, "Okay, I have given in the papers. Would say everything that I knew about George and Gigi in detail, with two pictures of the car that the person who came after me on the 8th May 2009, and one image of Zoi's vehicle, the Dodge Ram truck at the mechanic's repair shop at Ferrari Autoparts, the person who was a member of the criminal organization."

The police disappeared the two pictures of the Honda Accord, the person who came after me on the 8th May 2009, because he was a member of their criminal organization, and most probably he was sent by the police themselves. It's missing from my pictures, and the negatives I had are also gone from my house!

The information I gave the police I gave at no choice once I figured out that the safest thing for me would have been to tell the police everything I knew about these people and as much information as possible, so then the police could catch them and arrest them all together, and that's how I would be safe. I believed that the police, without the information, may not be able to arrest these people, and then I wouldn't have been safe at all. While the police had targeted these people after me, I had no choice but to do this. The reality was that they were partners in crime, and the police didn't arrest anybody, but they are still out selling drugs, not one of them in jail!!

The police in Montreal, Canada, were aware that I was returning to Montreal, and I intended to sue them. They overheard me saying that to my mother on the phone while we were talking. On September 16, 2009, upon returning from Greece at 3:15 p.m. at the airport in Montreal, two security officers instructed me to accompany them as I exited the airplane. They took me to the immigration office, where they took my passport and told me to wait. After half an hour, one officer instructed me to take my passport and then escorted me to the checkpoint, bypassing others in line.

When talking with her, she pretended she knew nothing about the case and that I had to tell her again what it looked like. I spoke a lot about the situation, and she kept asking more questions. At one point, she asked, "Why did you come back?"

I told her, "Mostly to sue the police!"

The other officers there seemed to go cold. They certainly didn't like that. I told her that things are all messed up: one police officer says this, the other one says that, one lawyer says this, the other one says that, it's too much of a mess.

She did not tell me the reason why they sent me to the immigration office, but she told me that the person who used my passport they are still being looked for, and that this will happen every time I come to Canada. When I told her it made no sense because my lawyer said to me that the person coming in with a stolen passport was deported immediately, she told me, "Yes, it could be so."

I responded, "Why are you saying he is on the loose?"

"That is not official what I'm telling you, but something that could be happening, not that it is happening," she said.

When I asked her how we could find out, she told me it's

tough to do so, and even if your lawyer inquires, the airport would not tell her.

When I was leaving, she noticed that my eyes didn't look blue in my passport picture. I looked carefully and told her that it had to do with the way the light was at the point of taking the photo. I really didn't know what to say to her. Maybe if I were a photographer, I would know. After checking my valise carefully, they let me go.

On the 17th of September 2009, at 9:45 a.m., I went directly to the police station at 7035 Parc Avenue near Jean Talon. I talked with police officer Mrs. Lambardi. It looked like they were waiting for me and lots of other officers, too. I got inside and told her hi, if she knows me, and that yesterday, when I came from the airport, the officer there had called the police station to tell them that I was at the airport and that I would be going there the next morning.

I noticed Officer Mrs. Lambardi had changed the name on the tag, and it now said Lampert. I told her that I'm back from Greece and that I'm afraid these people will be looking for me, and I want police protection. She got mad, and in a way told me that the police cannot protect me just because I think someone is after me.

I mentioned that I have visited here many times; she's familiar with the case. I've already shared all the information with Officer Guillaume, and I told her not to make those claims. She asked me who Guillaume was. I informed the police officer that I had reported the incident 3 days before I departed for Greece on 8th May 2009. She told me, "Oh, I remember. Now she says his name is Dion Desser, not Guillaume, like he had told me. He is not there, and he will be there around 3:30 p.m."

She continued, "Tell me the case from the beginning."

I started telling her what the case looks like and that George Papaspirou and Gigi, his partner, are after me. She told me, "How do you know they are after you? Did they tell you they are gonna kill you?"

Meanwhile, the officer was filling out an incident report and asked in an ominous tone if she should continue writing it, which made me fear for my safety. And if I were to write something they didn't like, she threatened to get me kicked out of the police station. It almost felt as if my life was in danger.

I kept telling her they never said it directly, and that when someone you know is a drug trafficker says, "If you talk, you know what's gonna happen," what more do you want from that? The officer still insisted, "But did they tell you that they are gonna kill you?"

I told her again that they didn't tell me directly. She said, "Oh, we are writing all this, you can't tell me if they're threatening you."

I filled out the police report based on the pressure the police officer applied to me, writing it in a way she preferred. When I went to start from the beginning of my arrest, she would change the conversation and go back to the fact that these people threatened me directly and that they told me they were going to kill me if I talked. I told her again and again, "No, they didn't say it directly."

She kept on telling me until I would write a softer report that would not show the police directly as the ones that have put me in this situation.

Every time I told her that since my arrest, George Papaspirou and Gigi had visited me at Café Cosmos, and then they started targeting me, the officer would always claim that wasn't the case! We were talking for about 2 hours. At 11:30 a.m., she finally made the police report and told me that if I want police protection, I have to declare that George Papaspirou is the one who has threatened to kill me and that they will go to arrest him, take him to court, and stuff. I told her, if you go and arrest George just like that, within 20 minutes, they will send someone to my door, pointing guns at me.

If they want to arrest them, they will have to arrest both Gigi, who is the drug trafficker, and George, his partner. I described to her Gigi (Steri Craciun) and told her again that I saw him at the Hudson Bay apparel store at the Rockland Shopping Center on the 3rd of April 2009. It was a Friday afternoon around 6 p.m. She told me that if there is something suspicious, I should call 911.

About the fact that on the 8th May 2009, when I went and talked to the police officer about everything, and that the drug traffickers came after me to kill me, she told me she has no information about that, no police report. I was surprised to hear that! They were trying to hide everything!

When I left the police station, although the police refused to give me police protection officially, they did so unofficially. The police had started on Wiseman (I still lived there, hadn't moved yet) from the 17th to the 30th of September 2009, putting all kinds of people with suspicious looks, horrifying and terrorizing me!

Two days later, on September 18, 2009, I went to see my lawyer, Sally Buttler, and told her that I wanted to sue the police. She told me that I can't do so and that I should just live like nothing is happening, and that I can't sue the police.

When I told her what to do, she said there wasn't much to it; just forget it and continue your life. This was so absurd; it made no sense to me. She also told me I can't sue the police; it's like a big shark eating a small one; they have more money than you do. I told her I would go and see another lawyer. She had a phone number handy to recommend someone else. It was crystal clear that the police had instructed my lawyers not to discuss or handle my case.

I told her I would go to see Mrs. Anna Colarusso, my

previous lawyer. Anna told me the last time I saw her to proceed with a lawsuit. When I went there, the police had already talked to her. She had the lights in her office closed, and the receptionist said she is not there, but I can see lawyer Nicholas De Tomaso. He was trying to say something, but I couldn't really understand what he was saying. He also said, "You can't do anything."

In mid-November 2009, I contacted lawyer George Peizler, who was recommended by Michael Stober, a lawyer I found in Old Montreal, and explained the case to him. He suggested Mr. George Peizler. I went to see him. I had made an appointment before, and he told me he takes these cases. The police, of course, had talked to him, and when I went there, I saw Mr. George Peizler. We sat down in the conference room, where a long table was situated, and to the right, he had some books.

He asked me what was happening. I started explaining the case to him. At first, he seemed friendly and made an effort to put me at ease, mentioning that I now live in Côte-des-Neiges, a place he had lived in for a long time. When I told him that I'm in big trouble now in the situation the police have put me in, and that I want to sue them to get some money to get out of this situation and my misery, his attitude changed.

He looked at me hostile and told me at the end that he doesn't take these cases, he only does business cases, which is false, a lie.

He told me, "Look at those books on my desk; they are all from businesses, and that's all I do!" He also told me that when he used to live in Côte-des-Neiges in the ancient years, where the plaza is now, there used to be a farm, and that there used to be dead bodies there, suggesting I have a connection to killing or something similar.

He finally told me he couldn't do anything and didn't charge me anything, just like Sally Buttler did.

After all this conspiracy with the lawyers, the police were now trying to put murder on me to put me in jail so I wouldn't sue them, and it wouldn't seem that they made a tragic mistake to go and trigger drug traffickers after me. In October 2009, during a conversation with my friend Sotiris from Greece, I didn't say good things about the police. Ever since, I noticed that the police would be after me, would apply psychological warfare with people working for them undercover, and I was wondering if that is ever possible. Not only was it possible, but that's what was happening. The police continued doing the same, terrorizing me. They were putting their undercover agents, applying psychological warfare, making it seem they would attack me or kill me, and others threatening that they would accuse me of murder.

Since mid-2009, THE GOVERNMENT OF Canada has been placed in THE CONSPIRACY BY USING its secret SERVICES. On 27 September 2009, I went to the police station on

7035 Parc Avenue near Jean-Talon to report that one mechanic, Dusep, from Garage Fujiaty on 255 Bates Street, had offered me 10,000 euros to sell him a passport. The police had told him to do so to see what I would do! There were two officers at that time, on Saturday morning. One police officer took me to the conversation room and asked me to explain the situation. I started telling him, but halfway through, I realized he was kidding, just like he had done in the airport when I arrived in Montreal. He later told me, if you know anyone involved with drugs in Parc Extension, you can become a teller to the police. You sign a paper, and after that, you become a number; no one knows you. The police wanted to show that the drug traffickers were not after me because the police, after forcing me to talk, went and triggered them after me, but because I was a teller! They wanted to portray me as a teller, someone who provides information to the police, as a pretext for their wrongdoing.

About a week later, I returned to the police station at 7035 Parc Avenue. I spoke with Officer Mrs. Lampert. I told her I'd like to talk with her for a while, if we could sit in the conversation room. I wanted to ask her what's happening and why they're doing all these things to me. I knew it was because I went to sue them, but I still wanted to talk with the police officer. She told me there is no need to speak; I should just go about my life as usual, avoiding the Café Cosmos, 880 Jean-Talon West, and Ferrari Auto Parts, 6484 St-Laurent. I left very disappointed and thoughtful. I couldn't understand how the police could be doing all this.

When I moved to 3435 Barclay, I went to apartment 10, and it was clear that at apartment 11 next door, there was a lady who was an undercover police officer. She started putting the TV at deafening volumes, and my mother called the police to report that these people wouldn't let us sleep because they had the volume too high. The police totally ignored us, and the lady next door continued the same.

When I knocked on her door and told her, "Madam, why do you keep the volume so high?" she would scream at me and was ready to start a fight. I left and went to sleep in another room. She continued doing so every night. I couldn't sleep at night, nor could my brother sleep in the same room. The police, while the secret services were involved, were still putting people who looked suspicious, appearing from the side lanes and from inside the building, terrorizing and horrifying me. This would happen every 2–3 days, and of course, the lawyers aren't talking, not saying what I should do or what the case is.

Although the police caught the drug traffickers red-handed doing illegal acts, after they accused me of it, like the building that I used to live in at Parc Avenue, they set a fire and then blamed me that I did it (11 May 2009). Theo Anastasopoulos was caught red-handed, admitting on the phone on 16 September 2009, a few days after I arrived from Greece, that he had lied by saying I had thrown eggs at his car and lit a cigarette on his front grill.

The police were watching me every step I took at that time. Still, the police didn't like that, but they found all kinds of people that I dealt with, people who would like to harm me because they don't like me, and started using them to find a way to say Christos has committed murder or something illegal.

In late October and the beginning of November 2009, a police investigator, Fred Chrarbonneau, called me at the police station located at 855 Crémazie Est. He instructed me to bring the information I had compiled about the criminal organization Papaspirou was involved in. I brought it with me, and he asked me what had happened. I told him. He told me to sign the information, and I did so. (I DID NOT ASK FOR MONEY AS LAWYER SALLY BUTTLER GRAND TOLD ME NOT TO ASK FOR MONEY!)

I also gave more phone numbers I had found in my phonebook: Emilios' (Gigi's partner) phone number, the person shown at the CNN TV station for credit card copying, Roxana's woman copying credit cards according to what George Papaspirou had told me, and Gigi's (Sterei Craciun), the person who operates the drug trafficking organization. I had kept these phone numbers because I had worked on their vehicles, installing alarm starters. Nobody thanked me. He told me we should contact each other once a week. He gave me a phone number.

Around the end of October 2009, a friend of mine, John Vlahakis, told me he was working for the police and secret services. He was asking me various questions to try to get me to say something, making it seem like I had committed a crime. He stated to me that Parasiris, one person, had shot the police when they invaded his home one morning, and at court, he was found not guilty. After that, while changing the conversation, he told me he had hunting guns at his home and that I should purchase one too.

One afternoon around 4:00 p.m., we were at the Eaton Center (downtown Montreal) drinking coffee with John Vlahakis and my brother George when John was trying to convince me to go to a store called Lebaron to go and see guns and that I should buy one, or another place somewhere at Notre-Dame.

I told him, "Ah, they sell guns there?"

He answered, "Yes, if you want, we can go to see."

I was not really interested in buying guns. I told him, "Okay, one day maybe we'll go." I tried to avoid him, so he stopped. He wanted to show that I'm related to guns, to make it easier to accuse me of murder, as they were trying to do so. My brother was looking at him with a question mark, like, "What kind of advice is this? You are telling him to get guns?"

While we were walking in the Hudson Bay Apparel Store at the Eaton Center and talking with John about the whole case, I told John that the police should compensate me. John turned around and told me, "How much, 70,000 dollars?" I told him, "What are you talking about? Are you joking? What's that gonna do?"

He didn't like the answer; he wanted me to agree. He admitted this in front of my brother George.

Little did I know it was about to get worse.

# Chapter 2

# Destruction of My Business in Montreal, Canada (2009-2010)

In mid-October 2009, I noticed that the police were sending their own people to install remote starters on their cars. The common thing was they would bring a Canadian Tire car starter in a bag. Cars would have baby seats in the back. They would start bringing defective units, and I would have to argue with them that the starter they got did not work (quite a few times). At this time, my customers had vanished, and my business depended on the cars the police were sending me.

Around the 5th of November 2009, a person arrived with his son in a 2004 Dodge Neon, red in color, with the license plate number 639XPN. The police sent them. When I finished installing the remote starter, the cluster (instrument panel) would not work, which I knew had nothing to do with my installation. I checked all the wiring, but there was no relation. I reset the battery, and the cluster started working, but the RPM meter did not. The person started putting pressure on me that I damaged his car and that I had to repair it now in a kind of threatening way. I told Vie, the owner of the car mechanic repair shop on 5760 Garnier, Montreal, to tell his mechanic to reset it.

I couldn't stay any longer and had to go back to the battery. If it didn't work correctly, he should take the car to the dealership or tell me, and I would fix it if it was related to the remote starter. The mechanic reset it and said, "Let's see if it would last," which made no sense because it should always work.

The next day, the man returned aggressively, blaming me and demanding, "Repair it now!" I wondered if he was sent by drug traffickers rather than the police and felt scared. I ended up removing the remote starter and refunding his money. He then claimed it was working fine, which was impossible. Meanwhile, all the mechanics at Auto Vie were watching me, as if questioning the situation.

On 16 November 2009, the police sent another car, a 2005 Toyota Matrix, plate 810ZQZ. The customer brought a Prostart alarm from Canadian Tire. I installed it, but the bypass for the key chip would not program. Technical support said the American model might not be programmable. The next day, I tried programming another bypass, but it failed again. I told him the only option was to put the second key in a transponder box.

He demanded I remove the system and refund all his money. I told Vie I couldn't refund everything, as I had worked about four hours on the car. The owner started a loud argument in the garage, accusing me of not knowing the job. His aggressive behavior made it clear he came to provoke a fight, possibly sent by drug traffickers.

While I removed the antenna, he insisted on covering tape with plastic and pushed me slightly while criticizing the panel alignment, saying it was "3 millimeters out." I stayed silent and finished the job, but he continued complaining. That's when I realized the police and secret services likely sent him. Vie, the garage owner, had been in contact with the police and was part of the conspiracy against me.

On November 18, 2009, a 2003 Toyota Matrix vehicle, license plate number 839ZVV, was sent by the police. One couple and a girl. They started telling me again why I don't know French, and the girl was also saying the same thing. I told them I can't know everything in this world and that I have to go to school. Their behavior towards me was again hostile. When she went to pay with a debit card to Vie, she told him, "My boss told me to get a receipt!"

The same night, the undercover police agent living in apartment 11 next door caused a loud argument at 4 a.m., waking us again. From 18 September 2009, the police continuously terrorized me without explanation and instructed lawyers not to handle my case. When I asked the lawyers what to do, they said nothing.

By this time, it was clear the police were trying to frame me for a crime to cover their mistakes and punish me, even though I had no involvement in any illegal act. There was no evidence against me, and the criminal contacts I shared with the police confirmed I had done nothing wrong. Theo Anastasopoulos, acting under George Papaspirou's orders, admitted over the phone that I had done nothing, although he falsely accused me of minor acts, such as throwing eggs at his car.

Despite all this, the police monitored me 24/7 and continued their harassment, attempting to create scenarios to accuse me of murder.

When I returned from Greece on September 16, 2009, I had asked John Koumparakos to store my car in the back lane of his building on De Lepee Street in Montreal. He and others from the criminal organization had removed my sound system from my car in a way that it showed that I did it for insurance purposes to make me look bad. I had basic insurance, only liability! They thought that I would claim it from my insurance, and the insurance company would assume that I had done it intentionally to get myself in trouble. One more thing they did to put the blame on me. I also understood then that John Koumparakos is a member of the criminal organization.

On 26 November 2009, around 1:00 p.m., I called police investigator Mr. Fred Charbonneau and left a message: "Hi Mr. Fred, I'm Christos Margelis. I would like to meet you to ask a few things and give you some information."

He called back around 3:00 p.m. I was working under a car dashboard and told him, "I can't talk now, Mr. Fred."

He replied, "Ok, I will most likely call at 5:00 p.m.; if not, we will make an appointment for next week." I said, "Ok."

At 4:15 p.m., I saw a suspicious person entering my building. Upstairs, I heard doors slamming. It was clear the police considered me guilty, interpreting my polite conversation and private meeting request as suspicious. At 5:04 p.m., I called him and he had the answering machine on, so I left him a message. I told him: "Hi Fred, the last 2 weeks I have understood that I have been accused of something. When you call me back, I want you to tell me WHAT."

A few days earlier, the police staged a segment on CNN with someone who looked like me, being interviewed by an army officer, admitting to a murder. I realized this was aimed at me, as the police often sent messages through TV, knowing which channel I was watching via their cameras in my house. I understood they wanted to charge me and were creating scenarios to accuse me of murder, making it seem they had done nothing wrong, and preventing me from suing them. Fred Chrarbonneau did not call back.

On December 1, 2009, at 10:40 a.m., I spoke with Bala, the manager of Auto Asha at 6820 Marconi, about checking a car or performing an installation. Neither of us remembered the appointment, so the conversation sounded suspicious. When I arrived, the customer had forgotten entirely. I noticed a suspicious person, likely sent by the police, wearing large black sunglasses, walking past me despite the garage construction. I feared a possible conspiracy to harm me and kept a close eye on him. After overhearing my conversation with Bala, he disappeared.

When I came back home at night, it was 7:30 p.m. I saw two people from the police in front of my building, where I lived, pretending that we were not bad guys (people who would do a criminal act).

On 2nd December 2009, I went to the Westmount Legal Clinic to see Ted Write for legal advice and to inform him that I had all the evidence needed to sue the police, while also showing him the terror they had been causing me. I gave my report to Ted to read, and we started discussing the events since the last time I saw him at the legal clinic, when he recommended that I see Sally Butler, the lawyer (which must have been in April 2009). I noticed he knew the case from the beginning in detail. I told him again.

I told him that ever since I saw some strange police events on the TV and one person lying down at the entry of my building where I live (the police one afternoon placed a person showing to have consumed alcohol in the entry of the building that I lived in, they were there checking him out and they wanted to see my reaction to consider it as a sign of guilt for murder, they were collecting points of guilt to accuse me for murder), I have understood that the police are trying to blame me for murder. I think I know what's happening.

He tells me, "What?" I told him that when I used to work at Ferrari Autoparts, there was a person named Macho, and George Papaspirou, the owner, would take his last resort financial assistance cheque and give him some money to buy alcoholic beverages. The person was there every day, and at night, most of the time sleeping in the garage. I had noticed that Gigi, George's partner in illegal activities, the last time I was going there, would pretend that he was wrestling with him for fun! He was trying to get him used to the fact that they were joking, so he could kill him easily one day. And then he looked at me, trying to do the same, when I gave him to understand (don't even think about it!).

After about 1–2 months, I noticed that Macho was no longer there. When I asked George Papaspirou, "Where is Macho? I haven't seen him lately." He told me, "Ha, we send him back to his country."

"Oh," I said, "and maybe he will have a better time there." But I thought and asked him: "But who is he going to find there?" He told me, "His mother." And after a while, he tells me: "And I think his sister."

"Ah," I said, I was glad he would live better like that. But it also went through my mind that maybe they killed him. According to them, they sent him back to his country. (I started wondering, though, and I would also bet anything that they killed him and they were trying to put the murder on me). Ted, of course, told the police the information.

In mid-November 2009, I consulted with a lawyer, Mr. George Peizler, and discovered that the police had already spoken with him. He informed me that he couldn't take any action, as he was simply following the police's instructions. When asking the police what the case is, they don't answer. When asking Ted Write, giving certain legal assistance at the Westmount Legal Clinic, Ted was telling everything to the police. Again, the answer I would get was no answer; he would not answer. When someone doesn't answer a question, either guns are pointed at him, or he is guilty. The police are trying to blame me for something I had no idea about at all whatsoever.

Furthermore, on Wednesday, December 23, 2009, when I visited Ted Write at the Westmount Legal Clinic and provided him with an email, I had a conversation with a member of a criminal organization, a customer of mine. I had installed a car alarm in his vehicle. Everybody found out what's happening. He admitted in an email that I have no involvement in anything illegal. AND WHAT IF I DIDN'T HAVE THAT EMAIL?

I told Ted Write to ship my report to the police, asking for explanations. Ted talked out loud: "NO, FORGET IT." The police wanted to put me in jail to prove themselves right, and I cannot sue them, and to punish me! The police were speculating that I was trying to blame them because that's what they wanted to do. If they had put me in jail, they wouldn't have had problems like that, and I wouldn't have been able to sue them, and they would have shown that I had done something illegal. We are talking about murder!

There was nothing to suggest that I had done anything wrong. They knew very well that I had nothing to do with anything. They had visited all my customers and spoken with them: Garage Fujiaty, Patel Garage, Auto Vie, of course, Auto Rajah, Auto Arcade, Automobility (where I purchase the remote starters), Platine Garage, and all the communities. A customer of mine, Simon, was looking to see what I'm thinking, giving information to the police and other customers of mine, and told them that I could have committed murder. The whole world now knows the police want to accuse me of murder.

On 28th December 2009, while I was installing two remote starters for customers working for the police, one at Auto Vince for a 2002 Nissan Xterra vehicle, and the other at Auto PNV for a customer, I saw her talking on her cell phone. I found out that the police did not like my behavior towards their undercover agents.

So, the police, later on, when I went to Touan (the address is Metropolitain Auto on Metropolitain, a car mechanics repair shop near Langelier on the Metropolitain), was not a coincidence. Two undercover agents were looking at me, hostile, and all of a sudden, their brown dog (which seemed small and menacing, being a pit bull) walked quickly and threateningly towards me, coming to attack. I went in the car that was in front of me in time, so he didn't jump on me. Then they took it and left!

I was very mad about this incident. Touan, the owner of the place, noticed it and tried to calm me down. They first said the dog belongs to the people next door. When I looked, nobody was next door with a dog. It was clear what was happening. The mechanic, whose name is Win, saw the scene. My face stayed red for 3 hours.

The next day, December 29, 2010, I submitted my official report regarding my case to the police. This report details everything about my case, which I have completed and shipped for explanations and to file my first complaint regarding all that is happening. Registered envelope tracking number 79445666497.

{This report, until this point, was sent upon my 1st complaint to the police at Archives/Document Management D'Iberville Street (door B-135), Canada.}

(According to the police, my first complaint was dated 11 January 2010.) When I went to get an envelope at the Uniprix

Pharmacy and Postal Office on Parc Avenue near Bernard (the post office I always visit), the cashier attempted to put basic stamps on it, so I sent the letter in a regular form. It was no coincidence. A letter was received, signed by Mr. Leboeuf, on December 30, 2009.

The police have answered my complaint and will refer it to the Access to Information Act. They did not respond to my complaint; instead, they changed the conversation. But by the time they had not gone looking for drugs at Ferrari Autoparts (as I mentioned at the beginning of this report), why didn't they answer that they didn't do so? The answer is that if they were to say so, then the question would be how Gigi (Sterie Craciun) and George Papaspirou learned that I mentioned them to the police. The answer is that by the time the police put me unofficially under police protection, it was they who told the drug traffickers what I mentioned to them. They screwed up!!

Also, majorly, WHY WOULDN'T THEY LET ME HIRE A LAWYER? WHERE IS MY LAWYER? This is the 4th piece of evidence that the police were in conspiracy with the drug traffickers!

On January 4, 2010, at around 6:30 p.m., I spoke with Ted Write. He told me to wait for a paper that confirms I'm a good citizen (the response from International Fingerprinting Services), and I informed him that the police have been bothering me. I will go to see lawyer Sally Butler. He told me not to go; it's meaningless. I wanted to consult with lawyer Sally Butler because she was familiar with my case and had some valuable insights about it that other lawyers wouldn't share. I knew they had told her not to handle my case, as they did with all lawyers. I was hoping maybe she would get to do something. The next day, I called Sally for an appointment, and I found that the phone directory was all mixed up! I couldn't talk to her. It was not a coincidence. They wouldn't let me call her.

The police have been interpreting and misinterpreting a lot of times, and after a while, when hearing me cough on the phone, they tried to interpret that as a sign of guilt for murder.

On January 6, 2010, I went to the Legal Clinic at Westmont to see Ted Write. I gave him a 5-page document on who could have murdered with proof. The person was threatening me via email, a member of the criminal organization that was a customer of mine. I had installed a car alarm on his vehicle, and he threatened me because I wouldn't repair his alarm system. Of course, Ted gave it to the police. They still put people who terrorize me, but this time, not too aggressive. They are doing everything to avoid compensating me.

On January 8, 2010, at 18:07, Vie, the owner of Auto Vie (located at 5670 Garnier, Canada, and other addresses), instructed me to call a customer to inform him of the price for a remote starter for a 2004 Honda Civic vehicle. The phone didn't answer, which I found suspicious because there was no real reason for me to call the customer. If this phone belonged to a drug trafficker, or so it's possible if this phone belonged to a drug trafficker, Vie wanted to show that I have relations with drug traffickers, or he was mixing things up. Vie is in conspiracy with the police. Vie has been working for the police and secret services since September 2009.

The month of November 2009, Vie, in conspiracy with the police, was bringing cars, and he told me to check the car to see if there was a Boomerang (tracking system) in. I checked 2 or 3 cars and after Vie told me to deal with the people who brought those cars and I told him, "Forget it, don't bother me with such things" (although I knew it was cars sent from the police I didn't have any other customers). Ever since I told him like that those cars stopped coming; it was no coincidence!

{This report until this point was sent to Vie Trung Ngo, the owner of Auto Vie at Garnier, Canada.}

{This report until this point was sent to Touan, the owner of Metropolitain Auto at Metropolitain, Canada.}

The 12th January 2010 I went to the post office and sent this 16-page report to Vie, the owner of Auto Vie, sent by registered mail confirmation track number 79445666191.

The 13th January 2010 I sent this 16-page report in a registered mail to Touan, address is in Metropolitain (the mechanics repair shop where the dog went to attack me), track number 79445666112.

The 13th January 2010 around 3.00 p.m. while I talked to Vie he admitted everything written on my report I sent him, that he worked in conspiracy with the police against me! Ty Fujiaty, the owner of Garage Fujiaty, also located at 255 Bates Canada (now at D'Iberville), participated in the conspiracy. Cars from the police are coming there all the time, trying to create signs of guilt in me for murder. They were bringing those vehicles when the police were telling them to do so, and they were trying to develop signs of guilt in me. It was noticeable on the phone as well.

On 14 January 2010, Touan called me at 10:43 a.m. and asked why I had sent him the letter. I told him I didn't like the story with the dog. He admitted everything! My report was delivered to Vie and signed by Nihn. In a strange way, Vie knew about the report before it was even delivered! The same happened with Touan also.

{This report, until this point, was sent to lawyer Sally Butler Grand at Place D'Armes, Canada.}

{This report, until this point, was sent to Ted Write at Westmont Legal Clinic, Canada.}

The 14th January 2010 I shipped the report to Sally Butler Grand, track number 79426745722. The 15th January 2010 I shipped this report to Ted Write, track number 79426745719.

The 15th January 2010 at 11:45 p.m., while I was going home with my brother, George Margelis, the police stopped me on Jean Talon just after L'Acadie. One officer said somebody had stolen my passport and they were looking for him. "What's the color of your eyes?" She told me to come out of my car. She looked at my driver's license and told me, "You filed a complaint?" After, she told me, "Did you report your passport stolen at the police?" I told her that I had gone to the passport office and reported that I had lost my passport. She went in the police vehicle, came out, and told me, "Ok." When I got in my car, she came and said, "Sorry!"

Lately, I also discovered that my home has installed undercover cameras to monitor everything happening in the house, including all rooms. There should be a lot more than one camera in each room.

On 17 January 2010 at 6:30 p.m., I called a former friend of mine, Costas Manolias, who was finally participating in the criminal organization. I knew his sister was a lawyer. I asked him about his sister; he told me she is now in British Columbia, where she is married, and that he had divorced his wife, hinting that it was all because of me (because I hadn't repaired his car alarm system!).

For one more time, people from the drug trafficking organization are trying with all kinds of hints to accuse me but never accuse me straight in my face of anything. He now wants to show me that I was guilty of the conversation we had about something and also pretended that he knew what I had done. He can't accuse me of being bad or guilty of something when he doesn't know what the case is or what has happened. Of course, somebody had talked to him; it was people from the criminal organization who were conspiring with the police. He had relations with the criminal organization. He made it clear that Peter Maltezos had spoken to him.

It's clear that Peter Maltezos, a member of the criminal organization, is friends with him and has told him that if Christos calls, he should portray him as bad and guilty. He also tried to suggest that I have a connection to Peter Maltezos by stating that the lawyer he will introduce to me is related to Peter Maltezos' daughter-in-law, who is a notary. When I told him I didn't need a criminal lawyer but one to sue the police, then he didn't talk. When I asked him what he meant by I had done something in the garage, he said, "NO, NOTHING, I'M SAYING WHAT I HAD WITH PETER MALTEZOS WHEN I WAS WORKING THERE!"

He said he would call me back to give me a lawyer's phone number. He called me back 15 minutes later, and I told him, "Don't give me no phone number, I understood your spirit." He agreed. I told him that it was not my fault that he divorced his wife because I didn't repair his alarm starter on his car, nor was it my fault that it had any relation to that, because we didn't have any relationship with his sister after she got married; she went to British Columbia. He agreed.

I told him that Peter Maltezos and George Papaspirou are gonna be caught and put in jail. In the meantime, the police were undercover before the conversation had even ended (at the first phone call when I called Costas Manolias); they had already come out talking loudly and had three small dogs looking at me from the next-door apartment.

I went to get some burgers from McDonald's. When I came back and Costas had called me back on my cell phone, and we talked for the second time, and I blasted him. One person in a green Sahara Jeep was waiting for me at the entry of my building, where I lived! Talking on the phone, they told him that this is one more person talking from the drug trafficking organization, or even a member who is trying to show me bad. Within seconds, all those speaking out loud from next door had the three dogs, pretending to smoke, and the person in the vehicle disappeared!

It was one more time that the police were interpreting and then calling back, misinterpreting, mostly trying to use it and say there, I have committed murder.

On January 18, 2010, at 12:00 p.m., I went to see a lawyer at IMK Irving Mitchell Kalichman. I asked for a lawyer and said that I want to sue the police. The lawyers had already talked to the police.

It was no coincidence. The name of the lawyer was Felix Lalond! I told him about the case, and he informed me that he cannot take it on and may send me an email to someone who can. Never did he. The police didn't let them take the case.

On January 19, 2010, at 2:00 p.m., the residents of Apartment 6, located directly below mine in the building where I lived, who were members of the police assigned there for "protection," deliberately played music on a sound system with hefty bass. The volume was deafening and clearly intended to disturb me and provoke anger. They kept the music on for more than two hours.

{This report, up to this point, was included in my second complaint submitted to the police at Archives/Document Management, Canada.}

I shipped this report up to this point, following my second complaint to the Archives Police on January 19, 2010, via registered mail with track number 79396207696. On January 18, 2010, around 6:30 p.m., Sally Butler Grand, the lawyer, called me on the phone to tell me she had received the report I sent her. She let me understand that the police won't let her take the case; she doesn't want no problems with them (it was a plot; she was the one that told me not to ask for money for the information if they would say to me to go to sign when I went to see her around the 18 or 21 September 2009, and after about a week I went again). We agreed on what's happening, and I told her that all the lawyers I consulted said the same thing: they don't do that kind of case. Lawyer George Peizler said so when I told him I wanted to sue the police. I described the conversation we had above, and lawyer Felix Lalond, and I explained what happened with the letters I sent him.

Lawyer Anna Colarusso did the same; she pretended she was not in the office when I went to see her, and when I sent her this report, she did not answer. When she told me, "Which other lawyer did you talk to?" I told her that I know him at De Maisonneuve Street; his name is Felix Lalond. Sally Butler told me I will have a hard time suing the police; of course, they talk to everybody.

On January 19, 2010, Vie (Trung Ngo, his name must be) from Auto Vie called me on my cell phone and told me that the police had gone there and asked him if there were some people they wanted to put in jail, and that Vie had cooperated with them. They also asked him to sign a paper, but Vie didn't. He told me the truth, that the police had spoken to him and that we had talked together, fearing that he might get in trouble. I told him I just want everybody to admit everything that happened. We agreed that everything is like that.

On January 15, 2010, I sent this report to Ted Write at the Westmount Legal Clinic in Montreal. The 18th January 2010, it was received, signed by M. Gabrielle, track number 79426745719. On 19 January 2010, I sent this report, the second complaint, to the police and received a signed acknowledgement from Ariste, track number 79396207696.

Last week, the police, with various methods, threatened to kill me if I went to sue them. Vie from Auto Vie told me that Gigi came there looking for me to kill me, something that had never happened before. Two days ago, while going home at night (one more death threat from the police) in the building, one person looked the same as the person in the Honda Accord vehicle license plate number 078 YYL that came to obviously shoot me last 8th May 2009 (which, after a while and after interpreting my report, I came down to the conclusion that it was him), walked in and went to another apartment. The person was, in fact, a police agent.

Wednesday the 20th January 2010, night around 8:00 p.m., when I went to Ted Write at the Westmount Legal Clinic at Westmount, someone there lifted a paper that was saying that a 22-year-old was killed (secret agent)! In the meantime, the major drug traffickers are on the loose, have not been arrested, and that scared me even more and depressed me that I will have to live in fear until and if they catch them. They will never catch them, though, because they are working in conspiracy with the police, selling drugs, and the police are harboring them!

Lately, I have found out that the police are horrifying me again by putting the ambulance coming after me with all the duty lights on and honking the horns; in some cases, police cars also follow me with their duty lights on. On the 22nd January 2010, there was an article on Yahoo, the internet website, that undercover police in British Columbia beat up a man for mistaken identity! They showed his eye was bruised. The police had put it showing that I would be getting a beating.

About a week ago, when the police stopped me on Jean Talon near L'Acadie, they told me that my identity had been used again, the same story they were telling me one and a half years ago. Now they were showing that next time you will get a beating from us.

The police are still applying psychological warfare by putting people following me, people dressed suspicious as members of a criminal organization, wearing hats, others with dark sunglasses, walking close to me, people behaving badly to me. The people living in apartment 11, which is beside ours, are making noise; their TV is playing loudly, they have loud conversations after 11:00 p.m., and even at 12:00 a.m. there is still noise. They are police undercover, and they do it on purpose to get on my nerves and drive me crazy.

On January 26, 2010, around 4:00 a.m., some police

personnel were making loud noises and screaming. My father woke up and wondered what was happening; he told me the next morning. On 26 January 2010, the law firm IMK received a registered letter containing a 16-page report, in which I accused them of conspiring with the police against me, thereby preventing me from suing the police. They didn't handle my case as the police instructed them to do, as evidenced by the signature of Rose Ann Cotturo, track number 79396207872. I also sent a registered letter with my request for a reward, based on the information I provided to the police and signed by Investigator Fred Chrarbanneau in late October 2009, with a track number of 79445668232. It was received, signed by Mr. Leboeuf, 27th January 2010.

On the 26th and 28th of January 2010, the police officers working undercover in the surrounding apartments from mine had all taken out garbage bags and left them sitting outside. I'm wondering why they would show that's what I am; they were showing that I'm worth nothing, that I am garbage. The ones at apartment 11 next door have been making noise often after 11:30 p.m. I have even told them, my brother, my mother, that they are disturbing us and not letting us sleep at night.

{This report, until this point, was sent to Lawyer Anna Colarusso at Montreal, Canada.}

On 29 January 2010, I sent a registered letter to Lawyer

Anna Colarusso, track number 79445668674. The same day, at 8:15 p.m., I was stopped by the police at the corner of Decarie and Jean Talon. The police officer asked me for my identification, and I provided it. The officer asked me if I knew the reason why they stopped me. I told her I guess something with my name in the computer. She told me yes, they are looking for the person walking around with my name, using my identity, because I lost my passport.

I told her, "How can you be looking for the person who had used my passport in my car out on the roads, by the time the person who tried to enter the country with my passport was arrested at the airport and deported back to their country?" When she asked me how I knew that, I told her that my lawyer, Sally Butler, had told me so. She told me that I have to contact the immigration authorities for this matter because it's not something that has to do with the police, but now it has to do with the government (as I've been saying since mid-2009, the government and secret services have been involved).

The 30th January 2010, the police and secret services put a show at the CNN TV station at 10:45 a.m., where it showed that in the United States there was an arrest of some people, one had some possession of marijuana, and that they beat him to death, where the mother of the person told them that she had a 41-page report (mine was 18 at the time, they knew that), and that the police attorney was saying that they just did their job! Showing me that I won't be able to sue them, and I will also be getting a beating.

On January 31, 2010, at 2:00 a.m., at the supper restaurant Tops in Laval, I was there with my brother, George. There were a couple of people who were working for the police, came in front of me and started kissing provocatively to make me feel bad. Another couple sent by the police arrived and did the same. Two other police officers were looking at me and nervously playing with their cell phones. When I went to leave, two cops were at the entry, looking on purpose to upset me. I have never seen the police there before; they were on purpose, of course.

The police had been putting women making me feel bad by doing and behaving in specific ways, and also embarrassing me. On the same day, in the afternoon, I saw several ambulances pass by while I was driving, with their lights and sirens on. They are piling on threat after threat, trying to discourage me in any way. Now the police have found a new way of terrorizing me; they put the fire trucks with all the lights on coming after me.

On 2nd February 2010, at 5:00 p.m., I installed a remote starter on a vehicle for Stephen, a car salesperson who was then working for the police. He was talking to someone on the phone when I finished and left. A few blocks down the road, a fire truck came behind me with all its lights flashing and honking the horn. When I went downtown to Zengin, a customer of mine who works at a parking lot on Drummond, one fire truck was running behind me on René Lévesque, and when I turned onto Drummond, another one was coming in the opposite direction towards me. I turned right to avoid it!

On 2nd February 2010, Anna Colarusso, a lawyer, received my report, signed by Kaperonis, with track number 79445668674. On 18 December 2009, Ted Write, following police orders, took me to International Fingerprinting Services Canada for fingerprints. The answer from there was to send me a yellow paper discussing a Canadian police certificate for employment. Upon filing my complaints with the police, they informed me that they would refer me to the Access to Information office to determine what information they have. Something that doesn't answer my complaint.

{This report, until this point, was sent to Lawyer George Peizler at Montreal, Canada.}

On 5 February 2010, I shipped this report by registered mail to Lawyer George Peizler, with track number 79445669799. Peculiarly, no registered letter was sent before the police opened it. Vie and Touan from Metropolitan Auto mentioned the report to me before it was even received from them.

On February 5, 2010, at 8:00 p.m., I went to see my doctor, Revilis, on Parc Avenue in Montreal, Canada. I told him that there is a case that has happened with the police and some people involved in illegal activities, where these people are after me, and the police are making my life difficult. I told him I'm having headaches, I'm shaking sometimes, and I'm having some depression symptoms. Doctor Revilis' behavior towards me became hostile, and he became unfriendly. He didn't want to hear anything; he didn't want to continue the conversation. When I asked him, "What do you suggest?" he said that I should just stay away from Café Cosmos, and everything would be forgotten. Something Police Officer Lampert had told me!

The police have been talking everywhere to treat me badly, people that I deal with in my small business, customers, doctors, even the employees at the local Tim Hortons restaurants did the same. They won't let me talk to others about what they have done to me. People working for the police, the undercover ones, like the mechanic at Garage Fujiaty, Bruno, if he heard that I'm telling someone what has happened, they would come close to me and start punching tires and doing things like that.

On 8 February 2010, Lawyer George Peizler received my report, which also indicated the relevant part to read, track number 79445669799. The police, after I have been sending my complaints, and since my business lately depends on their cars, have been sending me fewer cars. To the point that I can't make a living, and to make me feel bad, to punish me.

On 10 February 2010, I went to see Ted Write at the Legal

Clinic in Westmount. While we drove back on Sherbrooke, the police stopped me, asked for my registration papers, and I gave them to them. He told me, "We stop you because we are looking for someone who has used your identity, and that I should go to the International Fingerprinting Services to get a good identity so that we can recognize you better!" I told him that this is an excuse to keep bothering me; nobody had come into the country with my identity or passport. "No," he said, "this will always happen!"

{This report, until this point, was sent upon my 3rd complaint to the Police Archives/Document Management, Montreal.}

The 11th February 2010, I shipped my third complaint to the police once it reached 22 pages, track number 79442659611.

On 13th February 2010, one more undercover person working for the police, his name Pierre as he told me, not a tough-acting person, license plate number 888 TCK, came to Garage Fujiaty to repair his remote car starter that I had installed for him and tried to show that when I deal with someone not tough-acting I don't fear him and blackmail him by hiking the price or forcing him to install a new starter when I can actually repair the old one. If it's someone tough, I don't—which of course is not the truth. I always work the same way, fairly, with everybody. The day before, they sent someone pretending to be tough and didn't pay at the end for showing up, coming there, and providing an estimate to repair his remote starter. They try to show that I have murdered a weak person because that's my character (nothing to do with my character at all).

They have also been putting me in a weak position and forcing me to offer low prices or even do favors (work for free). Once my business depended on their cars, now and after interpreting that as a sign of guilt for murder, they were interpreting weakness that they were creating into guilt (this was manipulated) after sending me people terrorizing and horrifying me (that they will attack or murder me, others showing me that I'm guilty for murder!), creating a vicious cycle of horror and putting me into a weaker position to accuse me for murder by saying, "Ah, why are you scared? You are scared because you have committed murder!"

The police didn't let me hire a lawyer, they banned me from justice, and they were doing whatever they wanted; they were dancing! While doing this and making me work at low profits for some days, they would then send me not-acting-tough people who were willing to pay the price. I would tell them that I would go back to my previous higher prices. Then the police would interpret that when I deal with someone who is not tough, I hike prices, I'm aggressive, and if someone is acting tough, I don't. Trying to say that I have done the murder of a weak person because it was easy for me (that's your character)!

A weak person, though, was Macho, the person who used to be under the influence of alcohol all day long and at night sleeping in George Papaspirou's garage. If we consider this, we can come to my conclusion that the person who was murdered was Macho. That's why the police were always trying to show that when I deal with someone with a weaker character, I treat him badly, to link my way of operation to the murder of a weak person, and that was Macho. So here we see again the conspiracy that the police have with the drug trafficking organization. Both were aware of the murder, and the police proved with this tactic that they were following that Macho must have been the murdered person. They said, and in particular George Papaspirou noted, that they sent him to his country. I think they sent him DEAD!

THE POLICE, PARTICIPATING IN THE CONSPIRACY WITH THE DRUG TRAFFICKERS, DIDN'T WANT ME TO SUE THEM. THEY ARE TRYING TO PUT MURDER ON ME IN A SERIOUS WAY. IT WAS NO JOKE.

THE DOG WAS ABOUT TO ATTACK ME IN TIME; I WENT STRAIGHT INTO A CAR THAT WAS IN FRONT OF ME AND AVOIDED THE ATTACK.

While the police were trying to accuse me of murder, I thought they were doing it to scare me, not to stop me from trying to sue them. After I understood that they were really trying to accuse me of murder, I noticed they had some mathematical type, using and counting points of guilt for murder. They were translating confusion, politeness, weakness, etc., into points of guilt for murder, and after, taking them back when it wouldn't match very well for them. It became a horror and a nightmare. I knew they were doing it because I was trying to sue them, but I just couldn't believe it. With a method that was manipulated, as I mentioned above, by that time of course they knew I had nothing to do with murder or anything illegal.

After I had sent my first complaints to the police, I noticed that some people working for the police undercover had shown up for repairs or installations on their cars, where in one van I had to remove stuff, things he had from the trunk, and I saw a baseball bat, which I removed with my hands. On 11th February 2010, while I was working on one of their cars, a 1997 Corolla, there was a shuffle in the trunk that I had to remove in order to work. I also thought maybe they wanted me to put my fingerprints on it, and then they may accuse me of murder or so! I didn't touch it!

In October 2009, while I tried to find a job because I knew my business would be demolished (would be destroyed, customers would disappear) and it was not safe for me to run it, I saw that Future Shop, an electronics chain store, was asking for a car audio installer at every single store they had in Montreal, something impossible. When I applied, I got no answer! The same happened with Best Buy and another car audio store. The police were behind it, telling them not to hire me, to put me in a weak position, so I would have no choice but to work with them, so I would be even more scared, translating that as guilt, an excellent reason for them to come after me and do all these things, trying to press charges against me.

There is no more doubt, after all these weasel, cunning creations, malicious tactics the police have been doing, that they wanted to put me in jail or even kill me, so I cannot sue them.

The police were deliberately misinterpreting events and statements according to their own interests, rather than the truth. When those interpretations proved unsustainable, they would reverse or "un-interpret" them, often repeating this cycle, at least 20 times, from what I observed. Their purpose was clear: they involved people I knew who were unfavorable toward me, encouraging them to provide interpretations that would help frame me for murder. These actions were intentional, designed so that everything happening or being said could be manipulated against me and used to blame me for crimes I did not commit. The ultimate aim of the police was to fabricate a case of murder in order to imprison me, simply because I wanted to sue them.

At the same time, members of a criminal organization, capable of sending someone to kill me at any moment, were also connected. For example, Zois, with whom I had email correspondence, never accused me of anything. Another member, Peter Maltezos, whom I encountered at a Tim Hortons on Côte-des-Neiges around February 10, 2010, admitted his involvement when I asked if he was connected to George from Ferrari Auto Parts. During this meeting, he threatened me with death, making a gesture that indicated I was "already dead." He then told me he had to go to his grandchildren. Importantly, he did not accuse me of anything, nor did he create an argument, although under the circumstances it would have been expected for him to say something negative about me if the goal were to provoke or fabricate accusations.

Even before I submitted my first complaint to the police, I had already experienced threats. One individual working with the police, driving a Ford Windstar (1997 or 1998), came to me while I was installing a ProStart remote starter for him at Canadian Tire. He falsely claimed it was malfunctioning. Later, just before Christmas, he returned to Auto Vie (5770 Garnier, Montreal), repeating the same claim and then threatening me directly: "This damn starter is giving me problems, and I'm going to shoot you!" At first, I thought he was exaggerating, but eventually I realized he was serious. I was frightened, but I managed to calm him down.

When I returned from Greece on September 18, 2009, my lawyer, Sally Butler-Grand, admitted on our very first meeting that I should "just live my life and not bother." She said this because she already knew what was happening. The police were deeply involved with the drug-trafficking organization.

In November 2009, John Vlahakis (a police associate and former friend) openly admitted in front of George Margelis that the police were involved. He offered me $70,000 in compensation, which I told him was a joke. Then, in December 2009, he hinted over the phone that I would be going to jail, as if preparing me for it. At the time, I thought he was joking, but he was not.

Around the same period (mid-November 2009), I also spoke with lawyer George Peizler. As I previously reported, he indirectly admitted that the police did not want to be sued. When I told him I wanted to proceed, he made a disturbing statement: that where the Plaza Côte-des-Neiges mall used to be, "there used to be dead bodies."

Meanwhile, it remains unclear whether drug traffickers such as Gigi and others will ever be arrested. Although their whereabouts are known, the police continue to harbor and protect them.

[This report, up to this point, was submitted to the law firm IMK in Montreal, Canada.]

On 10 February 2010, I shipped a letter, including this report up to this point, which I have marked with track number 79445669533, to the law firm IMK, accusing them of conspiracy with the police. On 12th February 2010, it was received, signed by

Ross Ann Cotturo, track number 79445669533. On 11 February 2010, I filed my third complaint with the police, which is referenced by track number 79442659611 (mentioned above).

{This report, until this point, was sent upon my letter of complaint to the Department of Justice Canada.}

{This report, until this point, was sent upon my 4th complaint to the police Archives/Document Management, Montreal, Canada.}

On 15 February 2010, I submitted my complaints to the Ministry of Justice, Canada, with tracking number 79442659452, and my fourth complaint to the police, with tracking number 79442659466. On 16 February 2010, I received a letter from IMK. They shipped me back my documents (like garbage), saying that they don't wish to take the case and denying the fact that the police told them not to file the lawsuit. The letters I sent describe in detail what happened when I went to see the lawyer, and that downstairs, in front of the building, there were police cars and ambulances. On 17 February 2010, I sent a registered letter to IMK, telling them that the police were investigating them and that either they had been forced not to take the case or had done so voluntarily. On 17 February, the police received my fourth complaint, signed by Mr. Ariste, with track number 79442659611. On 19 February 2010 at 9:45 a.m., while I tried to place an order in my TD Waterhouse trading account 30BL35F, I noticed that a simple order to sell 3000 shares of Sirius Satellite (SIRI) wouldn't pass. There was no reason for that to happen. I called TD Waterhouse, the investment brokerage firm. The representative started asking me too many questions about my account. She wondered whose account, although I have been trading for more than 8 years.

She told me that when the automated phone recognized my identity by telling my month of birth and day, it didn't recognize it, which is false. I wouldn't be able to get through; it wouldn't connect to the representative. It accepted the passwords, which were the date and month of birth. She told me that I know my father's Social Insurance Number. I told her I have to check and find it. She told me, "Do you have power of attorney over the account?" I told her it's a joint account, my father and I! She passed me to another representative, who told me that the order didn't go through because I had to place it at 1.13 cents or 1.14 cents for sale.

When I passed it at 1.135, it wouldn't pass, which is false. I have passed other orders like that before, and the stock trades on those decimal numbers. When the price of a stock is at cents, of course you can place a trade at decimals. Of course I was seeing that the stock was trading at decimals. When I checked the TD Waterhouse page for the reasons why an order doesn't pass, it doesn't mention any of the reasons TD Waterhouse gave me. They were lying. When I asked him why the representative before asked me if I have a power of attorney, what does that have to do with an order? He told me, "I don't know." The police and secret services told TD Waterhouse to give me a hard time and not let orders be executed or delaying them for way too long, knowing that the last week I had made a certain amount in profits (I'm saying that the secret services were involved also because it was loud and one police officer admitted the involvement of the Government of Canada).

On 19 February 2010, I visited the car mechanics repair shop Platine, where George is the owner, and I installed an alarm starter for a van. I told George, "Hm, George, you work with the police, what did the police tell you to do?" George neither denied nor agreed; he looked at me only. He said something which I didn't hear clearly. I told him, "Conspiracy." I left.

While going down the road on Crémazie near Pie-IX Boulevard, one vehicle, a Honda Civic (2007 to 2010 year of manufacture), charcoal color, all of a sudden got in my way from the road, going across by a few meters. We didn't get into an accident. The driver was a person wearing the same hat as mine; the police and secret services sent him. I looked at him; he didn't turn, but looked straight ahead. When going home on the road, police cars and an ambulance were parked in the opposite direction of the road with all their duty lights on.

My fourth complaint to the police was received, signed by Graig on 18/02/2010, with track number 79442659466. My complaint to the Minister of Justice Canada was signed by H. Moore (what a name!), with track number 79442659452.

The summer 2009, and about 10 days after my mother gave to the police the information (the information I had been writing about the criminal organization since October 2008), that was about 10 days after I went to Greece, 11 May 2009 (around the 21 May 2009 my mother went to the police station on 7035 Parc Avenue, Montreal, to give the information as I told her to do on phone). About a week later, while I was swimming down the beach near a restaurant at the main beach towards the end of May 2009, I noticed two people who pretended they were after me came, started walking quickly towards me, and approached me directly. I pretended nothing was happening, that I was unaware, stayed calm, didn't move. They came around me, walked there around where I was, and disappeared.

When I mentioned that to Investigator Fred Chrarbanneau at the Montreal police station towards the end of October or beginning of November 2009, and told him that the drug traffickers sent them, he said, "Yeah, that was it!" He didn't ask anything nor pay attention. Those people were not sent from the drug traffickers but the police and secret services of Greece to force me to leave the country!

I also noticed somebody coming outside my house in Greece, pretending he was looking for something or someone, pretending he was from the drug traffickers looking for me. He didn't make it look like it was for me, but was looking suspiciously around. This happened around August 13, 2009. Around August 18, 2009, I went to the police station and spoke with an officer in the office. He was undercover. I told him about it and my case in Canada, and I asked him if I saw that person again, should I call the police to find out who he is and what he is looking for? He told me, "Yes, we will bring him to the police station and verify his identity."

I saw him again a few days later, not far from where I live. He pretended he was going to a café. As I understood, he was not a drug trafficker, but at that point, I couldn't understand what his role was. I also noticed two people who came just outside my store, which I had opened, pretending to look at me. One looked like a friend of mine, and the other was wearing a round hat, just like I used to. This scene, of course, was orchestrated by the secret services of Greece in conspiracy with the police and secret services of Canada, as I found out later on, to scare me and make me leave the country.

{This report, until this point, was sent upon my 5th complaint to the police at Montreal, Canada.}

On 21 February 2010, I sent my 5th complaint to the police,

track number 79452678270. Received and signed 24/02/2010 by Mr. Leboeuf. Ever since 21 February 2010, when the police heard through their secret microphones installed in my apartment that I'm going to go to Greece in the summer, they changed policy. Fearing that I might take them to the International Criminal Court in The Hague, they stopped sending me business and blocked me from finding a job, so they could financially cause me to struggle. They have put people showing up to me asking for money, showing me that's how I will be one day. Ever since then, I have had almost no income, no work; fortunately, I'm making some money from the stock market.

On 25 February 2010, the police again put people at Garage Fujiaty. I went to repair a 2005 red Caravan taxi with an intermittent problem with the headlights and the windshield wiper pump. I repaired the problem and charged them a certain amount, which was for half an hour of work. They blamed me for the parking brake lights on the dashboard that were always on, as well as the ABS (Antilock Brake System) light that was illuminated. I checked to see if it was related to my job, but it wasn't. I plugged in the scanner to see what it says for ABS, but it was not updated for that car. I told them I couldn't help them anymore and that they had to go somewhere that had an updated scanner for the ABS. Translating, they interpreted that I am confused, a sign of guilt for murder!

At the same time, I saw Bruno again, the mechanic undercover working for the police. I was glad he was there again; he had been gone for two weeks. The only thing that bothered me was that when I would talk about the case, he would get mad and start punching the tires. I felt safer with him there; I told him and shook his hand. When I went home, I saw one person at the entrance of the building, just like the one George Papaspirou had sent just before I left for Greece on July 8, 2008. At night, the police officers working at apartment 11, just beside ours, played music at a deafening volume and talked loudly on purpose from 11:30 p.m. until 1:45 a.m. I was shaking, I had cramps in my stomach, and my face turned red for at least 3 hours.

The next day, as I was leaving my home, I saw the person who lives in apartment 6, working for the police, providing protection (supposed to be police protection) in front of the entry door, looking at me. I turned back, retrieved the envelope I had for Sally Butler Grand, and went straight to the post office, where I sent it via registered mail with track number 79452676628. My letter urges Sally Butler to contact me and file the lawsuit. Sally Butler Grand, in conspiracy with the police, returned the letter to me, refusing to accept it.

From February 25, 2010, the police began sending me some work. On 26 February 2010, I had a conversation with an old friend of mine, Zengin, who now works for the police. He had told me that he had been in an accident with a car once because water had entered the brake system. He was the one who exchanged vehicles with me. Police told him that when they noticed I wanted to change my car. I now drive his car. On 23 February 2010, I exchanged my 1995 Honda Civic for a 1996 Acura Integra, which he gave me in green.

It was after the death threat I received from a member of the criminal organization, Peter Maltezos. At the same time, I saw him at a Tim Hortons restaurant on Côte de Neige around 10:00 a.m. on February 10, 2010. I didn't want to be detected. On Friday, I noticed that when I drove out in the morning and tried to brake at the corner of Barclay and Côte des Neiges, the brakes were frozen. I pushed so hard, the car wouldn't stop; I had no horn. It's good that no pedestrians were walking. The car finally stopped, passed the lines. If people were there, I would have hit someone.

The previous day, I lent the car to Koumar to get coffee, a person working for the police (a secret agent) and a customer of mine, who had added water to the brake fluid. The next day, I went to the garage at Kouan, bled the brakes, and removed the water that was in them. Since then, the brakes are good. I also replaced one ball joint (a part that holds the wheel) because it was dangerous; the wheel could have come loose, and both front link kits (front system stabilizing parts) were missing. Maybe all this is not a coincidence.

On Saturday night, 27 February 2010, I was at a supper restaurant on the 440 road in Laval. The police had put two women and some others there around the time I would leave, and they created a scene. When driving back home, we were talking with my brother, George Margelis, in the car. The police were listening to all conversations with some technology, and I didn't discuss that scene much. The police interpreted that negatively, and the next day, Sunday, while I was at the place Versales, a mall shopping center on Sherbrooke East to drink a coffee, a person sitting there from the police looked at me very angrily, and after he left, he continued looking at me angrily.

The police were the ones harassing and humiliating me on a daily basis and making my life miserable. They were using all kinds of people to harass me (without mentioning everything else they have done and are doing to me). Later, I went to the Hudson Bay Apparel store at the Eaton Center downtown Montreal. The address of the shopping center is 706 St. Catherine, Montreal. While I was walking just beside the Metro McGill going to the Eaton Center, the police put one person pretending, pointing his hand and saying, "You do this to me, you will see, you will see!" showing me that's how they will make me become.

# Chapter 3

# The Planned Volcano Eruption in Iceland (2010)

{This report, until this point, was sent upon my 6th complaint to the police in Montreal, Canada.}

On the 9th of March 2010, I sent my 6th complaint to the police, 27 pages, everything up to this point. Track number 79426694141. Sally Butler did not accept the registered mail I sent, urging her to file the lawsuit. Of course, the police knew what the letter said and did not let Sally Butler accept it. Track number 79452676628. The envelope has been returned; I have it in my hands. On March 11, 2010, complaint number 6 was received and signed by Mr. Leboeuf.

In the meantime, the police and secret services had gone to every single store that I go to and told them to mistreat me. The ones at the cash register would give me an ignoring and unpleasant look. They have been putting women everywhere I stand on the street and even while driving, and when I would look at them, they pretended to ignore me. To the point that I can't trust anybody, I am cautious with everybody. They want to show me now that all of a sudden, nobody likes me. It's their undercover agents they have been putting in place, and the people they have talked to. The police are trying to ruin my character, trying to make me impolite.

That's why it was easy for the police to create scenarios of guilt, translating my politeness into guilt for murder, a perfect way to make a vicious cycle of horror and terror.

On the 6th of March 2010, George from Garage Platine, Montreal, a person working in conspiracy with the police and secret services at Saturday noon, asked me to drive him home. Of course, he had cars. While driving, he told me, "Be careful here, the police give tickets when speeding." I was not going fast anyway. I told him, "Don't say that, because the car has microphones, the police are listening, and they will be after you like they are doing to me." (He wanted to show me that he doesn't conspire with the police.)

Saturday night, 6th of March 2010, around 10:30 p.m., I remote-started my car, and when I went downstairs toward my car, this lady (secret agent) came up to me, screamed, talked badly, and said, "Why did you start your car while I'm sitting near it?" She came up to me in a threatening way. I got scared. She came close and was looking at me like she wanted to attack me. I went to leave; she was always in front of me. I asked her, "Why are you following me?" She didn't answer. I stayed far and then left. I then understood that it was one of the police's scaring tactics. They like to keep a horror scene to terrorize me.

Later that night, I was at Supper Restaurant Moomba. When

leaving, around 2:00 a.m., one person from the police threw something on the floor near me that made a smell. Everybody noticed that, and the lady who hangs the jackets blamed me for it. She knew what the case was, though; she did it on purpose. They had talked to her to say so.

On Monday morning, March 8, 2010, around 9:45, my mother informed me about Sotiris and his daughters, a friend of mine from Greece, who wanted me to have a relationship with one of his daughters. We had quite a bit of a difference in age. To avoid this conversation, I don't enjoy these conversations with family members, I told her that I was joking and that nothing was happening. The police, again trying to find reasons to start harassing me and terrorizing me, made a loud noise from the downstairs apartment, and immediately, Stephen called me, a person who sells cars. I hadn't heard from him in at least 3 weeks, but he called me for a job, to do some work on his cars.

What they do is they call me early in the morning when my voice is not clear and sometimes sounds weak, to interpret that as a sign of guilt for murder! They also would tell the person calling me Lee, the manager of Garage Fujiaty—usually does that on purpose, to make a trembling voice which passes to the other side, to make my voice shaky and trembling as well. So like that they say, "There, his voice is not clear, it's shaking, he is guilty of murder!" Garage Fujiaty—Ty Fujiaty is the owner, and Lee is working there has taken part in the conspiracy, to their knowledge, by helping the police and secret services frame me, and by assisting them in creating evidence of guilt against me for any purpose.

They bring people, customers, from the police, into the garage, trying to start a fight, a conflict with me, cooperating with the police to terrorize me. One taxi driver almost started a fight with me and even created financial damage to me, doing whatever the police told them, sending business, then stopping business, doing whatever the police told them. Lee, the manager, is the person dealing with me; Ty is the owner.

On the 12th of March 2010, after the police had figured out that I may go to New York and after I could sue them from there, Lee called me early Saturday at 10:00 a.m. to tell me that I should install a radio on a vehicle, 2004 Cavalier, a car not favorable to me, not easy to work on. He wanted to see if my voice seemed shaky. His voice shakes on purpose, and he wanted mine to do so too, so they could find a reason to come after me, start terrorizing me, and interpret this as guilt.

One other incident I have not mentioned: when I was back from Greece and went to the police station the next day, 17th of September 2009, Mrs. Lampert, an officer, was there and we were talking for 2 hours and writing the police report. The police officer wanted me to write a report that didn't show the police as the ones who put me in this situation, and that George Papaspirou did not tell me by word that he was going to kill me. With the threat of being thrown out of the police station and not receiving police protection, she made me write a softer report according to what they wanted me to write.

When I saw lawyer Sally Butler Grand the next day, she told me that big fish eat small ones! When I told her I would ask a certain amount to sign the information (if they would tell me to go sign), she told me, "Forget about money."

I told her, "Now, the way things are, I cannot do anything."

She told me, "I know, but what can I do? Just live like nothing is going on!" She also told me that there was no proof that the police had arrested me. I told her that I still had the card from my arrest (26th of January, 2008) that the police officer gave me.

The officer at immigration at the airport, when I got off the plane on the 16th of September, 2009, when he saw that I was looking at the tag on his shoulder to see if it was police or security, they started misbehaving toward me.

They sent me to the immigration waiting room when I came from Greece on 16 September 2009 because the security officer saw that I was looking at the tag he had on his shoulder, understanding that I wanted to sue them. Lawyer Sally Butler had asked me before, when I visited her (likely in April 2009), if it was the police or security personnel who had spoken to me at the airport when I arrived from Greece on 5 September 2008.

The security officer at the airport told me that if I don't have the card the police gave me at the arrest, I can't sue them because I have no proof they arrested me. But I have the card.

On March 15, 2010, at 2:50 p.m., I called TD Waterhouse Financial Brokerage Firm from my home phone to place a trade on the stock market. The person I talked to gave me a hard time, asking too many questions about my account, and after that, said to me, "Good luck," the exact words the police told me around 2 July 2008, when the drug traffickers started putting people after me to kill me.

The police and secret services are trying to dent my psychology, to create a bad psychology while trading, so I can't make money, and even lose money.

Police Investigator Fred Chrarbonneau, when I went to see him as I mentioned above, and told him in detail what was happening, was not really concerned.

When I gave all the information that I had phone numbers of Roxana and Emilio, I had installed an alarm starter on Emilio's vehicle. Gigi at Ferrari Autoparts had told me to install one for him. George Papaspirou had told me Emilio was a partner in illegal activities with Gigi.

I saw Emilio at the CNN TV station a few months later. The police in the United States had arrested him for copying credit cards. I told the police also that they shall find Gigi; he is the leading drug trafficker and the person who operates and runs the drug trafficking organization, as George Papaspirou had told me and as I had understood also.

I used to see him at Ferrari Autoparts. He was friends and partners in illegal activities with George Papaspirou, the owner.

It must have been the first months of 2010 when I was at Café Dépôt on Prince Arthur, corner St. Laurent, Montreal, and I saw a woman. It was Roxana, the woman involved in the drug trafficking organization, whom I understood the police had put there so I could see her.

On the 18th of March 2010, in the morning, I told George from Platine, at his store (a car mechanics repair shop in Montreal), that if the police would compensate me, I would leave them alone. On the 18th–19th of March 2010, the police also put death threats by advertising on the radio and on email on Yahoo (the internet website) that Rizzuto (I never heard about him but only when the police wanted to pass me some message, right now I have not heard about him since 2010!)—that his criminal organization had an armed dispute with another criminal organization at Old Montreal, on streets that I go for a ride, and that there were four dead in a hail of bullets. (While talking about Rizzuto, I noticed it was directed at me, that's how they were passing the messages. It was just after I told George from Platine Garage that if the police compensated me, I would leave them alone.)

At 8:45 p.m., it must have been March 19, 2010, when the police had one ambulance, three police cars, and one fire truck downstairs at my apartment, and they pretended to be looking around for no apparent reason.

The apartment 6 downstairs from mine had the bass from his sound system loud from 8:30 p.m. to 9:15 p.m. The police continue harassing me, applying psychological warfare and making me live a horror by putting others to do so, and they continue, they do not stop.

On the 21st of March 2010, the lady working for the police from apartment 11 (the apartment next to mine) made a death threat, or made it clearer, saying: "I'm waiting for him to read the email so I know what to do!"

They want to kill me, as she was making it look like the email article (the one I have on file from Yahoo, the internet website), showing that I was shot with a gun in Old Montreal. It says: "An electrician was at the wrong place at the wrong time." This was the email article she was waiting for me to read! In any case of a shooting, the news would not mention the job that the person killed was doing.

On March 22, 2010, I went to pay a ticket at TD Bank, TD Canada Trust, located at 1555 Van Horne, Montreal. They asked me to pass my debit card, but I noticed it wouldn't work, it was new! (I had also used it.) The police had told TD Bank, TD Canada Trust to put it out in order! The police have blocked me financially, I have no access to jobs, no ability to do any business, and no customers. They are talking to everybody, not to deal with me.

I depend on the car mechanics' repair shops, which are in conspiracy with the police and secret services, and send me business. Call me for work if and whenever they want. They may send some customers in order to make me look guilty in a way (in order to create some sign of guilt). The police have gone to my major customers, where I go and install alarm starters and do electrical work on their vehicles—Garage Auto Vie, Fujiaty, Platine, Patel, Rajah, and every single customer of mine, and told them not to send me any business at all and not to call me for work.

On the 23rd of March 2010, at 10:50 a.m., while I called TD Waterhouse Financial Brokerage Firm to place a trade in the stock market for IMDS, an over-the-counter stock at 6 cents, the stock was on a rapid move. I asked the broker to be quick and make the purchase. When the stock started going a bit higher, I got a bit scared and told the broker, "Change the order, just buy now, so the stock doesn't go even higher." It went from 5.8 cents to 6.8 within 40 seconds. Fearing the stock might drop again, maybe lose value the same day or next, perhaps even half the value, I was a bit scared and in slight panic.

The police now interpret that I'm scared because I'm guilty, or so they think. Things that have nothing to do with anything, trying to pass the trade quickly so the price of the stock won't go higher, the police are trying to make it look like a sign of guilt for murder. They were slamming doors in the building where I live, and Lee from Garage Fujiaty called me immediately to go and remove a kill switch from a car the police had sent, trying to create signs of guilt. This was part of their method of trying to charge me with murder!

On my way there, I saw a police car issuing a ticket to a white Honda Civic. I used to drive a Honda Civic, too. One mechanic there at Garage Fujiaty, his name Alain, was trying to mix me up, trying to create signs of weakness, or translate it into guilt. The police now, once they couldn't threaten to kill me anymore (because I told my brother and family that if they kill me, they should take my report and the money I had in bank accounts, go to Greece, find a lawyer there, and sue them in The Hague).

On the 24th of March 2010, at 6:00 p.m., I went to see Ted Write, a person working for the police as well, at the Westmount Legal Clinic. He provides certain legal assistance. I got in the room, and Ted started talking about my stolen passport for the 10th time. I sat down and told him that I had found out what we should do here.

I told him: Why don't I sue the drug traffickers directly? We have 5 of them caught on phone conversations, and sending people to do some criminal act against me. As I describe at the beginning in this report, I mention on my 7th complaint the names: George Papaspirou, the owner of Ferrari Autoparts (I say everything about him at the beginning of this report; I used to do electrical work on his vehicles at his autoparts and car mechanics repair shop); Mike Plaras, who owns a car mechanics repair shop, Auto Adriatique, Montreal, Canada (I used to do electrical work and remote starters on his vehicles; a member of the drug trafficking organization).

At the time I was going there, I didn't know that at all. He had asked me quite a few times where I live in Greece after September 2008, with the purpose that whenever I go to Greece, they send someone there to murder me. Of course, with George Papaspirou, at that time, I didn't know that. He would make it look funny. I understood that around September or the beginning of October 2009, when he came pretending coincidentally to Garage Fujiaty and was asking me where I live in Greece. He admitted on the phone around November 2009 that he was asking me and said that he was kidding. It was very noticeable that he was guilty and got very mad at me. Right after, someone called me on my cell, telling me that he wanted to do some electrical repair on his vehicle and that he wanted to see me face-to-face. I didn't go, of course!

Peter Maltezos, also the owner of car mechanics repair shops, Docteur Silencieux, I also used to do electrical work on his vehicles. Around October 2009, he called me to show that we had a relationship and that everything was ok. I did not know that he was a member of the drug trafficking organization, but after that phone call, I understood that he was. Somebody had told him to call me.

Around the 10th of February 2010, I saw him coincidentally one morning at Tim Hortons restaurant on Côte-des-Neiges Street. I describe in this report that an undercover agent also witnessed the scene. When I told him that there are rumors that he is related to George Papaspirou, he made a death threat against me, showing me I'm dead. I ended up changing my car on February 23, 2010, so they couldn't detect me.

John Koumparakos, a person I knew for about 10 years, around October 2009, was calling me, told me to go for coffee (which we didn't), and was showing that he is terrified of me, trying to show that I'm some dangerous person, a murderer. He was acting on the phone, pretending he was terrified of me. He wanted to make me look like a murderer so that over the phone (phones are tapped) it sounds like I'm a murderer, so that the police can use it against me. This also shows the relationship that the drug traffickers had with the police, they were working in conspiracy.

The Global Conspiracy to Turn Me Homeless

I stopped having relationships with John Koumparakos after the 17th of September 2009, when I understood he was a member of the criminal organization. While they had removed the sound system from my car, he told me that he had asked George Papaspirou to find a place to store my vehicle. He called a couple of times in October 2009 to pretend that he was scared of me, and after he was calling me again in November 2009, telling me that he wanted to install a remote starter on his daughter's car, which I didn't do. He did that because he noticed that I knew he was a member of the criminal organization, to show that we had a relationship now, and that nothing was happening. He called again a couple of times, admitting that he knows what's happening at Ferrari Autoparts. I didn't tell him about his involvement in the criminal organization; I simply severed all ties with him.

Also, a person named Costas, a customer of mine, the owner of a printing shop, called me around December 2009 to show that nothing was happening, that everything was ok. He was also a member of the criminal organization, something I didn't know, and he wanted to check his alarm starter on his vehicle. These people appeared after the incident that took place on the 8th of May 2009, the person who came after me, obviously to shoot me, and I went to the police and told them everything I knew about the drug trafficking organization from Ferrari Autoparts.

Some members of the drug trafficking organization had mentioned to me some weird hints in the past that showed that they were related to George Papaspirou in the drug trafficking organization, but I never understood what they meant. I started understanding everything in late September or the beginning of October 2009, when Mike Plaras came, as he showed coincidentally, a Saturday morning at Garage Fujiaty, asking me where I live in Greece.

I understood everything at that point. Also, John Koumparakos, while I had asked him in the summer of 2009 to store my car at his building he had on De L'Épée Street (he had space there), had mentioned to me when I came back from Greece the 16th of September 2009 that he had brought my car to Ferrari Autoparts, I think to check my handbrake cable and to see if he had space to store my vehicle. When I told him, "You know what's happening with Ferrari Autoparts, why did you go there?"

He told me, "I went and asked him if he has space to store the car." Very clear, John Koumparakos was a member of the criminal organization. I never knew that. He had also told me in April 2008 that he would be going to Greece in the summer. He wanted to visit me at my house, most likely in August 2008. He tried to find out where I live so they could send someone to kill me at the same time. I didn't invite John to my home in Greece; for some reason, I felt uncomfortable. Also, Sterie Craciun, known as Gigi, is the person who runs the criminal organization.

Ted Write became immediately unfriendly and told me, "Put money in the envelope, put money in the envelope" for visiting him, and that it's going to be very hard (I had evidence the police saw also), and that I will spend lots of money on lawyers, and if I go to the police to get the information and reports for these people, "We will go to get what the police has for you, not for them!"

Hinting that the police had things to make me look guilty for something, it was very clear Ted Write was plotting with the police because the drug trafficking organization had relationships with them. He didn't want to pass them through trial. They did not want me to sue them, and it shows that he was just against me, of course, because I went to sue the police, which they wouldn't let me do either.

By the time, I had nothing, no involvement in anything illegal. The only way that the police could have had something against me was by creating it. He did not want me to sue anybody.

I went to see Ted Write to tell him to sue the drug traffickers for the simple reason that the police were talking to all lawyers not to handle my case before I even went there. If Ted Write had said he could do that and recommended a lawyer, that would mean the police would let me sue the drug traffickers.

Ted Write scared me, horrified and terrorized me, and was mad, saying: "Let's go there and you'll see what the police have for you!", because I was after the police to sue them.

I was looking at him, wondering: I asked for the reports to sue the drug traffickers, why is he going against me now?! Immediately, Ted Write tried again to create signs of guilt by horrifying me, the same method used by the police in the last 6 months.

{This report until this point was sent upon my 7th complaint to the police at Montreal, Canada}

On the 25th of March 2010, I filed my 7th complaint to the police, track number 79426693490.

This was police complaint number 7 up to this point.

In my 7th complaint, I also asked the police what I had been accused of, what had been said about me, and that I wanted to sue the drug traffickers. The police didn't tell me what they had been accusing me of. I got no answer at all, because the drug traffickers never accused me of anything, but they were working in conspiracy with the police! I wanted to sue the drug traffickers for their actions against me.

On the 26th of March 2010, the police talked to the cafeteria restaurant Rouge on St. Laurent, corner of Prince Arthur. When we arrived, the people at the door did not let us in because they required a reservation. Many people were going in, by the way, that was just an excuse.

On the 29th of March 2010, while talking on MySpace, an internet website, with a lady who was on behalf of the police or a police agent, she sent me a virus to my computer (sender port 182142220251 port 28434) and damaged my laptop. I took the computer to a technician at Jean Talon at the same time.

The technician had already been talked to; the police had spoken to him. Although my computer had antivirus software installed by Dell that said it had detected the virus, to repair it, I had to purchase and pay for the antivirus online. I didn't have a credit card at the time. The technician there told me I had to remove the Windows software system and reinstall it, so I deleted my police files.

When the other technician attempted to repair without updating the Windows software, he installed an antivirus program that didn't resolve the issue. He made it so that it didn't solve the problem. He tried to make me put my SD card, a chip I had with all my information inside, to store the information first to change Windows. What he wanted to do was delete all my information and my reports. I told him, "I can't give you my SD chip because I have critical information inside." He didn't like it. The next day, he installed new Windows software, and the computer was working.

On the 31st of March 2010, when leaving Platine Garage on St. Michel, they had one vehicle, a Honda Civic, smashed in an accident on the other side of the road on St. Michel with another car, and a police officer was going there, but looking for my reaction, most probably to interpret it as they wanted, of course.

The car I took to the mechanic's repair shop had a complicated electrical problem that took me about 1.5 hours to fix. They knew it would take that much; maybe I wouldn't even repair it. Maybe they put that first, and after the smashed car, to interpret it as a sign of guilt for murder. Complicated problems were interpreted as confusion, a sign of guilt.

In the afternoon, around 4:30 p.m., the police, using undercover agents, put outside my building where I live two people lying down on the grass, two police cars outside, and two police officers pretending to talk to them and looking at me. After, I understood they were trying again to create signs of guilt. The police, by putting people holding a yellow envelope, were showing me that I shouldn't send them complaints, that it bothered them. While driving on McGill Street, going to the Old Port, corner St. Antoine, one person who looked like Peter George Papaspirous, partner in crime and friend once, the police were showing a person who looked like him to me, who was holding that envelope, showing me that they didn't like the complaints. I'm dead. It's the envelopes I filed my complaints in.

On March 29, 2010, my seventh complaint to the police was received, signed by Mr. Leboeuf, with track number 79426693490. The police have been terrorizing me by slamming the doors and putting different people making noise in the building I live in, and babies crying.

On the 1st of April 2010, at 5:00 p.m., I went to Lambis Travel Agent at Parc Avenue near St. Viateur and asked him for a ticket for Greece. I noticed he had already talked to. He recommended a ticket with British Airways. He told me it was not that easy to pay the ticket in cash and that he could do so with a credit card. After I told him to get me a ticket, he said okay for the next day until 1:00 p.m., which I finally didn't purchase. He didn't want me to leave with Olympic Airlines or with Air Transat direct flights. Most probably, they wouldn't let me reach Greece but would somehow return me to Canada.

While driving downtown Montreal, they had been putting different people with dark glasses looking at me with a suspicious look, maybe I'm dead. The threats were serious.

At 9:00 p.m. on Friday, the 2nd of April 2010, I usually go out to eat or something. Before I went out, I looked out my window to see what was downstairs, and I saw one person coming to my entry with a suspicious, quite large, black cloth suitcase in his hand. When I saw him from the window, he turned around fast and left, going east on Barclay. I found that very suspicious. When I saw that, I told my family that if the police come and kill me, they should sue them at the Hague International Criminal Court.

On the 2nd or 3rd of April 2010, I went to get an air flight ticket for Greece. The police talked to all travel agents. I went to Olympia Express on Parc Avenue, at the corner of Fairmont. The travel agent named Peter let me understand that if I leave, I'm dead, I shall take British Airways.

I left and went to a travel agent at St. Denis called Voyages Forfait Plus, just after Sherbrooke, on the west side, upstairs, left door. A lady told me she could get a ticket with Air Transat or with Swiss Air for the 18th April 2010, and I told her I would take it on Tuesday, the 6th April 2010 at 1,024 dollars. I told her okay.

The 3rd April 2010, while I was driving my car, the police saw my facial expression and interpreted that I was mad at them and that I would sue them. They knew I wanted to go to the court in The Hague. When I went home around 7:00 p.m., one lady with black sunglasses, the same that the killer (the person with the Honda Accord vehicle, license plate number 078YYL, that came after me obviously to shoot me with a gun) was wearing on the 8th May 2009 just before I left for Greece, told me something bad and left mad towards the downstairs door of the building.

From the 2nd to the 4th April 2010, while driving downtown on St. Catherine Street near Peel in the afternoon, I saw in the crowd someone holding a big sign saying "Mafia" (secret organization engaged in illegal and criminal activities) and on the other side "Corruption," showing to me that even if I demonstrate, nothing is going to happen.

The 3rd April 2010, after the incident with the woman at the entry of my building, the building I lived in, around 7:30 to 8:00 p.m., it was shown on the CNN TV station that somebody had been thrown down from a hotel from the 5th floor! These were threats directed at me; it was noticeable!

The 6th April 2010, I went to get my air flight ticket for Greece at the travel agent Voyages Forfait Plus. She sold me a ticket with Swiss Air for April 21, 2010, although it did not have the exact name. According to the terms, if the name is not precisely the same, you cannot travel. It is an electronic ticket. The difference I was seeing was the "Jr." at the end of my name that stands for Junior. It ultimately made no difference. Now the police are threatening not to let me leave the country.

The 7th April 2010, at 10:30 a.m., the police stopped me with my car on Jean Talon near Côte-des-Neiges and told me immigration was looking for me and that someone was using my identity, the same thing they told me the 26th January 2008 at my false arrest. I said to them that that's not real. The person trying to get in the country with my passport, according to my lawyer at the time, around April 2009, Sally Butler Grant, was deported immediately.

Another thing here is, by the time the person who tried to enter the country with a forged passport was deported immediately, why did they arrest me, claiming identity issues, that I am Pavel from Romania? Pavel was exiled to Romania once he tried to enter the country with a forged passport, so this shows very clearly that the police had orders from Stere I. Craciun, the drug trafficker, to send me to Romania and then kill me there, one more evidence that the police had ties with the criminal organization!

The police had told me on the 26th of January 2008 that somebody named Pavel, Romanian, as they showed me on the computer, had come into Canada with my passport, which was a lie. I didn't know that then, and I believed it. When I had lost my passport, it must have been April or May 2006 or 2007. Within 3 days, I went and declared that I had lost it. It was humanly impossible that someone had come into Canada within that time.

The police stopped me that day, one day after I purchased my ticket for Greece, the 6th April 2010, in order not to let me go to Greece. They would have claimed identity issues at the airport, of course, fearing I would take them to an international court. While they had me under police protection and doing all these things to me, claiming an identity issue was something totally out of the question. It was a joke.

The police officer said, "We're going to the police station." We went on Decarie Boulevard, Montreal, Quebec, Canada. They looked at me and said no, it's not me they are looking for. We went to my home, and they looked at my identity. They said, "Now I need to go to a place and get a paper from immigration, so if they stop me, they can create a password." I didn't go. It was lies. They wanted an identity issue to exist. It's straightforward. They couldn't be wondering if I am someone that looks like me using my identity, by the time I was under police protection and all these things they were doing to me. They wanted to create an identity issue so that they wouldn't let me leave for Greece. They would have stopped me at the airport, claiming anything. They have tried another couple of times to create identity issues again.

The officer told me that if I didn't go, they would keep stopping me again and again. Lately, the police have been setting up new death threats, with people calling me and asking me to repair their cars in Laval. I found these invitations suspicious and didn't go, because I didn't trust them, like today.

On April 11, 2010, around 12:15 a.m., while I went for a

drink at Cafeteria Restaurant Rouge with my brother George Margelis, the police instructed the person at the entrance not to let us in, using the excuse that he only allowed his regular customers. An argument broke out, and everyone turned to look. When I tried to take a picture of the scene for evidence, the man objected, saying he didn't want to appear in the photo, so I removed it.

About 20 minutes later, while walking downtown on Crescent Street, a group of people approached me aggressively, as if trying to start a fight. I left quickly to avoid them. These individuals were connected to the police and secret services.

Every time I sat down to write my report on my computer about my case with the police, they would begin banging loudly on the walls of neighboring apartments to terrify me. They even arranged for babies in other apartments to cry loudly at those times. If I attempted to sue them, they wanted to portray me as their enemy and would then try to frame me for murder.

They also staged people passing by, talking to themselves in front of me, as if to show me that this was how I would end up. If I ignored them, they would escalate by making the death threats feel very real. With these tactics, they were trying to alter my character, destabilize me, or even drive me into mental illness.

On April 21, 2010, while I was driving, I noticed people deliberately carrying yellow envelopes—the same kind I used to send my complaints, signaling to me that this was the issue. They didn't want my complaints to be published or reach the courts.

Later, while driving on De L'Épée Street at the corner of Ball, I stopped at a stop sign. On the other side, a green Mazda MX6—driven by someone working for the police, ignored his stop sign and attempted to drive straight into me. Fortunately, I saw it in time and stopped. Had I not been paying attention, he would have crashed into me.

Whenever they suspected that I was considering taking them to the Hague International Criminal Court, they would immediately begin horrifying me again and escalate the death threats.

On April 22 or 23, 2010, while drinking coffee at Place Vertu Shopping Center in Côte-Vertu, John Vlahakis, a man working for the police, tried to manipulate me. He asked me to admit that the reason I didn't have a girlfriend was that I wasn't talking to women enough. He wanted me to agree that it wasn't the police doing all these things to me. If I refused to go along with what they wanted, they would threaten me all over again.

On the 25th April 2010, when I left the country, they took from my valise one small nail cutter knife I had and one other multipurpose nail cutter knife I had also at the airport to scare me that they would put something on it to accuse me of something, maybe for murder. Weirdly, I found them when I returned to my drawer at my new apartment in Montreal. I had put it in a pocket of a pair of pants in my valise myself. The police have been trying to show me as a pedophile now by putting girls, a lot under the age of 18, coming in front of me, acting weird.

They started doing this lately quite often, hinting to me that now I'm a pedophile! Science fiction scenarios, they have been trying anything to excuse everything they have been doing to me. The police have been threatening that they won't let me leave the country. That's why when they stopped me on Jean Talon with my car the last time, 7 April 2010, they told me I had to go to a place, immigration, where Mrs. Catherine was, and that they would give me a kind of password, so if they stopped me on the road, I would say the password.

Hence, they know it's me and not someone using my identity from my stolen passport. It was a scam. Nobody has ever entered the country with my passport. It's also possible that nobody ever attempted to come into Canada with my passport. They did that in case I left the country, they would arrest me at the next airport, or even at the Montreal airport, and send me back to Canada, or not let me leave, claiming identity issues.

After 6 April 2010, when I obtained my ticket for Greece with Swiss Air, the Montreal police, along with their secret agents, took every measure to prevent me from traveling to Greece, hiring a lawyer there, and referring the matter to the International Criminal Court in The Hague. They were putting their agents, threatening to kill me, and others, showing me that they wouldn't let me go.

In the meantime, the police gave notice to the government of Canada to do something in order that I wouldn't be able to hire a lawyer in Greece and refer to the ICC in The Hague. The government of Canada managed to come into contact with the corrupted government of Greece under George Papandreou. It came to light that the Greek government, through its secret agents and police, intended to prevent me from hiring a lawyer. In the meantime, the government of Canada under Stephen Harper gave notice to the government of Iceland and told them to erupt the volcano in order that they would cause flight cancellations. As a result, my flight would never go to Greece.

The government of Iceland was involved in the conspiracy, and on 15 April 2010, they caused the volcanic eruption, canceling many flights, including mine, which would have only taken me to Zurich and not to Athens, Greece. While I noticed this conspiracy, I canceled my ticket with Swiss Air for the next two days and got a direct flight with Air Transat.

While the police and government noticed this, they put on Plan B, which was that the government of Greece wouldn't let me hire a lawyer at all in Greece by putting the Greek police and secret agents in place, not letting me hire a lawyer. And for the reason that I would attempt to see a lawyer, the Greek government, for punishment, always in conspiracy with the Canadian government, they would both block me from doing any business of mine or finding a job in order to turn me into a homeless person as punishment.

On 19 April 2010, after the eruption of the volcano in Iceland on 15 April 2010, which was a manipulated volcano eruption, a conspiracy of the government of Canada with the government of Iceland so that they wouldn't let me reach Greece, I canceled my air flight ticket with Swiss Air for 21 April 2010. I got a direct flight with Air Transat on 25 April 2010, and that's when I finally left.

I noticed that with Swiss Air, they wouldn't let me reach Greece but would return me to Canada at the airport, claiming volcano problems. This I understood from an email I sent to Swiss Air asking if my flight from Canada was going to Greece properly, and they answered that it would go properly from Montreal to Zurich. No answer from Zurich to Athens, Greece. When I asked, "What about from Zurich to Athens?" they answered, after I changed my air flight tickets, that due to the volcano in Iceland, there had been flight cancellations. Usually, when the plane can make it to Zurich, it leaves the volcano behind, and it can go to Athens.

While I was likely to be unable to reach Greece, I changed my air flight ticket and booked one with Air Transat, a direct flight. They didn't want me to hire a lawyer in Greece and refer to the International Criminal Court, The Hague! Also, on TV, I don't remember the TV channel, but they showed an airport that was empty due to the volcano in Iceland and a Canadian flag hanging out, showing me who was behind it. It was something unbelievable.

As soon as I obtained my ticket for Greece with Swiss Air for 21 April 2010, the Montreal police issued a notice to the Canadian government under Stephen Harper, and also to the Icelandic government. They agreed to erupt the volcano in Iceland on 15 April 2010, most probably by putting a bomb in the crater, which caused the cancellation of a lot of flights for those 10 days. I noticed this and changed my ticket to a direct flight with Air Transat for 25 April 2010.

The police, in order to show that the flight wasn't direct, landed the plane in Toronto with the excuse that more passengers would get on the plane. Usually, the aircraft had to travel from Toronto to Montreal and then to Greece (or, more likely, it went directly from Montreal to Athens, Greece, which I know from previous experiences). They did the opposite, and that's when I left.

Later in this report, I mention how the Montreal police or government placed an article on TV to downplay the Iceland volcano eruption—clear proof they were behind it and are now minimizing it foolishly. The public must be aware that the government may have intentionally triggered a volcanic eruption that they witnessed.

On the airplane, I noticed flight attendants were undercover agents monitoring me to see if I would sue them at the Hague International Criminal Court, as I intended. One secret service agent, disguised as a flight attendant, was also on my 14 July 2010 Air Transat flight from Athens to Montreal. While serving near me, he angrily squeezed and broke a plastic cup, staring at me with visible rage and nervousness.

# Chapter 4
# Greece (Summer, 2010)

On April 26, 2010, I was in Greece. The Montreal police and Canadian government had contacted Greek police and authorities, instructing them not to let me hire a lawyer for my case or take them to The Hague, nor allow me to remain in Greece out of fear of the case. On April 28, 2010, at 2:00 p.m., when I deposited cheques and cash at the bank, they asked me to sign a paper for the 100-dollar bills and made copies of them. When I asked if this was done for everyone, they said it was standard for 100-dollar bills. I later realized Greek police and secret services were cooperating with those in Montreal and Canada, preventing me from contacting a lawyer, blocking legal help, and harassing me. They had people walk near me while checking cell phones, some behaving unkindly after looking at me, and others in red jackets watching me, the same tactics used before by Canadian police and secret services.

On May 3, 2010, at 1:00 p.m., I went to the police station and spoke with the commander (Dikitis) and brigadier general (Taksiarhos). They denied knowing about my case, but they were lying. When I asked the brigadier general if foreign agents were behind what was happening to me, he replied, "If we had evidence, you would be like this now," showing me his hands in handcuffs, using it as an excuse for their actions. He tried to make me admit that Canadian police would have jailed me if I were involved in anything illegal. I told him they couldn't have evidence against someone innocent, especially when police in Canada had already admitted this on the phone and seen it themselves. He gave no answer, avoided continuing, and said I was wasting his time. He did not want me speaking further because it would expose their role in the conspiracy against me and their plans to stop me from hiring a lawyer to take my case against the Canadian police and government to The Hague.

At first, when I entered the building, I went, it must have been the 3rd floor, and asked for the commander (Dikitis in Greek) of the police station. They mentioned to me, "On the door to the left as you get on that floor from the stairs." I went inside and asked for the commander. He said, "It's me," a person around 40 years old. When I told him that they had been putting people who bother me and that they had been cooperating with the police of Canada, he panicked and said, "Oh, I don't know, I didn't know about anything. You should go and see the brigadier general downstairs!" He also told me that I should sue the Canadian police downstairs on the first floor. He was kidding me.

I went downstairs to the office. I noticed no tag on the door. He was there. I told him that there is one police case in Canada that I have and told him, "I know that you have been cooperating with the police in Canada. Why are you putting people bothering me all over the place?" (At that time, the police of Montreal and Greece were showing that it was only them doing everything in order to cover up the governments, but later on, after paying close attention to my case, it was obvious that the governments were involved also.)

He told me, "It's not us that are bothering you. How do you say that we put people who bother you?" I told him, "And who are these people? Is it possible that foreign agents have come here doing all kinds of things to me, and they are after me, bothering me?" Then he told me, "If we had evidence, you would have been like this now," and showed me with his hands the handcuffs!

He was trying now to create an excuse for their doings, trying to make it look like I had done something illegal. Science fiction scenarios. I told him, "Evidence you can have for someone that has done something illegal, not for someone that has nothing to do with anything." He did not want to continue the conversation and told me that I should not be wasting his time.

About 10 days later, on the 20th or 21st of May 2010, while they had been bothering me and applying psychological warfare to me, I went to see him again. He did not want to talk and again was telling me that I should not be wasting his time.

The police undercover were doing all these things to me with the involvement of the secret agents, as the district attorney mentioned to me when I saw him the third time, that I went to the

113

court on the 17th or 18th of June 2010. The government was involved as well. They started the psychological warfare because I wanted to hire a lawyer, and they did not like that, nor did they want me to stay in Greece, fearing that I would try to go to an international court and also publicize my case, maybe on a website. They were acting according to the orders they had from Canada, and they wanted me to go back there. It was the Greek police and government that took action, utilizing undercover agents and secret services, which the government was also involved in.

Government services were participating in the conspiracy, as I mention later in this report: the taxi license office, which was delaying for an unknown time the issuance of my taxi driving license; the ombudsman, who did not want to look into my case; the airport, which put the stamps on my passport and my mother's, not showing the arrows if we were departing or arriving; and on my mother's passport, they put a stamp on a later page so it would not be noticeable that we left together.

The district attorney mentioned the involvement of secret services, something the police had admitted: a fake demonstration they had staged at the airport for Palestine, just at the Air Transat checkpoint where I was supposed to get my boarding pass to leave on the 14th of July 2010. Also noticeable, when I shipped my complaint to the Ministry of Public Security on the 14th of June 2010, the ELTA postal office was showing that the track number did not exist. Also noticeable, the Greek consulate in Montreal refused to give me a copy of a mandate I had written there for my aunt in Greece to discontinue my phone service in Greece, which was related to my case.

Alexis Alexiou from a financial brokerage firm in Athens did not deny the fact that the Greek authorities had talked to him. However, afterwards, he tried to deny the truth, but it was noticeable that he was lying. They had also put everybody participating in the conspiracy against me, even my friends and relatives, and they had also blocked me financially so that I would not have any income at all, not letting me work anywhere nor do my own business, of course.

The police at my false arrest at the customs in Montreal on the 19th of November did not deny the fact when I told them that they feared I wanted to go to the European Court of Human Rights against Greece. It is noticeable that on the 29th or the 30th of April 2010, at night, I sent my documents to Giannis via email. We had talked at a café that afternoon about the case (I had noticed, though, that they had spoken to him already), to give it to his lawyer. After that, I noticed that different people were bothering me a lot more, just as they had in Montreal, Canada. They did not like the fact that I told my accountant to find his lawyer.

On Monday at noon, the 3rd of May 2010, I got mad seeing

the same things happening in Greece also, and then went straight to the police station to complain around noon. On Monday, the 3rd of May 2010, in the afternoon, I told my accountant Giannis to find me the lawyer he had told me about. Giannis did not answer my phone that afternoon, although I called him 4 times. When I called him from a pay phone outside around 7:00 p.m., he replied and told me that his lawyer does not handle these cases and that it is unclear whether I will win. I had noticed they had talked to him, of course, he would not find me a lawyer!

Everybody has admitted to everything. Police did not let me sue them. Giannis was telling me it is not clear if I am going to win! Then Giannis turned around immediately and told me, "Your income tax, your income tax, you have to file for your income tax, we need some papers." He is my accountant.

While driving down the road, they saw someone walking mad with a valise, showing me that I am angry, and I leave the country! At the same time, as soon as I got in my car, someone was on the same phone, wearing a red shirt, looking at me. The police of Greece are collaborating with the police of Montreal, Canada, in a joint effort, and the secret services are also working together.

The 4th of May 2010 at 11:00 a.m. I went to see a lawyer in a building, it's all lawyers, near the court. On the door to the left, weirdly, there was no name, no tag, no firm on the door. I found out the police had put someone walking around there on purpose so that I would ask him about a lawyer, and I did. He told me, "I know someone here." He introduced me to a lawyer, the one with no tag on the door, who told me, "You can't do a lot from here." He had already been talked to. The person left the place with a peculiar look, so I asked another lawyer in the same building, and he advised me to contact the Lawyers' Bar Association in Athens. I thanked him. The police of Greece, undercover and secret agents, have been following me discreetly.

May 5, 2010, at 1:30 p.m. I was drinking a coffee at a café with Sotiris, an old friend of mine who the police had also talked to, participating in the conspiracy, and Mike. While we were talking, people from the police were listening to the conversation. I told Sotiris and Mike that I would put a lawyer from Athens to claim the compensation from the police of Canada, the compensation I had asked for, and that the case could go to the International Criminal Court at The Hague.

After a while, while driving home on the road, I saw a military ambulance, and the soldier was looking at me. I understood what they meant: it's not gonna happen!

When I went to the building with the lawyers—must have been number 36, to see which lawyer told me I can't do anything from Greece, on the 4th or 5th of May 2010 at 9:00 p.m., I found out there was no sign on the door, lawyer's name, or law firm where I had gone to ask. People from the police, undercover, and secret agents were following me.

The 7th of May 2010 at 11:00 a.m. I visited the Lawyers' Bar Association on Akadimias Street in Athens to find a lawyer to review my case. They were following me, and when I got inside, the undercover people, secret services, were already on the ground floor. I hadn't gone upstairs yet. All the way to the right, I asked for a symvolos (advisor) lawyer. I asked first for a lawyer, and they told me to ask for an advisor to get advice. They told me they don't know anyone. I wandered through every office in the building for a lawyer or advisor. They pretended they didn't know, and they were trying to make me leave.

One person was waiting for me (waiting to see what I'm going to do) with a cell phone in hand, their signal. I told him that I'm trying to find a lawyer, I can't find one anywhere, and that nobody is telling me where I can find one, and that I have a case in Canada. I wanted to see what he was going to say, also, and he told me, "You can't find a lawyer here, and you should ask a relative who has a lawyer to ask him which lawyer takes these cases."

They had heard from my house in Canada when I told my mother that if the police did something to me, she would find a lawyer in Greece. They knew about that. They did not want me to see a lawyer at all, although I was at the Athens Lawyers' Bar Association. When I asked other offices, they told me that they didn't know where to find a lawyer and suggested I look in the Yellow Pages. One office told me the same thing.

While leaving the place, undercover agents and secret agents holding a yellow envelope were walking in front of me. The yellow envelope was the envelope that I was sending my complaints to the police in Montreal, Canada. At the same time, driving down the road in Athens around 1:30 p.m. I said to myself in the car out loud, "If they are doing these things, I will refer elsewhere to the court to complain." They heard that because they have a special microphone that records my conversations in my rented car. I knew that, and while driving, one big truck coming the opposite direction came close to me, and when he passed, he came all the way to the other lane, doing zig-zag, showing me they will crash into me, one more death threat.

The same day, while I was visiting a friend of mine, Mike, I noticed he had a second phone number as well. The police of Greece and secret agents had put a lady dressed in black, pretending she was crying. That's one more death threat. When I looked at her carefully, she changed her attitude and started smoking a cigarette.

The 8th of May 2010 at 12:15 a.m., on a Friday, and while I was driving home, the police stopped me to do an alcohol test.

Sotiris was with me, although they did not prevent anybody else; they stopped only me, hoping they would catch me with alcohol higher than the limit. I was with Sotiris. Of course, they didn't, and I was let go.

In my rented car, the police had placed secret microphones or were listening with other technology to my conversations. The vehicle I rented was an Opel Corsa. Every time I would say something they didn't like, they would start doing all kinds of things, like putting people in wheelchairs passing by to show me they would hurt me, do bodily injuries, and put me in a wheelchair. Others, with a small valise, showed that I was leaving the country. Other ladies dressed in black, noticeably looking at me with a glance, signaled that I was dead, to terrorize me.

I knew they had put the person there by the police because of the noticeable way they would behave and look at me. Due to the fact that I had been seeing too many of them, I noticed them very easily. Kostas had said in the email conversation that nobody had put any device in the car. Of course, I saw that the car had a hidden camera watching my facial expressions all day long, and it was also listening to my conversations.

The instrument panel, also known as the cluster, had been modified. While I was driving, when they figured out that I was thinking about something they didn't like, they would make the indicators, speedometer, and RPM indicator go all the way down, and the handbrake light would come on, telling me to stop thinking. At the same time, cars from the secret services were passing by, where a lot of times they had a license plate number passing me a message that if I attempted to go to the European Court of Human Rights in France or elsewhere to sue them, they would not let me.

On the 10th of May 2010, while I went to the DOY (Public Revenue Agency) at the Department Mitroou (Registry Department) to get a paper they needed at the unemployment office, they had put someone in front of me in line with the purpose of not letting me get in line and to start trouble, fearing that if I found a job in Greece then I would sue them or stay there. He came on purpose in front of me and pushed me to the side. The following person tried to do the same. When I told him that I had priority (at 10:45 a.m.), I got mad because they were not letting me get my paper. Then he stopped.

At around 2:00 p.m., I went to the OTE phone company to see Sotiris, another friend of mine who has been working for the police, who also tried to convince me that I should go and see the Eisageleas (District Attorney) and say my life is in danger. I did tell Sotiris that I should tell the District Attorney everything regarding my case if the District Attorney looks after these cases and could help me out. He told me, "Tell him that your life is in danger."

So, I saw Mike, a friend of mine, coming down the road. All of a sudden, he was told to pass at the time and told me we would go for a coffee, but now he is busy! Hinting that because I got mad at the police and I will find a lawyer to sue them, he doesn't want to drink a coffee with me, no friends! Of course, they had isolated me from everybody and everything.

Mike is working at a hotel; he is the manager at the bar. When I applied for a job, I asked Mike to hire me, and I was willing to do any job. He told me that now he is hiring waiters and waitresses, and I mentioned to him any job I would do. He told me "Eh" and moved his hand, letting me understand they told him not to give me a job. He was able to hire me within days. I understood and didn't tell him anymore.

The previous day, a friend of Mike and his neighbor, Thanasis, a person working for the police and secret services, also told me that he has a lawyer, the President of the Lawyers Bar Association, who is going to tell me what's the story happening with my case. Basically, he would tell me that I can't do anything and that I have to end up begging for food as punishment from the police and government because I tried to hire a lawyer to look into my case. He said that on the 10th of May 2010, the next day, I would meet him at Mike's house to go to the place where the lawyer is.

What they had done was talk to the lawyer beforehand to

discourage me, participate that way in the conspiracy, and then make it look like the lawyers don't get involved in my case because he told them so, and not the police with the government. Of course, I didn't go, it was a conspiracy.

I have recently discovered that they have installed microphones and cameras in my home in Greece. On the 11th of May 2010, at 9:20 a.m., when I woke up, Sotiris called me immediately after at 9:24 a.m. to tell me that I should go and connect my telephone. He works at the telephone company, which means they saw me waking up, they had hidden cameras in my house. When I walked out the previous day, I noticed someone fixing and combing his hair noticeably, just as I did in my home.

In the summer of 2009, around the 10th of August, when my brother George Margelis came to Greece, I noticed the police had put someone (a secret agent) to go out of my house to pretend he was looking for me to scare me, make me leave the country. I told my brother and my mother about it on the phone while talking with her (phones are tapped).

In September 2009, the police in Greece sent more people to come and scare me when I saw three people pretending they were looking for me near my house, when I told my mother again on the phone that it's not sure that it's safe here and that I saw some weird, suspicious people around again.

By the time I was under police protection, these individuals had been sent by the Greek secret services. I noticed it was not from the drug traffickers, but that it was something else, which at that time I was trying to figure out what was happening.

I obtained a phone number of a lawyer in Athens from the internet, and on May 10, 2010, while I was at a café, I called him from that location around 3:00 p.m. He answered the phone, and I told him I'm having a case with the police, that they are making death threats, and so on. He was telling me "Yes, yes" all the time and was interested to sue them. I made an appointment for around the 11th or 12th of May 2010.

At around 3:00 p.m. on May 11 or 12, 2010, I visited the law firm in Athens. On my way there, the police and government of Greece were putting people in wheelchairs, showing me that's what they will do to me. I saw lawyer Xrisanthis.

Mr. Xrisanthis told me to sit down in a room on the left where there was a long table. We sat down. I noticed they had talked to him already. I told him everything that was happening, and he told me we don't have proof that the police are putting death threats against you, nor for anything else. If the police had caused bodily injury, then we would have proof (he said maybe broken legs or hands or perhaps a broken face!).

On the phone, he had told me, "Yes, yes," he was interested in suing them. Now, all of a sudden, he was telling me this. His phone, of course, is tapped, we can listen to the conversation we had, of course.

Once I noticed the police and government had talked to him already, fearing heavy retaliation in the form of torture from the police and secret agents of Greece, because I went to tell the lawyer to sue them, I couldn't talk to him as I wanted. I understood he was not going to handle my case, and I had to be careful. I also made a joke of it, and I also pretended and asked him at the end what he thinks, where there was nothing to think about—I just wanted to sue them and look and proceed with my case I have with the police of Montreal, Canada, to sue them also.

He told me his partner was going to review the case, and I gave him my SD (Secure Digital) chip, which contained all the information related to this report. He didn't feel comfortable taking the chip; he didn't want to take it, but he took it at the end. I was hoping maybe they would get to do something.

I also informed Xrisanthis that we should send a letter to the Government of Canada, detailing what they have been doing to me and requesting compensation. He said, "And what do you expect— that they will give you money?" I told him they have to compensate me. If they won't, we go to the Hague International Criminal Court or wherever we are supposed to. He did not want to talk about the case but was giving me to understand, without speaking, not to continue the conversation!

He did not ask me for money—no receipt, nothing like that, which he was supposed to ask for once the visit was done. We were talking for about half an hour. He also told me not to go to another lawyer because they will take my money for nothing! Of course, they would have been talked to, not to do anything. I understood that they couldn't let a lawyer sue them.

When I was about to leave, we went towards his office. Opposite the conference room, on the left, was a kitchen. He showed me an email where I had asked for an appointment.

Later, at 7:00 p.m. the same day, the police put on the news on TV that a person, 35 years old, was shot with a machine gun outside of Athens, and he was a person who had a case from last year! The person talking on the TV, his name was Giorgos (my uncle's name!). This was a death threat directed at me.

On the 14th of May 2010 at 11:00 a.m., I applied for work at a place. They had already been talked to—I noticed the undercover agents had already told them not to hire me, because they didn't want me to find a job and stay there.

On May 10, 2010, I visited the unemployment office to apply for a job, look for work, and obtain my unemployment card. They asked me what jobs I do and told me that if they had something, they would let me know. The police did not want me to go there, creating scenes to prevent me from registering.

When I went to the Tax Department (Public Revenue Agency), they tried to make me start a conflict with someone. And when I was in the OAED (Manpower Employment Organization) unemployment office, they put some people near me behaving strangely. They gave me an unemployment card dated May 10, 2010, where I noticed that the police and secret agents had also spoken to them and instructed them not to find me any job.

On the 12th or 13th of May 2010, a person I had known for many years, Mike, who was working for the secret services of Greece, and another person—his neighbor, also working for them, whose name Mike told me was Thanasis, told me he was going to find me a job because he knew the person at a car dealer. This place sells new Renault cars.

On the morning of May 13th or 14th, 2010, we accompanied Thanasis to the dealership. I found out they were only kidding me. The manager of the garage, someone named Tasos, was joking, saying that we had an economic crisis. They had already talked to him, and he was just acting. Also, one lady from the police got a coffee from the coffee machine and spilled it all over, showing me "the coffee is spilled" and not to bother.

Thanasis was joking around at the places, trying to show me they would never let me work again, and that I would end up begging for money and food because I went to find a lawyer to sue the police and the government of Greece.

He then sent me to Toyota. We went there with Thanasis, but the police and secret agents had already spoken to the manager. He told me, "We don't need anybody now." When I asked him for an application form, he told me he didn't have application forms, but that I should bring my own paper with my experience and knowledge, and just give it to the office.

At the same time, while we were talking, they brought in a customer who pretended to have a problem with the car alarm, giving the mechanic the remote control to check the car, a job I was doing in Montreal, to bother me and make me feel bad.

Thanasis was just taking me all over the place to show me that they wouldn't be giving me work anymore, to make me feel horrible and depressed. They made me cry.

The police of Greece, undercover as the police admitted, and secret agents, as the district attorney mentioned, were also involved. They have been applying psychological warfare to me every day. Whenever they noticed I was thinking of suing them, they started putting death threats, putting people in wheelchairs driving in front of me, and people with no hands or no legs, horrifying and scaring me.

On May 15th, 2010, while driving around 6:00 p.m., I showed Mike a person in a wheelchair in front of me, I have it on picture, and told him that's what the police and secret services have been doing. They did that because they saw me looking at the currency exchange rate at Alfa Bank, interpreting that I was going to exchange dollars for euros to sue them either myself or through an international court.

The police and secret agents in Greece have told my friends—one person is Sotiris—to act according to their interests. One time, they tell them, "Talk to Christos (me)," after they tell them, "Don't talk to Christos, now try to make him spend money." They used to do this with Mike, or try to make him say things that show the police were not at fault. The same applies to Mike, he also participated in the conspiracy and was working for the police.

Now they have placed a big blue garbage depositor next to the existing green one in front of my house to make me feel bad.

On the 17th of May 2010, at around 6:45 p.m., fearing again that I would try to sue them, they put another death threat from the TV station ET3, where George (my uncle's name) is the person talking again, saying the news that a person 22 years old was shot with a gun with one bullet for something related 2 years ago!

Just an hour earlier, I had sent an email to Ted Write from the Westmount Legal Clinic, a person working for the police in Montreal also, where we were negotiating on email for a certain amount of money that the police would give me to go there, telling him that these people—undercover agents, are bothering me continuously. They were applying psychological warfare, calling them my neighbors!

At 8:20 p.m., while I was going home, Padelis, a mentally ill person, passed by in front of my house, talking out loud to himself, hinting that if I did something, he would be the one to attack me. They were thinking maybe I would go to the court to sue them myself or to an international court.

The police have even put my relatives against me, working for them, like my Aunt Patapia. When I went to her home on the 18th or 19th of May 2010, around 2:00 p.m., she was telling me that I should go to a lawyer, one that she knows! Of course, they had spoken to him; the police and secret services had contacted all lawyers and talked to them. She said I should tell him to check why they are following me and harassing me. Of course, that's not the subject. They do that because they don't want me to sue them, also because I went to hire a lawyer to look into my case, and also, they wanted me to go to Canada.

They didn't want me to hire a lawyer to look into my case I

had with the police of Montreal, Canada, nor stay in Greece. The way the case was, fearing international courts or whatever else could happen, they had to keep watching me. When I went and asked a lawyer, they unleashed brutal psychological warfare on me and blocked me financially (from doing any business and the job market) so that I didn't have any income.

When I came to Greece, they had already started harassing me, and they were showing me that I should go back to Canada, something I didn't want. My aunt told me to ask the lawyer why they are applying psychological warfare on me, simply because now they wanted to create a scenario that I had done something illegal, and that's why the police and secret services are doing these things to me, which was the only way to excuse their actions to me. Of course, if somebody read this book, they would understand that very easily. They wanted to excuse themselves.

I should also try to find a job doing delivery or so, somewhere far away! She also told me, "You can't go against the police or the government, and you are not gonna find the end of this story," something I had said in my rental car.

They have also placed a camera in the car. Her son-in-law, George, would get very mad when I would talk about the case. They wouldn't let me talk about it! My aunt also told me how I can prove that the police are sending people after me, and that maybe it's my fantasy!

On the 19th of May 2010, around 2:00 to 3:00 p.m., I went to see Kostandinos, the owner of a retailer of electronics and home appliances. He kind of panicked. I told him, "Hi Dino, how are you doing? If he has done any sales of remote starters," he tells me, "Oh, I have to go now," and turns his back to me and leaves. He was told by the secret services not to do any business with me, nor hire me to work at his shop.

It was noticeable sometimes Kostantinos would call me on my cell phone pretending he wanted to repair his remote starter on his car, and after, at the end of the conversation, he would say, "Ok, we will see." The police and secret services had told him to do so, kidding me.

In the summer of 2009, I noticed that although Kostantinos had asked me the previous year (2008) to bring remote starters to sell in Greece, when I arrived with them in 2009, he refused, offering strange excuses. Greek secret services had influenced him and others I worked with not to do business with me, aiming to push me out of Greece and back to Canada because of the case.

Around late May 2009, his business advisor, Vasilis, mentioned a case involving someone in Montreal's Parc Extension, where I had lived, connected to the wife of a man involved in illegal activities, hinting at trouble. This was strange and not my case, but somehow related. When I asked how he knew about Montreal and Parc Extension, he said he had lived there until about 1982 before moving to Greece.

They have been making death threats against me if I see a lawyer to sue them, even on my way to the lawyer in Athens, and after that, all the time. They have been putting people on the road everywhere doing strange faces at me, odd facial expressions, behaving and acting weird, applying psychological warfare every second passing, all day long, trying to drive me crazy, create health damage, and mental problems. And they have been putting people pretending to be begging for money or food, showing me that's how I will be soon.

On the 23rd of May 2010, at 8:30 p.m. news, they showed on Alter TV that a murderer had killed a taxi driver and he would do so again. The person they drew in the sketch looked like me! It looked the same as the sketch they had shown me at the police station on 7035 Parc Avenue, Montreal, during my false arrest on January 26, 2008, which I described at the beginning of this report. That's because I said that I would be buying a taxi and driving it in Athens. They did not want that, as they wanted me to leave the country, to end up begging for money and food there or here.

Last week, once I had mentioned the fact that I would go and see the eisageleas (district attorney) at court, the police, with the involvement of the secret agents, launched a massive psychological warfare against me. Every second, people were passing by in front of me acting weird—scratching their head or their nose, laughing the way I do, pretending they were talking to themselves, passing me messages continuously that I'm dead, that I will be begging for food to survive, while the public was aware of the scene and everybody was watching, as they had talked to everybody.

They were putting people pretending to be begging for money or food, showing me that's how they will turn me into; walking handicapped people, others in wheelchairs, or others fishing, showing me that's how they will turn me into—that's how I will have to survive, by fishing. They wouldn't even give me food because I tried to hire a lawyer to investigate my case and file a lawsuit. And that it's a matter of time before I become like this.

They are trying to make me feel desperate, or even drive me crazy, create mental problems, or put me into depression. Also, they were putting on the radio the ad that if you feel like you want to commit suicide, call this number, knowing that when I'm listening to the station, by the secret microphones they have already placed in the car or other technology, they were advertising this all the time. As long as I was in Greece, they would put it maybe 15 times a day. The police have been doing this psychological warfare with the secret agents. Also, they didn't want me to go to the eisageleas (district attorney) to testify and complain, because there could be an investigation. Then maybe I would be able to sue them (something that I thought, which was not the case at all).

On the 23rd of May 2010, while I called Sotiris for a coffee at 12:00 p.m. at Flocafe, I asked him if I should go to the district attorney. He told me yes, I should, and also told me, "Don't feel desperate, you will find a job. Look also in the local newspaper or ask the mayor." When I tried to find a local newspaper, they had disappeared them all!

At 3:30 p.m. on May 23, 2010, I went to see my aunt, Pagona. The police had also spoken to them about participating in the conspiracy. My mother's sister was at a village; my cousin Christos was there also, my aunt's son, and his sister Katerina with her husband. My cousin Christos and his mother were trying to convince me, after I told them what was happening, to go and see her cousin Eugenia, a notary who had her office somewhere at the back side of the courtroom, a person that I did not know at all and had never heard about. They tried to convince me that I should not go to the district attorney at court because I should be advised by her first! She is a notary; she doesn't know about these cases anyway. I understood that the police and secret services had also spoken to them. It wasn't very sensible for me to go. He told me the district attorney is for small things only!

I noticed they did not want me to go to the district attorney because that could mean a court case, and maybe I could sue the police! (Something I was hoping, but it was not the case at all, finally.) My cousin and aunt are in a conspiracy.

When I came back home and went to Mike, he told me, "Let's go to a place, I want to get something." When we went there, he showed me a small market store that was for sale and told me that if I wanted to buy it! That way, I would spend my money there, rather than in lawsuits! Of course, it would end with me closing the store and losing my money because they would tell everybody not to come to the store.

The psychological warfare they had been doing to me the previous days had now changed their behavior, and they started behaving better.

On May 25, 2010, at 11:00 a.m., I visited the district attorney at the court. He was on the second floor at door 5, a person around 55 years old. I told him that there is a significant case happening and that the police, because of this, were applying psychological warfare to me now. I told him what was happening, and he told me, "OK." He told me I have to sue them. He can't do anything; I have to find a lawyer.

When I handed him my file with my 36-page report, he did not accept it. He told me, "I don't know English." I didn't tell him it was in English.

While I was telling him what had been happening in my case and that the police of Montreal, Canada, tried to charge me with murder, he told me, "They didn't attempt to charge you with murder. There was nobody dead; how would they charge you with murder?"

While I understood that they had talked to him also, I pretended that it was OK and didn't continue talking about it, fearing heavy retaliation in the form of torture from the Greek police and the secret agents, since they were listening to everything.

I left. Walking downstairs, I saw several lawyers all pretending to take my case. It was very noticeable they were there on purpose, participating in the conspiracy to stall the case or just take my money and do nothing. Of course, while they had blocked me financially, what they wanted to do was leave me with no money and no income either. Of course, they wouldn't do anything with my case. I noticed that, and after looking for a while, I said forget it and left.

It was something out of the question. The police and secret services of Greece had blocked me financially (from doing any business or getting a job) so that I would not have any income. It was remarkable—one time, a person who was selling CDs with songs on the road, I called him and asked if I could do the same job. I asked him where he got the CDs from so I could go and buy them to sell. He was kidding me; he told me, "in Athens somewhere," and then he continued to tease me again. The answer was: forget about it.

Another time, although I knew they wouldn't let me do any job, I saw a person selling lottery tickets out on the streets. I approached him and told him that I had no job and that I wanted to sell some lottery tickets as well. The person was kidding me, and at the end told me to get lost, that they wouldn't let me do any job. After a while, a truck passed by with a big sign saying "boofos"—in Greek it means "stupid." They were calling me stupid because I tried to get a job to do.

After all this, I decided to go and get a license to drive a taxi. I passed the exams on the 1st of June 2010, and they told me (the teacher Giannis from the driving school) that in order to get my license, they had to check my background from the Canadian courts (to get a paper stating that I don't have a criminal record). It might take a month or even six months, in other words, I would never get my license!

Of course, the ones at the prefecture taxi license office, when I went to ask when I should be getting the license (I went more than two times between the 3rd and 10th of June 2010 in the morning towards noon), avoided telling me and let me understand to forget it, that they would not be giving me any license. This is what Giannis told me, participating in the conspiracy. He said that's what they told him at the prefecture taxi license office, where I had done my exams and where they issue the taxi driving license.

The owner of the driving school, Giannis, of course, knows better than anyone else that I didn't need any paper from Canada. On the 9th or 10th of June 2010, I went to the Nomarxia at the prefecture taxi license office around noon. The person in charge, Paulos, told me he had sent the request to the Ministry of Justice to get one paper (a paper that I don't have a penal record), and also that he was waiting for the police to give him the new driver's license.

There is no request or anything needed from Canada; it's clearly the national papers they need. After I went there more than a couple of times and he did not want to tell me when I should be getting my taxi license, I asked him to make it written what he was telling me. He finally told me what was happening.

The police of Greece had told them to create some reason or excuse in order not to give me the license and told Giannis to lie and convince me that I had to wait for a paper from the government of Canada stating that I hadn't been charged with anything criminal, something they could have kept saying forever, just to continue causing financial damage to me once I had no source of income. In that case, they could say month after month that Canada was sending no papers, so I would never get my taxi license!

Around June 8, 2010, I consulted with a couple of lawyers to consider suing the police and the Greek government. I was hoping I would find someone they hadn't talked to, and I found out that the police had already spoken to them all beforehand. Of course, I left; they didn't want to look into my case and pretended they didn't handle these cases. It was very noticeable, they had been instructed not to deal with my case at all, and they would say so even before we sat down to talk.

On Monday, the 7th, or Tuesday, the 8th of June 2010, I attempted to send a fax of my case to the Citizens Advocate/Ombudsman office in Athens, which handles citizens' rights, addressed to Hatsigianni Mexi. I went there in person, finally, from June 8th to 10th, 2010, around 1:00 p.m., and they didn't review or handle my case. The fax would never go through; when I tried to send it from my home, it just rang forever. We had a conversation over email before I went.

When I tried to call the Ministry of Justice around the 10th of June 2010 from my home to request a paper regarding my taxi license, the certificate that shows I don't have a penal record, once I noticed that the taxi license office would delay it for an unknown time, as they didn't want me to get my taxi driving license, the phone would just ring on any of their numbers. I tried maybe six or seven numbers, but there was no answer.

When I called a number I had elsewhere, they answered, but they were not the ones to provide information about that paper. The ones who could tell me were the Ministry of Justice in Athens, but they were not answering. On June 11 and 14, 2010, I visited the Ministry of Justice in person to obtain the certificate. They did not want to give me the certificate, finding excuses, and kept telling me that they would call me. I told them that I needed it, and after they said they would send it to the taxi license office, they still refused to give me the paper. The police and government of Greece are not only listening to my phones but also manipulating them!

{This report, until this point, was sent upon my complaint to the Ministry of Public Security, Police Department, Athens, Greece.}

On June 14, 2010, I sent a registered letter from the ELTA Post Office with my complaint to the Ministry of Public Security, track number RE826027665GR. The other registered envelope I sent was to immigration lawyer Boyd Campbell for asylum, track number RE826027679GR, addressed to Montgomery, Alabama, USA. On the same day, I sent a registered letter to the Prefecture Taxi License Office, requesting the date they would issue my taxi driving license, with tracking number RE826027651GR.

After I sent the registered mail, the complaint to the Police Ministry of Public Security in Athens and the letter to the Taxi

License Office on the 14th of June 2010, asking when they would issue my taxi driving license, they called me within two days to say that the permit was ready.

On June 4, 2010, I sent an email to the Citizens Advocate (Ombudsman) in Athens, Greece, informing him that the Greek police were not allowing me to hire a lawyer, as they were in communication with the lawyers. I asked him to investigate the case, as it involves a police matter that originates in Canada and extends into an intergovernmental conspiracy.

The Ombudsman told me that I should go there and fill out my application or send it by fax. I tried to send it by fax, but the fax wouldn't work. From June 8 to 10, 2010, I visited around noon. The address was Hatzigianni Mexi 5, Athens, Greece. It was a building with two security guards at the entry. I went to the third floor using the elevator, then turned right from the entrance.

Downstairs, on the street where you park your car, there was paid parking where you could purchase a time card at the small market store. I went inside and, after talking with a lady around 40 years old, I noticed that they had already spoken with her. She didn't want to hear the case and told me that I should go into a room, fill out my application, and give it to them. The room she referred to was to the left, a few steps ahead, and then to the right. It was pretty big.

I took the paper, wrote what was happening, and when I went to give it to them and talk about the case, they wanted me to leave and not discuss it. They didn't want me to sit down at all. When I told them to take my application, a person in his 40s, sitting at the right desk, informed me that they couldn't investigate the case and that I should send a registered letter to the police and the Taxi License Office as a complaint. Only after they responded should I return to them.

I also showed him the receipt the driving school had given me (which has since disappeared). It stated 80 euros, but I told them that the school had charged me 250 euros. He replied that something was amiss there.

The owner of the driving school, participating in the conspiracy, charged me more than he should have. He did not look into my case but was simply trying to make me leave, and refused to take the application I had filled out. The Ombudsman was very nervous about my case. He told me to send a complaint to the police and the Taxi License Office and to get a response from them first. The police and government had instructed him not to handle my case.

On the 18th of June 2010, while I was going into Athens in the morning, a truck pretending that the road was narrowing came toward my side at high speed, and another car coming from the left almost caused an accident while I was traveling at 100 kilometers per hour. I was going to get my taxi license.

When I returned home, I found a cat with a large wound on its side near the leg, as if cut with a knife, walking in my yard, I captured a picture of it. They continued issuing death threats by approaching my house and firing a gun; they repeated this a few days later.

During the email conversations I had with immigration lawyer Boyd Campbell from the Immigration Law Center in Montgomery, Alabama, he initially intended to take my asylum case in the United States. However, the police of Greece and the government of Montreal, Canada, intervened and told him not to take it. Later, he demanded $10,000 just to advise and communicate with me. Initially, Boyd Campbell had asked me to fill out and send the application form to him via email on June 9, 2010, after which he would determine whether to handle my case. After the authorities intervened, he created the excuse on June 15, 2010, that he wanted $10,000 to advise and speak with me, in order to avoid taking my case.

On June 14, 2010, I emailed him to inform him that I had shipped the application form and asked where to deposit the funds. I wanted to talk to him over the phone, but then he told me that he wanted $10,000 just to advise me and to speak with me. He did this because he did not want to talk on the phone, the phone conversations are recorded, and it would be noticeable that he took part in the conspiracy. He also mentioned that one of his bank accounts, where I could deposit the funds, is in Birmingham.

Undercover agents in Greece first showed me that I was lucky to have found a lawyer in the United States. However, after a few days, they revealed that I was no longer so fortunate, as they had spoken with him.

Under conditions of extreme fear and panic, and with all these things happening, I decided to go to the United States, where I know the language, to apply for asylum. I did not know that I could live in a European country as a Greek citizen; I found out about this afterward (anyway, it would have been the same story in Europe as well).

In mid-June 2010, while I was under persecution from the global governments, I decided to go to the United Nations office in Athens for refugees to explain what was happening. The Greek government notified the person responsible there not to accept me. I went in my rented car, and when I saw the building, the person was already outside waiting for me. The big gate was closed and locked.

I told him that I was having a big problem with the Greek and global governments and that I was under persecution for a case I had with the police in Montreal, Canada. He told me, "Get out of here, I can't do anything." I understood that he had already been spoken to.

Meanwhile, as I was heading toward the United Nations building, a group of cars and motorbikes from the Greek secret agents followed me. At some point, I lost my way, and one person in her vehicle was left behind me. I asked her for directions, and she told me, ironically, that I was totally lost. I understood that all those following me were indeed secret agents, which was also noticeable from the way they were driving.

On June 22, 2010, around 11:00 a.m., I went to apply for a job at another location. I filled out my application, and very close to me, a security guard was standing and showing me his gun in a very noticeable way in its case. I understood what he meant, they would never hire me, and that I was "dead."

The police had sent their agents and had instructed my neighbors to have their kids pretend to play and scream right outside my house, applying psychological pressure. They were using psychological warfare on me all day, everywhere I went, every second. They were continuously passing messages that I would soon be begging for money and food, threatening me, and making people behave around me as if I were already doomed.

They have told every single person I know—friends, relatives, anyone, not to associate with me, in order to leave me isolated. Even when I met someone, they would look at me and behave as if I would soon be begging for money and food.

They continue putting death threats to me in various ways, as I describe in this report, including placing people—primarily women dressed in black, showing me that I am "dead," and threatening that they will hurt me badly by putting handicapped people in wheelchairs or others with broken hands or legs in front of me, all because I tried to find a lawyer to look into my case and file a lawsuit.

I obtained my taxi license to drive in Athens on June 24, 2010. I went in person to places in Athens that rent and sell taxis. At one place, the name was George. The person I was talking to, who seemed to be the owner, was George, a man around 30 years old. I went to his place about three times, around noon, from the 17th of June 2010 until the 5th to 7th of July 2010.

The first time I went there, I asked him to explain how the taxi works, the expenses, and everything related to it. He told me he would rent me a taxi. I knew, of course, that the police and government had talked to him, but once he told me he would rent one, I did not worry. It seems, however, that they were only pretending. When the Greek police realized I was going to rent it, once I went to get my taxi license for Athens on the 24th of June 2010, I received it, and then they told him not to rent it to me. He refused, saying he did not have a taxi.

He even told me this over the phone when I called him toward the end of June 2010. Two more people were working in that place. It was a small building with two offices and possibly two or three taxi vehicles in front, plus one that seemed almost totaled, likely showing me what would happen if I rented it.

From around the 17th of June 2010 until the end of June 2010, when I went to see George to rent the taxi, I was receiving threats from the Greek police and secret agents. They warned me that if I attempted to rent and drive the taxi, I would get into an accident and not survive. They were placing accidented taxi cars close to me, or others with freshly painted bumpers or sides, as a warning.

George, of course, participating in the conspiracy, was telling me he would rent me a taxi for the simple reason that they didn't want the cameras and microphones recording the conversations to show that he didn't rent me one. After I got my license for Athens and told him to give me a taxi to work, he told me that he didn't have one. Most probably, they thought that I wouldn't rent one, fearing the threats they were putting on me that I would get into an accident. However, it was a matter of life and death: if I didn't go to work with the taxi, I would end up with no money, no income, and would have to beg for money and food.

That's what they wanted to do to me, as they were blocking me financially. I had no choice but to go and see what would happen.

Just before I got my taxi license, George started telling me, during our conversations, that if I got into an accident, I would have to pay for the damage with my own money, something he hadn't told me before. When I asked him, "Doesn't the taxi have insurance? If I have an accident, shouldn't the insurance pay?" he told me only if it was the other side's fault, and that it would be hard to prove. Most probably, they wanted me to drive the taxi, get into an accident, and pay for it myself. The conversation took place in his office. I went to every place in person; nobody would rent me a taxi.

Over the phone, whenever I tried to rent one, I couldn't. They had talked to the owners beforehand; they knew which newspapers I was looking at, and they would notice me and tell me they didn't have a taxi to rent. In a couple of cases where it seemed they hadn't spoken to the owners or hadn't noticed me, they contacted them afterward. When I called a second time to see them, they would tell me they didn't have a taxi available or give some other excuse. The phone numbers I got were from a newspaper, and I called them from my phone.

I also visited a place called Christos Ilias around the 21st of June 2010, and I went again from the 5th to the 7th of July 2010 in the afternoon. They sell taxis, and he told me to buy half a taxi to be a half-owner. He wanted more than half the money as a deposit at the same time I was receiving serious threats from the police and secret agents of Greece—threats that they would get me into an accident, as they almost did a couple of times, and that they wouldn't let me work with the taxi.

Buying it was complicated and risky. Under normal conditions, it would have been something straightforward. Most probably, I would have lost the money, and they wouldn't have let me sell it afterward. They were also putting threats in place that I wouldn't be able to rent my parents' house, even with their authorization, in case I went to live in the village at my grandmother's house, where they were threatening that they wouldn't let me live either.

I was scared to go to Canada because the police and secret services there would be doing the same, especially now that I had tried to sue them in an international court. Also, I had exposed them in Greece, while they had to inform the police and government of Greece about my case in April 2010 and told them to plot with them not to let me hire a lawyer to look into my case, and also force me to go back to Canada, fearing the case.

When I sent my complaint to the Ministry of Public Security, Police Headquarters, Athens, on the 14th of June 2010, I received it around the 23rd of June 2010. Things were worse, they were showing me "I'M DEAD." They did a trick: they put on the news, showing on the Greek TV stations for one week, that someone had sent an envelope with a bomb inside to the Ministry of Public Security in Athens.

If somebody paid attention, there was no explosion! While showing the Ministry of Public Security, they were passing messages to me that they would crucify me and torture me. They were calling my complaint a bomb, and that it "exploded" and killed one police headquarters. They said it was an act of terrorism, and by the time the whole Greek parliament knew what that was, they were all together condemning the terrorist act. I saw some ministers very mad, also!

I was trying to negotiate with Ted Write, a person working for the police in Canada, for a certain amount of money in exchange for my visit, so I wouldn't end up with no money and no income, as they would block me financially if I went there. Under these circumstances, this is what I tried to do.

The conversation is written in an email. We called that amount "INSURANCE," which Ted Write never confirmed that they would give me, and people working for the police of Greece showed me that I would not get anything. The police and government of Canada were fearing that I might sue the police and government of Greece in court myself, and that's why Ted Write was negotiating a certain amount of money to give me, called insurance, on email. When they noticed that I would be going to court, Ted Write sent me an email saying, "Call me right now."

The conversations we had with Ted Write on the phone were noticeable. While he noticed that I would not be able to sue the government of Greece, he didn't confirm anything, and in the last email, he didn't answer. At the same time, people working for the police and secret agents were showing me the same thing, that I would not be getting anything. This occurred around June 17, 2010.

I visited the District Attorney on June 17 or 18, 2010, around noon, at Door 5. I told him my case with the police. The District Attorney did not investigate my case, told me to sue them, and also mentioned the involvement of secret agents. Of course, the police were doing these things and directing the operations; they admitted to that when I went to complain at the beginning of May 2010, two times at the police station, and talked to the Brigadier General I describe in this report, the 3rd of May 2010 and the 20th or 21st of May 2010.

The government, of course, was involved also. It was noticeable with the airport, the taxi license office, the Ombudsman, the Ministry of Justice, and other places. The police were always using undercover people, and they had put everybody conspiring with them. They had also put my friends and relatives.

The police of Greece conspired with the police of Montreal, Canada, where the governments were also involved. They had put everybody to participate in the conspiracy against me. By that time, the District Attorney would not investigate the case, and they were talking to all the lawyers not to handle my case. Of course, under these circumstances, it was impossible to file a lawsuit.

On the 27th or 28th of May 2010, I tried to file a lawsuit myself. I went to the court, to the office where lawsuits are filed, and entered the court through the right upstairs, to the first office. They knew that I was going, of course, they had cameras in my house everywhere, watching every move I made. I went and told them that I wanted to file a lawsuit; I tried to sue the Ministry of Public Security. I noticed they had talked to them. They told me, "Leave your envelope and go." I looked to see a lawsuit form to fill out. They wouldn't give me anything. Of course, I couldn't leave my envelope just like that—this is not how to file a lawsuit. So, I took my envelope and left.

The police of Canada had notified the police of Greece, where the governments were also involved, to cooperate with them. In the summer of 2009, when I was in Greece, it was noticeable that they would put people there close to me who looked a lot like me, which was finally from the police as police protection. I noticed that around July–August 2009.

One day, after my brother George Margelis came to Greece, around the 10th of August 2009, a person came to my neighborhood near my house, pretending he was looking for someone or something. But he was actually there for me. When I went to the police station around the 18th to 21st of August 2009, around noon, I told them about my case and that I had seen someone suspicious pretending to be looking for someone in my neighborhood. I asked what I should do if I saw him again. They told me, "We will bring him to the police station and check his identity."

A few months later, I realized that they had already been aware of my case beforehand, having previously conspired with the Montreal, Canada, police. Also, the undercover police officer that I talked to looked at me with a kind of surprise, it was noticeable behavior. At that time, I didn't pay attention; of course, they had sent him. That person did not come around my house again.

That person and others that I saw were sent by the police and secret services of Greece to scare me into going back to Canada for police protection. I also saw some people, who must have been there since June 2009, in the afternoon at a café, acting suspiciously as they looked and talked on their cell phones, pretending to look at me suspiciously.

After careful examination, I noticed that they were not affiliated with the criminal organization; they stopped and, after a while, disappeared. These were similar behaviors to those people working for the police in Canada often employed. I couldn't understand what was happening, who had sent them, or why they were doing these things. It seemed that they could be police officers from Greece, but I wondered how that could be and why they would be doing this.

I found the answer to what was happening in the winter of 2009 in Canada, after the conversation I had with police investigator Fred Charbonneau. When I went to see him at the police station mentioned in this report, I mentioned it. In the summer of 2010, they had put everybody participating in the conspiracy against me, and they had left no one excluded.

It was either May 20th or 21st, 2010, around 1:30 p.m., when I went to the police station to complain for the second time. The Brigadier General told me that I should not be wasting his time. He did not want to talk and start a conversation because it would show in detail what was happening and what they had been doing. Also, he knew what was going to follow, what they would be doing to me, and he didn't want me to be going there to the police station, of course.

When I left, on the next corner, they had put one person on a red motorbike; he had two bags of potatoes, which looked very noticeable.

After the second time I went to the police station to see the Brigadier General, it became meaningless for me to go there again to complain. They had conspired with the police and government of Canada to block me financially and torture me as punishment because I had gone to hire a lawyer to look into my case, because I had exposed them with my complaint sent to the police of Greece containing my report, and because I had gone to Greece while the police of Canada, undercover and secret agents, were showing me not to go.

Also, they wanted to force me to go back to Canada, where they would do the same. The Montreal police in Canada didn't want me to travel to Greece in April 2010 to find a lawyer to investigate my case. They wanted me to stay in Canada, and now I had demonstrated to the police and government of Greece that they had to tell them about my case and plot with them not to let me hire a lawyer, and also force me to go back to Canada, fearing the case that I may go to an international court or anything else. Because I showed them a bad example by going to Greece, and I also tried to hire a lawyer, they would now punish me.

On the 21st of June 2010, I went to the bank to set up my bank account at my address, and they gave me a tough time. They continued doing psychological warfare on me every second passing by putting people doing strange facial expressions, others looking at me weird, others acting in different ways, others pretending to be begging for money or food, showing me that's what I will be doing soon. Others on the road pretended they were fishing, showing me that's how I will live from now on. They were showing me that they would let me find a girlfriend in 30 years, also putting people wearing black clothes, showing me I'm dead.

They spent a lot of time with vehicles, each one having a special meaning; the colors also held significance. In places that I would go, they would behave like soon I would be begging for food and money. I went to a store; they sent one person in, pretending to ask for meat for his dog, showing me that's what I will be eating soon. They were putting others on, showing me that I will lose a lot of weight. Others were showing me that I will be living in a car; they were putting some people in a van vehicle that had a mattress inside! From what I had understood, there was some fraud they were going to do to seize, suspend, or make me lose my father's house. It was a reality; they would do it. The law did not exist anymore. It was impossible to reach the court.

They used to put people screaming in my neighborhood, showing me that from the torture I would be screaming. Beginning in July 2010, they were putting a new threat, and they would do it. They were about to discontinue the electricity and water supply at my home. They would put small trucks with some bottles of water in the back, and someone would be unloading madly while noticeably looking at me, showing that I would have water only in bottles. They would put someone talking about electricity and saying, "Eh, around October," then stop, hinting that around October they would have discontinued the electricity supply at my home. They did that around two times.

In a phone conversation with my Aunt Patapia, she mentioned that around October 2010, while I was in Canada, there was no electricity in my home in Greece, while she went to get the business cards from the taxi places I had gone to, and there was electricity in the house. She said that, hinting that they would have discontinued my electricity if I had been there.

They wanted to give me health problems. When my mother, Eugenia Margelis, came to Greece on the 8th of July 2010 so we could leave together, as she knew I was not able, scared, and horrified to leave due to the threats I was receiving from the police and government of Greece, their undercover agents, who wouldn't let me leave the country, they started applying psychological warfare to her also. When my mother came to the airport in Athens, they had intentionally put a strike on the Proastiakos trains. She took a taxi to the bus station; the taxi driver took her through other roads deliberately and charged her a high price.

In my house, my mother, while she knew that there were cameras everywhere, put her pills that she takes for her kidney transplant, which she had done, on a small dish and on the table so the camera could see them. She was telling them not to kill her. Also, they would put women showing to be with their son near us, dressed in black, showing us we are both dead, and other times that they are sitting down, showing to be very thoughtful and distressed, showing that we wanted to leave but they didn't let us leave the country. My Aunt Eleni told us, in a conversation on July 11, 2010, that the government provides a pension to individuals over 60 years old, hinting to my mother that she should take a pension because she would not be leaving the country; they wouldn't let her.

It must have been around June 2010, and while I was driving on the old highway I mentioned earlier, the police had an accident involving a truck and a car, where the car was almost totaled. There was a police vehicle where the officers were looking at me, showing me what would happen if I tried to sue them. They were still fearing at the time that I might be able to sue them either in Greece, the European Court of Human Rights, or The Hague-ICC. Behind the accident was one woman dressed in black, pretending to be walking suspiciously and noticeably, on purpose for me to see her.

Towards the end of June, beginning July 2010, around 5:00 p.m., again driving in Athens, at a curve where it goes to the old highway, the police had placed an accident on the left side where one car had hit a tree, like a side accident. The officers there were looking at me very noticeably and nervously. This was a threat in case I tried to go to the European Court of Human Rights or The

Hague. They did not want me to go to the airport. It was the time they started putting threats that they wouldn't let me leave the country. I understood that clearly around July 3, 2010. They were putting cars that had a big dent on the hood, showing me that the gate at the tolls going towards the airport would not open, they wouldn't let me go. They were also putting other accidented cars.

They were passing me messages, threatening that if I attempted to go to Canada, they wouldn't let me, and after that, they would torture me with no food. They now wouldn't let me leave the country, holding me as a homemaker beginning July 2010, not letting me work anywhere, and not letting me do my own job, financially struggling me.

After doing all these things to me and not even letting me rent the taxi to work, fearing international courts, they wouldn't let me leave the country. I thought about calling the European Court of Human Rights, but they were showing me not to try—I would fail; they wouldn't let me. I was also wondering if the phone number I had was the right one with the country code. If I attempted to call and failed, the retaliation would have been heavy in the means of torture. They were showing that they wouldn't even give me food whenever I ran out of money. I was scared and horrified.

It was noticeable when I tried to send a fax to the Ombudsman in Athens, it wouldn't go through. When I tried to call the Ministry of Justice for a paper regarding my taxi driving license, I called about six phone numbers, none of which answered. I had tried to send an email to the European Court of Human Rights, where I noticed that I couldn't. I had noticed they had been manipulating the internet. If I tried to send my application form I had prepared by mail, they would never let it go, they would change the content and the pages and send something else. The registered mail I had sent on 14 June 2010 was opened while I was driving. Someone showed me the pages in their hand, they had opened the envelopes!

On the 4th of July 2010 at 9:00 p.m. (the police of Canada and Greece may have changed dates or even sentences in this report, and this may not be the correct date; if it is not the 4th, it is the 5th or 6th), I went to see Mike, a person I had known for 20 years, a person that was working for the secret services of Greece that summer. While talking, I mentioned to him that I would be going to Canada, where my parents live, regardless. At least I would attempt, of course, to try to go to another country. It was impossible, they wouldn't let me. They wouldn't even let me go to Canada because they were fearing that I might end up going to another country. If I were to take a direct flight, I would probably do something, such as pretending to have health problems, to make the pilot divert the airplane to a different location. They were fearing that I would file my case at the European Court of Human Rights or The Hague.

Immediately, he got a message on his cell phone that we had to go right away to a place with cafeterias and get a cell phone. He told me that I would take the cell phone and give it to Mike, a cousin of his, at the store. The stores at that time were closed! I didn't want to drive there, but he told me we had to go. On the way there, as I noticed what was happening (they tried to put my fingerprints on the cell phone that must have been involved in illegal activities), I told him that he would deliver it himself and not me. He didn't like that at all because he wanted me to give it. I didn't make it look like it was a trick from the police in order to create a scenario to press charges against me, because if I had said something like that, they would never have let me leave the country.

In the meantime, I noticed panic in Mike. He told me not to worry. On the way there, just beside the coast, the police had a fake scene with duty lights on, where they were showing that they had two kids to arrest, threatening me that if I attempted to leave the country, they would create some reason to arrest me, the reason would have been made with the cell phone.

We went to the place. Mike went into a café and, after a while, came out. In the meantime, a person I knew from the past, Trouboukis, came into my rented car suddenly (I hadn't invited him, nor had I seen him outside). When Mike arrived, we left and drove around, going towards his house to drop them off. They were continuously looking at me, trying to interpret what I was thinking and wondering if I was planning to escape somehow. I understood that, of course, it was another way the police of Greece were threatening me not to attempt to escape or leave the country, and they were in a kind of panic condition.

Mike finally didn't deliver any cell phones anywhere! What they wanted to do was have me take the cell phone. That cell phone would have been involved in illegal activities; my fingerprints would have been on it, and afterward, they would have arrested me, claiming that I was involved in illicit activities. Once I understood what they wanted to do, they didn't do the trick.

Another way they were threatening me not to escape or leave the country was through the TV. Beginning in July 2010, a TV channel reported on the news that someone or some people had escaped from jail by climbing out of a building's roof, and that someone was waiting for them on the road with a vehicle, something that couldn't happen either. Also, one person in the past had escaped from jail, and it was planned from before to escape in September; he finally did escape, and the police headquarters afterward resigned. I knew it was meant for me. They were continuously showing things like that; it was noticeable to me.

On July 14, 2010, at 11:00 a.m., as my mother and I were leaving for Montreal from Athens Airport, the Greek police, with the government's complicity, staged a fake demonstration. They were demonstrating for Palestine just in front of the Air Transat check-in counter, where we would obtain our boarding pass and check in our valise, although I didn't have mine with me because I didn't believe they would let me go, and I was not wrong at all.

It was about 15 people, and from the whole airport, they had gone only in front of the Air Transat check-in counter, not letting anybody obtain a boarding pass or check in a valise for Montreal! From the time I arrived at the airport, they stayed there for about half an hour. They were watching me to see if I was about to create a scene on the airplane, to pretend I was having health problems in order to make the airplane land somewhere after departure, with the purpose of filing my case at the European Court of Human Rights or The Hague, and staying in another country.

If they had noticed that I was going to pretend I was having health problems to make the airplane land somewhere, they wouldn't have let me go. They would have kept the demonstration there until I missed the flight. Also, one thing they were expecting was that maybe I would leave the airport while seeing the demonstration, considering that they wouldn't let me leave the country. If my mother had not been with me, they would not have let me go, finding some excuse or creating some reason.

When we went into the airport, I noticed that at the place where there were some airline office counters selling flight tickets, they had put some people pretending they were there to buy tickets, showing me not to go there to get a ticket for another country, they wouldn't let me. It was very noticeable.

At the end of May, beginning of June 2010, Mike, a person I knew for many years, along with Thanasis, his neighbor, people working for the police and government of Greece that summer— were telling me to have a cigarette that, as they were showing, contained narcotic substances, which they called "za" or "stou." They did that on purpose, trying to make it look like I smoked cigarettes with narcotic substances. If I had smoked a cigarette like that out of curiosity, it was a police trick. I have never smoked these kinds of cigarettes, of course.

In a conversation with Mike on Facebook, the conversation started on 17 May 2010, I told Mike, "What happened? Did the police tell you not to associate with me?" He did not deny the fact and gave an excuse that he was going to see a friend to drink a coffee. When I asked him a second time if the police had told him not to associate with me, he did not deny the fact and pretended to change the conversation.

After I told him, on purpose, if he had those cigarettes he was telling me to smoke, calling them "za" or "stou," I told him like this, of course, on purpose, to show in writing that they did tell me to smoke these kinds of cigarettes. He understood why I asked him and never answered or talked again on Facebook; he knew I was collecting evidence.

They started doing anything just after I left the place they rented a taxi in Athens, where I went to ask, but they didn't rent me one. From the 5th to the 7th of July 2010, around 3:00 p.m., they put some people on a motorcycle, and they tried to start a fight, claiming they didn't like the way my car was standing on the road, an excuse.

On July 14th, 2010, when we went with my mother to the airport in Athens to leave the country, it was noticeable that, as we got into the airport, at a counter to the left where airline offices were selling tickets, they had placed people on purpose, acting to show me that they wouldn't let me get a ticket to go to another country. From the psychological warfare they were doing to me, it was very noticeable on my face. My mother saw that; she was highly distressed and mentioned this to me. It was very noticeable, my head was leaning forward. My father mentioned that to me when he saw me at Trudeau Airport in Montreal on July 14th, 2010, and he was crying.

After a few weeks, I came back to about normal. Everything was happening in public, while they had talked to everybody to participate in the conspiracy. There would have been much worse things happening when I ran out of money. They were talking to all the lawyers in Greece not to handle my case. To some, I had sent emails, like the ones where I also went in person—ENA Law Firm, AVG Law Firm, Adrikan Law Firm, and lawyer Boyd Campbell from the States, when I asked for asylum. Anywhere I went, they were not looking into my case. In many instances, fearing retaliation, I would not ask for names or office cards.

I continued writing my report about three months after I was back in Canada on July 14th, 2010, due to the fact that I was receiving indescribable psychological warfare from their people working for the police, undercover, and secret services.

On the 9th or 16th of May 2010, a Sunday afternoon around 5:00 p.m., while I was drinking coffee with Mike, the Greek police, with the government conspiring, had placed numerous people all over the place, acting strangely and passing messages to me, as I describe in this report. They had managed to talk to everybody there. Also, I could not stand the psychological warfare they were doing to me, my face was red. When we went to drink a coffee, I couldn't stand there to drink it because every second that passed, they were all over me, passing messages to me, showing me all kinds of things, that I was dead, that they would break my hands or legs, that I would be begging for food, that I would be sleeping on the streets, and a lot of other things.

In the café, they had put their people there, also one undercover agent that I saw was holding and looking at his cell phone and moved his head toward me, hinting "good luck!" Mike was seeing everything, of course, and knew what they were doing to me. Shortly after, within 20 minutes, when I told him that we should leave the place, he said immediately, "OK." Of course, he was aware of what was happening; he was also working for the secret services.

They were trying to create health problems for me, especially to make me suffer mentally. They were acting like this all day long, everywhere I went, sometimes to a massive extent. They had also put my mother's sisters and brother in a position where they were behaving as if they were not relatives. They were seeing my mother like, "Soon your son will be begging for food," and that she might have the same luck as me because she came to Greece to pick me up.

Her sister Filio, when we went to see them on the 9th or 10th of July 2010, my mother said that day over her sister Filio's phone, talking to her other sister, that she didn't like the things she was seeing. They were also passing messages to my mother that I would be begging for food and that she might have the same luck with me. My mother told me out loud afterward, "If they are like this, you know what I'm going to do? I'm not going to talk to them again."

My mother told her mother, Sofia, to stay at our house while we were there. She hadn't even seen her for a few years. Her sister Filio and all her family, participating in the conspiracy, took my grandmother to their house and did not let my grandmother stay with us on purpose so that my mother wouldn't have her there together, and so that I couldn't find my grandmother after my mother would leave on July 14th, 2010, to get from her the keys for her house at the village and go stay there, as she had told me to go. I wanted to go there because of the public humiliation and the psychological warfare they were doing to me, and at my house they were going to discontinue the electricity and water supply.

They were counting on the fact that at the airport, they would have created a reason not to let me leave, like they almost did with the demonstration they had staged, or that I wouldn't dare go to the airport at all.

My mother in Canada mentioned the demonstration at the airport in Greece. Of course, she knew the police were listening to everything we were saying in the house. Fearing retaliation from the police, she tried to downplay the event and pretend it was a coincidence. I was recording her, but I didn't tell her, so that I would have it on my cell phone as proof that these things happened. I tried to make her at least mention the demonstration at the airport.

The fear of saying the truth was noticeable. My mother and father kept saying it was a coincidence—about six times, to avoid showing that it was deliberate. My father claimed it was a coincidence even though he didn't see what happened. Both my father and mother are unable to speak the truth while they are terrified, distressed, and horrified by all these events. They were also being blackmailed.

When the police at customs at 400 D'Youville in Montreal arrested me on November 19th, 2010, it was intentional. They wanted to press fraudulent charges against me. They had taken my birth certificate, my cell phone, and my pair of sunglasses from my valise. They tried to claim identity issues, but in reality, they wanted to accuse me of something criminal. While I was in a room, my father was speaking to the police and security officers. He later told me that he had told them I had lost money and was very distressed, which was entirely false. Everything that actually happened is documented in this report. He lied, thinking that the police would leave me alone.

He knew everything that was happening. He was the one who even paid the airfare for my mother and me to come to Greece to pick me up on July 14th, 2010. While he was petrified to say the truth about what the police had been doing to us, he told them lies about my financial distress, hoping that would protect me.

Also, on the morning of July 14th, 2010, while my cousin Christos, along with my mother's sister Pagona, was driving us to the airport in Athens, the police were listening to everything we said and watching me. They were interpreting my behavior to see if I intended to go to another country, and whether I might claim a health problem on the airplane to force it to land elsewhere. The demonstration at the airport was designed to prevent me from catching my flight.

From July 5th to 6th, 2010, I went to the Parliament in Athens for a hunger strike. I felt I had no choice after all these events and the isolation they were imposing on me. At some point, I would have ended up with no money, begging for food to survive. Of course, I would not have waited until that happened; this was how they intended to make me live. After that, further punishment would follow, and rumors circulated that I would end up sleeping on the street, as I mention in this book.

Two police officers reported the situation on their handheld communication devices. I told them that they should let me work or allow me to leave the country. While the government was also involved in the conspiracy, I did not tell them more, under these circumstances, I was just trying to save myself. Letting me work or leave the country would have meant that they would stop all the harassment and psychological warfare directed at me. Of course, they would never let me hire a lawyer to handle my case.

The government's involvement was noticeable everywhere I went, especially in places connected to or under its jurisdiction. The conspiracy I mention in this book was known and participated in by these entities. One district attorney even mentioned the involvement of secret agents. The police were using undercover agents, which they admitted when I went to file a complaint at the police station, as I describe in this report.

I frequently refer to these individuals in this report as those working for the Canadian police, used for protection and other purposes. Secret agents were also involved, working together with the police, while the government was participating as well. The police were placing people to apply psychological pressure on me, which they admitted to, and I describe in detail in this book.

They did not want me to return to the police station to file another complaint so that they could continue their harassment. Undercover and secret agents were officially involved, and the police had spoken to others, asking them to participate in the conspiracy against me. The police contacted a few people I mentioned. They did not deny it: Mike, a person I had known for 20 years in Greece, did not deny that the police told him to avoid associating with me during a conversation on Facebook.

That conversation later disappeared from my account. Sotiris, another person I knew in Greece for 8 years, also did not deny it in a conversation we had in early June 2010. Alexis Alexiou, a financial services broker, did not deny via email that Greek authorities had tried to influence him regarding me. He attempted to hide or deny it, but it was clear he was lying. I have that email conversation printed; my email is christosmargelis74@yahoo.com.

I also noticed that my neighbor, Stelios, was instructed to install an intense light at the back of my house at night so I could see if someone from the criminal organization in Canada came with the intent to harm me. In 30 years, we never had a light there, and we had no intention of installing one. After researching, I learned that the people working for the police in this way are called undercover agents. Secret agents from the police and the national intelligence service were also involved, as both the police and the government were participating in the conspiracy. Nothing secret.

While I was on hunger strike, someone drove past in a taxi to suggest that I could rent a taxi to go to work. I left to do so, but when I went to taxi rental places, no one would rent me a taxi. I also went to George to ask; he claimed he didn't have any, even though he had three taxis parked outside his building, which was deliberate. I went to George because he was cooperating with the police, if he had rented me a taxi, it would have meant they were allowing me to work. They did not.

At the same time, I also went to the place Christos-Hlias had suggested to inquire about buying half ownership of a taxi. He told me he wanted more than half the deposit and expected very high payments, likely knowing that I would have difficulty meeting them. The threats they had been making, that they would cause me an accident—felt very real. One thing was sure: they would not let me work. They wanted to punish me brutally because I had gone to hire a lawyer to look into my case.

At the same time, I also visited two other places. At first, the person there refused to rent me a taxi, saying he wasn't the right person to help and that I should call someone else listed on a business card he gave me. I called the number from my cell phone the same day, but no one answered. I still have that business card at home. At another place across the street, I was told that all the taxis had been rented and none were available. It was very noticeable that they were lying, participating in the conspiracy. I left the place.

I called many taxi rental places listed in the newspaper from both my home and my cell phone. Most of them refused to rent me a taxi, claiming they had already been rented or that they would call me later. It was clear that they were monitoring my calls and had instructed these businesses not to rent to me. They even seemed aware of the specific newspaper I was using.

In a few cases, when they overlooked me the first time, I called a second time to make an appointment. By then, they had already spoken with the owners and told me no taxis were available. I called these places again the next day, but both repeated that no taxis were available. I understood very clearly that everyone was talking to each other and that they would not allow me to rent a taxi to work.

Although the newspaper listed around 30 taxi rental places, and under normal circumstances, anyone could easily rent a taxi to work, they managed to block me from all of them. Even when I kept trying, it was meaningless, they would not let me work. There was one place at Plateia Batheis in Athens that appeared promising. However, based on my phone conversations, someone would instruct the owner to pretend to help me, saying they would call me at a particular time, then never call back. It was clearly done on purpose, just to frustrate me.

On June 23, 2010, for about a week, all Greek TV channels were showing news about a bomb in an envelope delivered to the Ministry of Public Security in Athens at Kanellopoulou 4, allegedly killing a police general who was a friend of the minister. They showed how the bomb had passed through the scanners at the airport and reached the minister's office. But there was no bomb, no explosion, and no one died. It was entirely fabricated.

This coincided with a complaint I had sent on June 14, 2010, which the ELTA Hellenic Post Office confirmed was received on June 24, 2010. About four days after sending it, I checked the ELTA tracking website, and it showed that the letter had not yet been received, only sent for delivery.

I then sent an email, my email is christosmargelis74@yahoo.com to the ELTA Post Office on June 22, 2010, asking why my mail had not been received, even though the tracking system said it had been sent for delivery. The next day, all the TV channels were showing that a bomb in an envelope had been sent to the Ministry of Public Security and exploded, allegedly killing a police general.

When I checked the tracking number on the ELTA Hellenic Post Office website again on June 23, 2010, it showed that the item had been received. They called it a terror act and claimed the sender was from abroad. They were making it look like a major terror attack to make me panic, even though I was only stating the truth. Although I saw it had been delivered on June 23, 2010, the ELTA Post Office later stated by email on January 24, 2011, that it had been delivered on June 24, 2010. I understood that they did this intentionally so that it would not appear that my complaint coincided with the bomb report, allowing them to claim it was unrelated.

While the TV coverage of the "bomb" at the Ministry of Public Security was airing, messages were being sent to me indicating that I would be punished severely and tortured. The messages were noticeable in the broadcast.

The ELTA Post Office later disappeared the tracking number RE826027665GR from their system. When I checked their website toward the end of September 2010, it said the tracking number did not exist. I sent an email on October 1, 2010, inquiring about the nonexistence of the tracking number, but I did not receive a response. When I emailed them on June 22, 2010, asking if the item had been delivered, they also did not respond.

On January 24, 2011, I sent another email asking why the tracking system showed that the tracking number did not exist. The system was showing SQL (Structured Query Language) errors. I had printed the page. The Post Office replied that there were temporary technical problems and that the item had been delivered. They stated that to get information regarding its handling, I would have to complete an inquiry form within six months. They knew this was impossible, in other words, nobody could verify who had received my registered mail.

On February 22, 2011, I again checked the delivery status of the registered mail I had sent to the Ministry of Public Security. The system still displayed the same SQL error and did not show the delivery status. I asked the Post Office by email why it still did not show the delivery status. They replied that it had been delivered. They were lying; when they claimed there were temporary technical problems, they were actually hiding the registered mail.

On September 12, 2011, I checked again. It now said "no information found," although for other registered mail I had sent to the Taxi License Office, the system correctly showed that it had been delivered. I printed those pages.

When I emailed the Post Office on October 1, 2010, asking why my registered mail did not show delivery status, they did not respond. This was because I did not have the receipts from the Post Office. They could have falsely claimed that my registered mail had never been delivered or did not exist. My aunt, Patapia, sent me the receipts around January 18, 2011, although she initially tried to hide them, claiming she could not find them at my house in Greece. Once I had the receipts, the Post Office replied to my email, saying it had been delivered, but I would never know who the recipient was.

They also tried to make it seem as if I had some sort of psychological problem so that my account would not be believed.

There were also times when they would put women behaving in a kind of provocative way, most likely to tempt me into having an affair with them. Later, they would claim that I had raped them to get me into trouble. Sometimes, it was a woman I already knew, with whom I had no significant relationship.

When they suspected I might leave for Athens, thinking perhaps I was going to the airport, the police would place damaged cars in my way to show me what could happen if I attempted to leave. Other vehicles had a big dent in their hoods, indicating that the gates at the highway tolls might not open properly.

On July 11 or 12, 2010, just before my mother and I were to leave Greece, my cousin Sofia came to our house to stay the night. I tried to figure out why they sent her; it was a sudden and unusual visit. Later, I understood that they wanted to imply that I had harassed her in order to put me in trouble.

Kostas, the car rental agent from whom I had rented a car that summer, was aware of my case with the police in Canada. He told me, "Oh, it's worse here!" He knew what might happen later and did not deny saying this in our email conversation. When I asked him to send me the bank receipt for the 300 euros I had transferred on August 13, 2010, from Canada, he told me to "send it scanned by email." He feared that if I sent it by fax, I might also send my application form to the European Court of Human Rights in Strasbourg. He never answered when I said I could only send it by fax.

Although I sent 300 euros to his account, only 260 euros arrived. The banks deliberately did this to cause trouble and make me keep spending money. It was likely TD Bank that did this.

It is very noticeable on my passport that on July 14, 2010—the day I left Athens, they put a seal showing the date, but it does not indicate whether I was departing or arriving; no arrows are shown. On my mother's passport, Eugenia Margelis, her address is the same as mine. When we left Greece together on July 14, 2010, the airport did not put the seal on page 7, where it should have been, but on page 12. Again, no arrows indicate whether she was departing or arriving. Both the Greek and Canadian police and governments know everything on my computer, as they hacked my laptop and can also interfere remotely.

They know that my emails and conversations are truthful; *I am not a liar.*

My cousin Christos, the day before we left Greece—July 13, 2010—told us, along with his mother, that we should sleep at his apartment and go to the airport from there the next morning. Instead, he took us to another location, not his apartment. He did not want me to know where he lived, fearing that I might ask him one day to stay at his place in Athens.

There was a café near my house in Greece that I used to go to. The owner, Giannis, and his brother Stelios, neighbors of mine whom I had known for many years, had been approached by the police. While talking to Stelios one day, he implied that soon I would be asking to borrow money, likely begging. I asked him, "Will it really be that bad, Stelios?" He looked at me and nodded slightly.

When I went to the café, the customers would scream on

purpose and, while watching TV soccer games, swear at the players. They were looking sideways at me, and I understood that this behavior was directed at me.

# Chapter 5

# Montreal, Canada (After 14th July 2010-2011)

On 20 June 2011, I talked on the phone with Stelios. He admitted that customers were screaming in his café when I was there and that things were suspicious. When I asked him more, he said twice, "Me, I don't know anything!" He also mentioned the earth placed in front of my house (hinting at my grave), with a white box as a coffin. He claimed, "It was not for them!" That meant it was for me.

In May 2010, my Aunt Patapia told me, "Should we be leaving you a container with food on your window?"

I laughed and asked why. She replied, "Oh, I'm just saying." She knew the truth, the police and government would not let me work, wanting me to beg for food because I hired a lawyer to look into my case. She later admitted this on the phone in October or November 2010. Who knew what would have happened if I had run out of money?

My conversation with my brother, George Margelis, on Facebook in the summer of 2010 clearly showed what happened while I was in Greece. I printed the conversation. In Canada, Bell did not connect the phone in our new apartment on 1 July 2010; they connected it only on 12 July, preventing conversations from being recorded.

During early July 2010, while planning to leave Greece with my mother, I had to pretend in conversations with relatives that maybe all this was my imagination, just to loosen the grip of Greek authorities so they would let me leave.

My Aunt Eleni tried to show that I had psychological problems. I had to pretend I accepted it. Even with my aunt Maria's boyfriend, Nikos, one night I agreed with him when he said nothing was going on, and it could all be in my mind.

The Montreal police and secret services threatened me, hinting that I should become like Martin Luther King if I tried to leave the country. They also threatened jail, showing people in white shirts with black stripes, or holding Foot Locker bags (white with black stripes), signaling what would happen if I went to the European Court of Human Rights or similar courts.

I also noticed that the police station at 7035 Parc Avenue, Montreal, where they took me at my arrest on 26 January 2008— was no longer there, now moved to Beaumont Street.

In late July 2010, my Aunt Pagona called me on the phone to inform me that she had arranged to pay the money I owed to Kostas, who had rented me a car in Greece. But when I emailed Kostas, he said, "It's not all right. You owe me money." The trick was that while I thought all was fine, he could sue me and force me back to Greece for court. In his email, the proper amount was missing: instead of 300 euros, he received 260. Either he lied, the Greek bank hid the amount, or TD Bank in Canada withheld the transfer. The banks were clearly part of the conspiracy.

The Canadian police and secret services showed me, through various ways, that if I went to another country, they would block me financially, just like in Greece, keeping me trapped.

From 29 September 2010 to 2 October 2011, the tracking numbers of the registered mails I sent on 14 June 2010, one to the Ministry of Public Security in Greece (RE826027665GR) and the other to immigration lawyer Boyd Campbell in the U.S. (RE826027651GR)—did not exist on the ELTA website.

The Montreal police blackmailed my parents, Eugenia and Christos Margelis, to say I had psychological problems and to participate in the conspiracy against me. They wanted to cancel my report, calling it imagination. But everything was proven—there was no imagination.

The police admitted everything in response to my complaints by saying they would "check with Access to Information," which had nothing to do with what I reported. The governments of Greece and Canada never answered my complaints.

They also told my mother to go to Dr. Thomas Kolivakis, a psychiatrist at Royal Victoria Hospital (687 Pine Avenue), and claim that I was "seeing all kinds of things." They even made an appointment on 2 September 2010 without informing me, so he could claim that I was fantasizing or hallucinating. I did not go, knowing what they planned!

By mid-2009, my brother George Margelis had been working with Montreal police and Canadian secret services. They blackmailed him to obey, showing me wrong and them right, pretending everything was my imagination. He did not work but stayed home as ordered.

At the end of August 2010, they blackmailed my mother, Eugenia Margelis, threatening to change her kidney transplant medication and send her to hemodialysis unless she obeyed, using George as an intermediary. She then tried to show that I had health problems and that nothing was happening. They also blackmailed my father, threatening to cut his pension and force him back to work, and he acted the same way.

I contacted law firms in Athens—Adrikan Antonios D. Andrikopoulos, AVGLAW Avgerinos & Partners, ENA Law Firm, Lykourezos Law Offices, and Professor Hrisanthis (whom I visited in person). Many refused before we even sat down, as the police had already spoken to them.

I collected photos of threats: a cat in my yard with its side cut open, likely with a knife; after I photographed it, the body disappeared. Another photo showed a white box (my coffin) with soil beside it. People in wheelchairs signaled threats of injury. In a rental car, I photographed all indicators (RPM, kilometers, fuel) dropping to zero, with the handbrake light flashing, while police vehicles drove past, showing it was them.

I also saw a black Cadillac Escalade without plates in my neighborhood, the same type driven by Gigi, a Montreal drug trafficker, who had threatened me in May 2008.

On 29 September 2010, I emailed Alter TV in Greece (from my address: christosmargelis74@yahoo.com) asking about the terrorist attack on the Ministry of Public Security in Athens with the bomb in an envelope. No reply. On 1 October 2010, I inquired with Elta Hellenic Post Office why the registered letters I sent on 14 June 2010 did not appear in their tracking system. No answer.

In summer 2010, Alexis Alexiou from a brokerage firm began emailing me, urging me to open an account and attend seminars. On 13 July 2010, the day before I left Greece, he emailed again, trying to persuade me to stay and risk losing my money. He kept writing until October, when I told him to stop. On 6 October 2010, I confronted him in an email, saying the Greek government had put him up to it. He did not deny it, only replied, "Sorry, sorry."

The Montreal police made loud threats that they would create a reason to jail me if I tried leaving or filing my case with the

European Court of Human Rights in Strasbourg or the ICC in The Hague. They used signals: people with black bags labeled "This bag is green," Foot Locker bags, or other staged signs.

They allowed me to work only at Fujiaty and Auto Vie garages, which were part of the conspiracy, sending me cars and controlling how much I earned. My business was destroyed, my finances controlled, no chance of other work since they warned others not to hire me. They threatened that I would end up on the streets, begging for food, or crippled in a wheelchair.

They had hidden cameras in all rooms of my home, and undercover agents followed me everywhere, five to fifteen at a time, passing coded signals.

On 27 October 2010, I discovered TD Waterhouse had withdrawn small amounts from my trading account. At their Eaton Center office, they lied, claiming my U.S. stock "Research in Motion" was in Canadian dollars. On 16 November 2010, I noticed that they had charged $8.95 in fees to my checking account; when I inquired, they refunded it.

When I returned from Greece on 14 July 2010, I confirmed George Margelis was indeed working as an undercover agent, as I had suspected since March. He passed messages from the secret services, always siding with them. John Vlahakis, another agent, often pretended to speak to George but was in truth delivering messages.

On 19 November 2010 at noon, my father and I went to Old Montreal customs to process a valise sent by my Aunt Pagona. After two hours, the police suddenly arrested me. I asked, "Why are you arresting me?" The officer mumbled something about my identity. I wondered again clearly. She answered, "There is a problem with your identity."

It was the same trick: creating an identity issue to block me from leaving, fearing I would go to Strasbourg or The Hague. I told her, "How can you be looking for someone using my identity when no one entered the country with it, and I'm under police protection?" She gave no reply.

I reminded her that on 7 April 2010, before I traveled to Greece, they had done the same thing, trying to stop me from leaving, until it proved false. She said immigration would see me. An officer arrived, said little, and let me go.

They still charged me $70 for my valise, which I had left in Greece when I departed on 14 July 2010, because undercover Greek police and secret services had shown me death threats and made it impossible to go with it.

The Montreal Canadian police were now trying to show me as a pedophile, I wondered where that even came from. Before, they had wanted to charge me with murder, and later with rape. They kept inventing accusations as excuses for everything they had been doing to me. They threatened not to let me leave the country and hinted they might put me in jail and even kill me there, making it look like "maybe it's an accident."

In September 2010, I had told my Aunt Pagona to include my taxi driving license when she shipped me my valise, reminding her not to forget because it was important. My mother also asked her the same, but Pagona did not put it in.

Around the same time, my Aunt Patapia paid an insurance bill called TEVE that I had had since 2009. It was not necessary to be paid then, it cost €450. Afterward, she asked my mother for the money, expecting reimbursement. That bill had been sitting unpaid at the post office, where I could have paid it at any time with interest.

On 10 December 2010, I told my mother to call Pagona again to remind her to send my taxi license. She promised she would and finally sent it in February 2011.

In August 2010, I tried to send a message from my mother's cell phone to my cousin Christos in Greece, but it would not go through, it was blocked.

Meanwhile, at Montreal customs, when I went to sign the papers for my valise, the security officer told me she would send me home with the police report from my arrest over the so-called identity issue. I only received it later after submitting a written request. The report falsely stated it was for "identity purposes," even though I was under police protection and they knew very well who I was.

That officer had also asked me, "Do you want a lawyer?"

I replied, "Which lawyer?"

She answered, "Call the 1-800 number."

Of course, there was no lawyer, it was just for show, to pretend they were not blocking lawyers from handling my case.

On 16 December 2010, I sent a message from my cell phone to Koumar, an undercover police agent, inquiring why he had tampered with my brakes before my trip to Greece on 25 April 2010. The message would not send, it stayed saved as a draft, even after I tried twice. The police and secret services were controlling my phone.

A couple of hours earlier, I had spoken to Koumar, and he told me he no longer went to the Fujiaty garage because of "a problem with one mechanic." That was not true. The real reason was to avoid my confronting him about the brakes. After that, he disappeared, though I used to see him once or twice a week.

At the beginning of October 2010, I asked my Aunt Patapia by phone to send me the addresses of some places where I had tried to rent a taxi in Greece. I told her the business cards were on the bookshelf in my home. She agreed. By mid-October, I called again, and she told me the address, but when I asked her to send the business cards, she avoided it. On 7 November 2010, I called again to remind her, and she claimed she thought I only wanted the address, not the cards. That was a lie. I had clearly asked her to mail them. She was avoiding it under orders from the Greek police and secret services. Later, she did finally send them.

On 23 December 2010, at 10:30 a.m., I visited the Greek Consulate to collect my new European Greek passport. A lady asked me to sign, which I did. Then I asked her for a copy of the mandate I had made in September 2010 for my Aunt Patapia to discontinue the phone service in Greece. She refused, saying, "We don't have a copy. The mandate wasn't written here, you brought it from home."

I replied, "No, the mandate was made here, on this computer," and pointed to it with my hand.

Still, she refused, saying, "You should have kept a copy yourself."

It was clear they were participating in the conspiracy. My mother later told me that when we sent the mandate in September 2010 to my Aunt Patapia, instead of discontinuing the service, she had paid the bill and let it continue, just as the Greek police and government had ordered, to cause financial damage to me and my family.

My cousin Christos was also involved. When it was time for us to leave Greece, even though he knew we were leaving within a day or two, he kept taking us around to restaurants. He was showing us, symbolically, that we should stay in Greece and they would "give us food." I understood what he meant, but what could I say?

In my online conversations with my brother George Margelis on Facebook in summer 2010, it was very noticeable that he continuously tried to underestimate the situation and change the subject, making it seem like nothing was happening. Whenever I mentioned that a disaster was unfolding, he switched the topic to "our friends," so the conversation would look harmless. He lied that my claims about the police had no basis, even though he knew the truth. He was working as an undercover agent and knew precisely what was happening.

On 6 January 2011, I called my Aunt Pagona, my mother's sister, to remind her to send me my taxi driving license and the two books of my bank accounts in Greece. She told me she could not send them the previous month (since I had already discovered they were missing from the valise she shipped me in September 2010) because she was "busy."

I then asked her why she hadn't included my cell phone and sunglasses. She said she had put them in the pocket of a jacket and told me to check there. I searched everywhere, but when I received my valise from Greece on 19 November 2010, the sunglasses, cell phone, and even my birth certificate were missing. Most likely, they had been removed at customs in Greece or Canada. The plan seemed to be to use them as supposed "evidence" to charge me with something. When that failed, they changed the story and said they arrested me for "identity issues."

Strangely, in March 2011, my cell phone and sunglasses suddenly reappeared, placed inside my jacket. It was apparent someone had planted them back.

Pagona kept avoiding sending me my taxi driving license, so I would not have proof that I had tried to rent a taxi. They were not letting me get a job anywhere. I also spoke to her son, my cousin Christos, and told him, "Didn't you see they wouldn't rent me a taxi in Greece to work?"

He replied, "Ah Christos, it's the bad economy in Greece, that's why everybody is crying, they are not busy."

He deliberately changed the subject, avoiding the fact that the rental agencies were refusing to rent me a taxi at all.

The sunglasses, cell phone, and birth certificate had been removed by Greek and Canadian authorities to fabricate a scenario of guilt, planning to use them as evidence for false charges. The cell phone had no real value, it was worthless.

On 10 January 2011, at 2:30 p.m., I received a phone call from my Aunt Patapia. She told me she could not find, at my house in Greece, the three postal receipts from 14 June 2010 when I had sent my complaints by registered mail to the Ministry of Public Security in Athens, the taxi license office, and immigration lawyer Boyd Campbell in the U.S. I told her to check every drawer and every place. Later, she admitted she found them. It was clear that the Greek police and secret services were destroying evidence.

My aunt also tried to send me the wrong file (a dossier). Instead of the one I had requested, which contained documents in English related to my case against Greece before the European Court of Human Rights or the ICC at The Hague, she sent me one in Greek that was for income tax purposes. She claimed she did not take the English one because she "couldn't understand what it said." I told her to send me both. A few days later, I asked her again about the three receipts, and she admitted that she had found them, fearing she had been caught hiding evidence. I also told her to send me my last phone bill, but strangely, that bill disappeared from inside my house in Canada.

She wanted me to be left with only the income tax file so that I would lack the evidence needed for international courts.

Ted, a man working at the Westmount Legal Clinic, who also worked for the police, had been negotiating with me on behalf of the government in June 2010 for a supposed "compensation" he called insurance. Nothing was ever confirmed. In October or November 2010, he admitted he had participated in the conspiracy with the police, claiming it was "in a non-harmful way."

On 6 or 7 January 2011, I called the National Bank of Canada from home with my father to request a credit limit increase on his card. They refused, saying Equifax had reported bad credit. What had actually happened was in September 2010, my father did not pay a bill on time because they never sent it to him. They then used that to put bad credit on his record, which blocked him from obtaining a credit increase.

On 11 January 2011, around 8:00 p.m., in a conversation I had with my brother George Margelis, he admitted, like my mother had—that if they had left me in Greece during summer 2010, I would have died of starvation. George was a secret agent.

On 16 January 2011, at 1:30 p.m., I called Pagona again to ask if she had sent my taxi license. She lied once more, saying she had forgotten. But as soon as I pressed her about when she would send it, she quickly said, "Oh, I will be sending it tomorrow." When I asked if I should call her again to confirm, she replied, "You don't need to—it will be sent tomorrow." She only promised because I had caught her in a lie about the delay.

Immediately afterward, I called Patapia and asked about the

dossiers and the receipts for the registered letters I had sent on 14 June 2010. She claimed she had sent them. While we were talking, I reminded her of what happened in summer 2010: "Didn't you see I tried to rent a taxi and they wouldn't rent me one?"

She asked, "You had a taxi driving license?", trying to confuse the situation.

I told her, "You were the one who recommended where I should go and ask for a taxi to rent. Now you tell me I didn't have a taxi driving license?"

She started making excuses. Pagona had avoided sending me my license since September 2010, and Patapia pretended I never had one.

She also admitted that she told me they would bring me food in a plastic container and leave it on my window. At the same time, the police of Greece and the government, involved in the conspiracy, never let me work, so I would have no money and be forced to beg for food.

My Aunt Pagona refused to send me my taxi driving license. On 16 January 2011, when I called her in Greece to remind her again, she told me, "You shall be strong, and you shall not fear anybody!" They had already spoken to her (secret agents), and she was participating in the conspiracy. The case we had involved the police in both Greece and Canada, as well as the secret services, and what they had been doing to me, that's who she meant.

On 23 January 2011, I called her again. She started to say the same thing suddenly but then stopped, knowing exactly what that meant. She knew very well who was behind everything: the police of Greece (with undercover agents, secret agents, and sometimes the police themselves), threatening me and passing messages, while the government was also involved. Still, she denied that they had spoken to her.

That same day, 23 January 2011, while reviewing my passport, I noticed that the stamp from when I left for Greece on 8 July 2008 was missing. Only faint black dots from the seal remained, but nothing was visible. I also noticed there was no stamp for my return to Montreal on 5 September 2008.

There was a conspiracy between the Montreal police and secret agents, possibly even the governments of Greece and Canada. In August 2008, I noticed a man following me. They created a scene with a woman pretending to fight, waiting for me to intervene so they could stab me, and no one would ever know what happened. The same person later followed me into a club, but when I told my friend Mike in Greece that he was stalking me, the man disappeared. The Montreal police and secret agents had planned to kill me in Greece, but they failed again.

On 24 January 2011, at noon, I went to Alcyon Olympia Express travel agency in Montreal and asked for a copy of my air ticket for 11 May 2009, when I flew to Greece with Olympic Airways. They refused. On 31 January 2011, I went again, and they gave me a hard time before finally giving me a poorly printed confirmation, not the actual ticket, clearly part of the conspiracy.

A few weeks later, I went to Voyages Mont-Parnasse in Montreal, where I spoke to Bill Tsoukalas, who was also part of the conspiracy. I asked for a copy of my ticket for 8 July 2008, when I traveled to Greece with Olympic Airways. He only gave me a copy of the invoice, not the ticket. When I insisted, he again gave me the same type of poorly printed confirmation I had already received from Alcyon Olympia Express. He told me, "That's all I can get. I can't find an actual copy of your ticket."

In early January 2011, I also went to Voyages Forfait Plus to ask for a copy of my 25 April 2010 ticket with Air Transat. Instead of the ticket, they gave me an invoice. By late March 2011, after much difficulty, they finally gave me a copy of the ticket, but it was missing one page, clearly removed on purpose. The travel agent, Yvonne Iskenian, told me not to bother them again and said Air Transat would never provide another copy. She, too, was part of the conspiracy, trying to block my case from reaching the European Court of Human Rights.

In March 2011, I asked another travel agency for copies of my tickets from Greece to Canada (5 September 2008 and 16 September 2009). They faxed them to me, but also gave me a hard time.

In December 2010, I discovered that my birth certificate was missing—stolen from my suitcase. I applied for a new one at the Centre Administratif Services Quebec in late December 2010 or early January 2011.

On 6 February 2011, I called Sotiris, a man I had known for eight years, who worked for the Greek secret services. I told him about my case and how the police and secret services in Greece had spoken to everyone, though he denied they had spoken to him. When I asked for the address of the courthouse, he said he would ask a lawyer at a nearby café. I told him, "The lawyers are all talked to—don't ask them."

He also told me he passed by the court every day. I replied, "While you're passing by, look for the number."

He said, "They have no number." I told him to go inside and ask. I also explained that I was preparing my case for the European Court of Human Rights in Strasbourg, but since I wasn't a lawyer, all my information came from the internet, which wasn't easy.

On February 10, 2011, around noon, I visited NLP Technologies, a certified translation service, to translate my airline invoices and police letters. They deliberately mistranslated the documents three to four times across all pages to prevent my case from being accepted at the European Court of Human Rights. That morning, I accused the translator of conspiring with the Montreal police to mistranslate the documents. He did not deny it and even said, "Here we work for the government."

On April 4, 2011, I called Textronics Translation Office to ask about my translations. At first, one person answered; suddenly, someone else came on the line, proof they were manipulating the phones. They made it difficult to find proper translators.

By April 2011, I found Asiatis (Word of Excellence Inc.) in Montreal and spoke with Jean-Philippe. They completed the translations, but I noticed they had outsourced them. The printing was poor, and the translations were inaccurate. I had to return them for correction, and I kept the bad versions as proof. They also refused to give me a receipt.

In May 2011, I gave documents for translation to an office called Mona Rassem. Like the others, their translators were part of the conspiracy, misleading me with bad translations. The person I spoke with, Frank Michael, who I understood was a secret agent, kept misleading me about which documents needed a commissioner of oaths stamp for "true copy." I always had to read and correct their errors, which were done on purpose.

In March 2011, I also gave documents to Integrated Consulting Services, owned by Anastasios Moussas. His translations were full of deliberate mistakes. Even after returning them for corrections, he still did not fix them properly.

On March 23, 2011, at 5:45 p.m., I went to make copies at Copie Express. All three printers produced very noticeable defects. Only after I insisted did the clerk use another machine, which finally made acceptable copies. Similar problems happened at other stores, too.

On March 31, 2011, during a phone call with my Aunt Pagona, she did not deny telling me, "You should be strong and fear nobody," nor did she deny that the Greek police and secret services had spoken with her. She simply changed the subject.

On May 9, 2011, I transferred funds online from my TD Waterhouse trading account to my bank account. The next day, the money wasn't there. When I called, they claimed they would do the transfer manually, but it still hadn't arrived by May 15. Only after I called again at 1:30 p.m. did they complete it, making the process unnecessarily difficult.

On May 31, 2011, at 2:00 p.m., at Rosemont Metro station, the police staged a man lying on the ground, hinting they would leave me homeless and starving.

On June 7, 2011, at 10:30 a.m., I messaged Vie at Auto Vie

about work. He told me to come, but when I arrived, there were no cars. When I called, he shut off his phone. At 11:37 a.m., I texted that he had plotted with the police to block me financially. Two minutes later, he called back, saying, "Now I really have cars. I don't plot with anyone." At 12:19 p.m., he sent another message insisting he needed me and wasn't plotting, though it was obvious he was.

That same day, my mother complained that buses were unusually delayed. From April to August 2011, more than half the time, buses never came when I was waiting. I often had to walk to the metro.

On June 13, 2011, at Jean-Talon station, the police placed someone pretending to beg for money, showing me that was my future. On June 14 at 4:00 p.m., at the same station, another man with walking sticks pretended to beg. These psychological tactics happened every day once I left my house.

On June 17, 2011, my father called from Greece, where he and my mother had gone for ten days to sell the house. He said the National Bank of Greece told him he could not transfer money to Canada by check, only by wire transfer, another lie. Real estate agents also claimed the house, worth about €160,000, was only worth €50,000, clearly conspiring with the police.

That same day at 3:00 p.m., I called TD Bank in Canada. The representative first said checks from Europe could not be deposited in Canada, then contradicted himself, admitting that money orders were possible. He was avoiding the truth.

On June 15, 2011, at 3:48 p.m., at Acadie Metro, police placed someone who looked like Martin Luther King Jr., showing me what they wanted to turn me into.

On June 18, 2011, my mother confirmed from Greece that real estate agents were all quoting one-third of the home's real value.

On June 21, 2011, I called Lee at Garage Fujiaty to ask why he wasn't sending cars. When I told him he was conspiring with the police, he pretended nothing was wrong.

On June 22, 2011, my parents returned from Greece and confirmed agents had been quoting only €50,000 for the house.

Back in October 2010, undercover police agent John Vlahakis, a friend of my brother George, was seen at Place Vertu mall petting a cat near its leg, the exact spot where they had once left a dead, mutilated cat in my yard in Greece as a threat.

On June 20, 2011, at 12:51 p.m., I spoke with Stelios, a café owner in Greece. He admitted that customers had been shouting and swearing at soccer games whenever I was there, but twice said, "I don't know anything," to avoid trouble.

On June 23, 2011, at 4:55 p.m., John Vlahakis called me. I mentioned the dead cat and how he had once told me to live on the streets begging for ten years. He did not deny it.

In March 2011, lawyer Anna Colarusso told me she did not have the original letter from police dated February 24, 2009—only a copy, which was a lie. The letter she sent to the police on February 18, 2009, asking for the report of my January 26, 2008 arrest, was also not what she claimed. Lawyer Nicolas De Tomaso's English translation was missing seals and seemed unofficial, with errors throughout.

On June 26, 2011, I went to Bureau en Gros for a laptop. They claimed they didn't have the one I wanted, and when I used their printers, every copy came out defective. Staff pretended not to hear when I asked about it.

On June 27, 2011, at Best Buy in Carrefour Angrignon, they tried to push me to buy a poor-quality discounted laptop. When I asked for an Acer Aspire, they said it wasn't in stock, then refused to give me a business card.

On June 28, 2011, at another Best Buy, I found an Acer Aspire AO522 at the regular price. The salesman lied, saying it was a liquidation, and told me the only one available was the display model. They were clearly participating in the conspiracy with the police to stop me from getting a decent computer. I asked customer service to bring me one so I could buy it. They said they couldn't. When I asked for a business card, they refused: "We don't have business cards."

Around July 6–7, 2010, I tried to get an airline ticket from a travel agent near my house in Greece. They refused, saying their computers were not working. That same day, before noon, they called my cell phone in Greece and said they had found one at a very low price with Air Transat, hinting that something was going to happen, that I wouldn't make it to Montreal. When my parents were in Greece from June 12–22, 2011, I told them to obtain the address and phone number of that travel agent. They told me it was closed; it didn't exist anymore.

In July 2010, my father went to the post office in Canada to register our change of address so letters would be sent to our new home. The post office, participating in the conspiracy, did not update the address correctly, so that letters would not be delivered properly. We had moved from 3435 Barclay, Apt. 10, to Champagneur, Apt. 6, on July 1, 2010. Yet the post office repeatedly—six times—mixed in our previous address at 7045 Wiseman Street (where we lived July 2007–September 2009), which had nothing to do with the current change. From September 30, 2009, to June 30, 2010, we lived at 3435 Barclay, Apt. 10. From July 1, 2010, we moved to Champagneur, Apt. 6. The postal office did not want to write the change correctly. One reason was that the government of Greece might reply to my complaint by sending letters to my Canadian address, and they could then claim I never received them because the change of address was recorded incorrectly.

Another thing: when I was preparing to go to Greece in April 2010, Montreal travel agents—after being contacted by police and secret services—kept telling me to fly British Airways. In other words, they wanted me routed through England. Why? The answer is clear: the British government, contacted by the Canadian government and police, would send me back to Canada and not let me go to Greece.

The financial services broker, Alex from Greece, who had been emailing me since April 2010, urged me to attend stock-market seminars in England. From what I understood, there was a plan to kill me there. There was no reason at all for me to go to England, trading seminars can be attended in Athens or Montreal. Why was he continuously telling me to go to England?

Other countries, I noticed, took part in the conspiracy as well. Through TV messages, I was warned not to seek asylum in France or Germany or else I'd be turned into a homeless person.

On June 29, 2011, I saw President Obama speaking on CNN. He said some people can't find a job for a year or more. From his tone and facial expression, the message felt directed at me: don't go to the United States, they won't let you work. I already suspected this; now it felt confirmed. Secret services pass me messages in ways you wouldn't imagine, including TV.

The Canadian police and government consider that I embarrassed them by sending my complaint, detailing everything since 2008—to Greece's Ministry of Public Security. It shows clearly what they've been doing and who they are. Lawyer Nicholas De Tomaso, partner of Anna Colarusso, refused to give me his bar number or hers.

On August 13, 2010, when I wired €300 from TD Bank to the car-rental owner in Greece, the bank entered his correct address even though I had an incorrect one—how did they know? Because they were already monitoring my computer and emails. In my email thread, Kostas gave me the wrong address; that is what I supplied. The bank "knew better," which means police told them.

In August 2010, I drafted (but didn't send) a letter to Greece's Ministry of Public Security with my change of address, due to death threats from Montreal police and Canadian secret services.

From December 2010 to June 2011, MétéoMédia (Videotron Channel 17) kept showing houses being demolished, mostly by floods. These were threats that they wouldn't allow my father's house in Greece to be sold. TV was used constantly to send me messages.

At my false arrest at D'Youville customs in Montreal on

November 19, 2010, around 2:00 p.m., they placed a water bottle in front of me to drink, a hint that soon water would be the only thing I'd have, not even food. They wanted me to die of starvation.

Montreal police also instructed bus drivers passing my house to rev their engines loudly, telling me to go live and sleep on buses. Other times they placed people nearby grinding metal to scare me.

On July 9, 2011, at 11:00 p.m., at Café Dépôt on St-Laurent, Montreal, secret services staged a woman crying to another woman at a table, the same scene they'd staged before I left for Greece on April 25, 2010, around April 20 at 3:00 p.m., at Côte-Vertu Shopping Centre near the Royal Bank. Back then the message was: they're "sorry" and I shouldn't go to Greece. I don't know why they repeated it in 2011, but I know what it meant in 2010.

On July 15, 2011, at 3:45 p.m., in Jean-Talon Metro (direction Snowdon), they placed two people posing as beggars, showing me I'd soon be begging.

On July 17, 2011, at 10:30 a.m., I called Lee at Garage Fujiaty to say buses 160 and 161 hadn't come to Van Horne & Outremont; I'd be late. This happens often, they skip buses when I'm at the stop so I arrive late.

On July 23, 2011, Lee brought in two undercover "customers" to fix their electrical systems, then ordered defective parts on purpose to make it look like our work lost clients. The cars were a Honda Civic and a Honda Accord.

On July 25, 2011, at 10:30 a.m., I phoned lawyer Nicolas De Tomaso about the letter Anna Colarusso had sent police and how to certify true copies. He dodged straight answers, wouldn't even clarify what a commissioner of oaths certifies.

On July 26, 2011, at 4:40 p.m., near Parc Metro on Hutchison by Ogilvy, I ran into George Margelis. I pointed out the undercover agents passing messages. He tried to excuse everything. Within four minutes, two police cars pulled up, and between them a gray van marked "Messages Courier." At least they admitted they were sending messages, trying to show it was "police," not the "government," protecting the government.

On July 22, 2011, around 11:30 a.m., translator Mona Rassem spoke strangely on the phone, as if participating in the conspiracy.

On July 28, 2011, at 10:00 a.m., TD Bank on Jean-Talon W. refused to submit my line-of-credit application, saying I needed "more documents," though I had everything. Fifteen minutes later I asked for a credit card application; they refused that too. I went to Scotiabank and got one.

On August 1, 2011, at 10:30 a.m., a mechanic from Auto Vie Ducep called me to repair a vehicle. When I arrived, Vie's wife, Min, said there was no car and refused to pay me for my time. She's done this many times to block me from working.

On August 2, 2011, I went to get the bar numbers for Anna Colarusso and Nicolas De Tomaso. Lawyer Ilias Kaperonis told me, "You don't need bar numbers. The European Court of Human Rights asks the Government of Canada to verify the lawyers."

On July 3, 2011, in Parc Metro, they placed a person with a broken hand—warning what would happen if I tried to submit my case to international or local courts.

By late 2010 I learned Café Cosmos on Jean-Talon had changed ownership; later it moved to Beaumont.

On August 10, 2011, at 5:23 p.m., bus 179 on L'Acadie never came; I left on foot.

On August 16, 2011, in the morning, Vie Trung Ngo had his wife call me to come work. When I arrived, they didn't pay me and told me to leave. I told Ducep by phone.

On August 18, 2011, at 5:45 p.m., I tried ten times to text Frank Michael (from translator Mona Rassem's office) about my translations messages wouldn't send. He is an undercover police agent, but I have no choice but to deal with him because police talk to everyone.

On August 31, 2011, at 3:40 p.m., bus 80 at Parc Metro didn't arrive; I walked home. This is constant, buses come an hour late or don't come more than half the time when I'm waiting.

On September 3, 2011, I visited several garages—Roza, H.K. Auto, and Auto Rajh—to collect business cards and accuse the owners in writing of conspiring with police and secret services to block my income. I mailed letters, too. No one replied, because they were involved. I had worked with these shops for years; suddenly, since September 2010, they stopped calling.

On September 3, 2011, at 12:21 p.m., at Saint-Michel Metro, I saw a man identical to someone who used to show up near my home at Jean-Talon & Wiseman (Oct 2008–Mar 2009), posing as a street dealer. He entered my metro car, then moved to another. In September 2009 I had mentioned him on the phone to John Koumparakos; soon after, another undercover in a red shirt waving a newspaper hinted we'd be "in the news."

That day I went to Auto Vie to work. Vie wasn't there. Ducep told me to work on a car; I did. They didn't pay me, and Vie never appeared. I texted him that he owed me for the work.

On my way home, at 5:37 p.m., I saw a man pretending to sleep on the bench at Jean-Talon Metro, now on the opposite platform (toward Montmorency). I mailed more letters to the other shops accusing them of conspiracy.

They also staged couples with children around me, signaling I'd never be allowed to have a family.

On September 11, 2011, at 4:15 p.m., I waited for bus 80 at Ogilvy & Hutchison (downtown direction). It comes every seven minutes; none came until 4:45. The driver lied "traffic," but it was a quiet Sunday, clearly deliberate.

On September 12 and 13, 2011, both Lee (Fujiaty) and Vie (Auto Vie) called to say they had cars for me. When I said I could come, each replied, "Okay, I'll call you back." They never did. And since then, they've never called me again.

# Chapter 6

# Into the Psychiatric Clinic (2011-2015)

On 13 September 2011, around 3:30 p.m., my father, who had been blackmailed by the police to participate in the conspiracy—told me that nothing was happening with the police and that everything was fine. He looked very unhealthy from the pressure and blackmail. I shouted at him to tell the truth instead of hiding what was happening, reminding him that the police were recording the conversations. He knew this, since he was saying and doing whatever they told him through my brother, George Margelis, an undercover agent.

I told him, "The way you are listening to them, you won't live much longer. They're going to kill you like this."

About 40 minutes later, at 4:15 p.m., four police officers entered my house and told me they had a court order to bring me to the Royal Victoria Hospital. They said, "If you don't go voluntarily, we will force you."

I told them, "You've been bothering me for more than two years. I want a lawyer right now to sue you."

They answered, "Ok, we'll find you a lawyer."

But they never did.

They handcuffed me, took me downstairs, and brought me to the Royal Victoria Hospital on Pine Avenue West, Montreal. They wanted me to see a psychiatrist. I realized it was a scam, a trick to make it seem like I had psychological problems in order to cancel my report and everything I had written.

The police had been trying this scam since September 2010, when they told my mother to make an appointment with psychiatrist Thomas Kolivakis at the same hospital. I knew their fraud back then and didn't go. Now, I couldn't escape because they forced me.

Everything I wrote in my report was proof. The police themselves had admitted much of it in my seven complaints. Yet they wouldn't let me sue them, instructing lawyers not to proceed. I told them again I wanted a lawyer to sue them, but they refused to provide one.

From what psychiatrist Gerald Wiviott wrote in the motion, and from what the police hinted to me, it was my father who had called the police on purpose, under their instructions through George—to send me to the hospital and cancel my report. Both acted under police orders, with George working as a secret agent.

The goal was to make it look like everything I said and wrote was untrue. My parents, blackmailed and brainwashed, ended up doing and saying whatever the police told them. They were even deceived into believing it was the right thing to do.

Around 5:30 p.m. the same day, a psychotherapist came to see me for five minutes and filled out a report. Shortly after, I spoke with another psychiatrist in a conference room for about 15 minutes. I told him about my case with the police and accused him out loud of conspiring with them to make it look like I had psychological problems. He never wrote any report.

The next morning, 14 September 2011, psychiatrist Silvia Monti de Flores spoke with me while standing for no more than four minutes. She told me, "Take pills."

I replied, "There is nothing wrong with me. Why should I take pills? This is a conspiracy with the police."

She left, went into her office, and another person came out, telling me to lie on a bed so they could tie me and inject me. I said, "If it's voluntary, I won't go. If you're forcing me, I will."

They told me they were forcing me. I went to bed, they tied me down, and injected my right leg. Whenever I spoke about the police, they would inject me without knowing my case, clearly conspiring with them. Other people were present, so even if I had resisted, they would have forced me.

They did this because I told Dr. Monti de Flores that it was a conspiracy. On the motion, she even wrote the diagnosis: paranoid state. But I was speaking the truth. How could I be paranoid when everything I wrote and said was backed by my complaints, which the police had admitted to? They kept me tied for about half an hour.

An hour later, they transferred me by ambulance to another facility of the same hospital, the McGill University Health Centre, Allan Memorial Hospital, in the Brief Therapy Unit. It was a psychiatric clinic. Meanwhile, they told me to do a CT scan of my head. I refused, saying, "If you adjust the machine according to your interests, it can show anything." I did not trust them; it was all a scam.

The first two days, they kept me in isolation for no reason. Later, I was moved to the general rooms. On 15 September 2011, in the morning, a nurse told me to take pills. I answered, "There is nothing wrong with me. This is a conspiracy with the police while I have a case against them."

He insisted, saying, "Because you don't let us finish talking."

Another person came and told me they would give me another injection, and if I refused, they would force me. They ordered me to lie down, and I did. They injected me again. Around 8:30 p.m., they forced me to take pills, which I swallowed with no choice.

At 2:00 a.m. the next day, 16 September 2011, while sleeping, I felt my mouth and throat were very dry and uncomfortable. I woke up, went to the washroom, lost consciousness, and fell to the floor. I got up, drank water from the sink, and felt a bit better. A nurse came, measured my blood pressure, and it was 5/8 when it should have been about 8/12. The injection, combined with the pills, had caused it. It was not impossible that they had wanted to kill me. They gave me two cups of apple juice, and I eventually fell back asleep.

On 15 September 2011, around 2:00 p.m., they presented me with the motion papers, requesting that the court order my confinement at their health center for a maximum of 30 days. The hearing was scheduled for 19 September at 10:00 a.m. On 17 September, someone stole the motion papers from my bed, they are now missing.

On 19 September 2011, I went to court in Montreal, room 14.11. A lawyer standing outside told me, "I can represent you."

I said, "If you want, you can represent me, but I will speak in court."

She agreed. I knew they had already spoken to her, but I thought I might need some technical help.

In court, I told the judge, "This is a conspiracy with the police from an ongoing case I have with them." Still, the court decided I should be confined at the hospital for up to 30 days.

I also told the opposing lawyer, "If this is my imagination, why didn't the police let me sue them, and why did they tell lawyers not to proceed?"

There was no answer.

When the judge asked my lawyer for her opinion, instead of saying this was a conspiracy, she simply replied, "I leave it to the court to decide," which made me look wrong and implied that I was participating in the conspiracy.

That night, the nurse told me that if I did not take the pills, they would take me back to court and force me to take them. They also said, "If you don't take pills, we will never let you leave the hospital." Under that pressure, I finally took the pills with no choice.

Gerard Wiviott was supposed to be my doctor at the Brief Therapy Unit of the McGill University Health Centre, Allan Memorial Institute. In the motion, it was written that Christos Margelis underwent two psychiatric assessments: one by Dr. Silvia Monti de Flores and one by Dr. Gerard Wiviott. However, as I mentioned earlier, I spoke with Monti de Flores for no more than four minutes, standing, and with Wiviott for only about six minutes, also standing. We never even sat down to talk. Yet, Wiviott wrote in the motion a diagnosis of "delusional disorder," even though he knew nothing about my case with the police.

They simply wanted to show that what I had written in my report was false. But how could they do that, when the police themselves had admitted their actions in the seven complaints I had already sent? For the psychiatrist I spoke with in the conference room on 13 September 2011 for about 15 minutes, they mentioned nothing at all, precisely because I had accused him of conspiring with the police to make it seem like I had psychological problems.

On 21 September 2011 at 5:10 p.m., I saw on CNN a report about a person about to be executed by injection. While they were speaking, someone walked past the camera with a sign saying "not enough evidence." The message was clearly directed at me, implying that I did not have enough evidence against Greece for the European Court of Human Rights, when in fact I had more than enough.

That same day, Dr. Wiviott told me, "You will do injections. If you refuse, we will take you to court and force you, instead of just giving pills." Around 3:00 p.m., a nurse injected me. Around 7:40 p.m., another nurse tried to give me the same pills that had previously dropped my blood pressure to 5/8. I refused to take them.

Inside the Brief Therapy Unit, patients were working for the police and secret services, or at least influenced by them. Nurses and doctors were also participating in the conspiracy. What they wrote in the motion was all lies. Dr. Monti de Flores claimed that I had threatened to harm my parents and that they were afraid of me. This was utterly false. My parents visited me almost every day, and each time they kissed me. When I left the health center, they took me straight home.

It was also very clear that my father had been pressured. He had told me he was willing to come to court, but in the end, he did not. Who told him not to come? The police and secret services, of course.

Psychiatrist Gerard Wiviott lied again in his report, writing that my mental state made me a danger to myself and to others, and that I required close treatment. This was untrue. I had never threatened anyone or done anything dangerous. If I truly were a danger, it would have been obvious, and they would not have let me leave the health center so quickly and without problems.

On 22 September 2011, Dr. Mathieu Sloan changed the story. He told me that I had to continue taking pills "for a little while." After the injection of 21 September, my blood pressure dropped again to 10 instead of the normal 12, even though I had also taken pills.

On 29 September 2011 at 11:00 a.m., they finally let me leave the hospital. I walked out at 11:30 a.m. I had an appointment with Dr. Sloan on 5 October 2011. I went, we spoke, they gave me the injection I had brought with me, and they set my next appointment for 20 October 2011. I kept going to these appointments with no choice.

The police and secret services had blackmailed my parents. They were doing and saying whatever the police told them, essentially working for the Montreal police. The secret services were, of course, involved as well. They kept repeating that nothing was happening and that it was all my imagination.

But this was false. My mother was the one who came to Greece in the summer of 2010 to save me. My father paid for both her ticket and mine, even though I had money for my own. He knew what was happening—that they wanted to force me onto the streets, begging for food, as punishment for hiring a lawyer to investigate my case and sue them.

My father even had a secret plan to sell his house in Greece in December 2010 or January 2011 without the Canadian and Greek police noticing. He informed his relatives over the phone that he would be moving there permanently. He planned to return in summer 2011, pretend he had changed his mind, and quietly put the house up for sale. But the police, through secret agent George Margelis, found out. They warned him not to dare.

When my father went to Greece for ten days in June 2011 to try to sell the house, the police had already spoken to the real estate agents. They blocked the sale by insisting the home was worth only one-third of its real value or less. In this way, they prevented my father from selling his own property. He could not sell his house.

The police and secret services had been telling everybody what I was doing in my house. They had also put airplanes, from July 2010 until July 2011 and at other times, flying low and making loud noise. The entire area had been hearing that, applying what seemed like psychological warfare on me, so that I would take the plane and go to Greece to be tortured.

The police of Montreal, Canada, together with the secret agents, had been applying psychological warfare on me all day, every day, telling me that they would make me become homeless and beg for food and money on the streets, and that they would cause me bodily injuries if I attempted to file my case with the European Court of Human Rights against Greece and other courts.

The police and secret agents in Canada had been manipulating and misleading the internet websites so that I could not know or trust the information they provided. For example, as I saw around August 2010, the Inter-American Court of Human Rights website said that Canada belonged to the Commission. They had also made it clear to me that if I attempted to file my case by mail, they would alter the papers at the post office so that the incorrect case would be sent to the Commission, and my case would be dismissed.

On 10 October 2011, I noticed that they had stolen my unemployment card, which I had obtained in Greece on 10 May

2010, from my documents. The official card had been stolen from my files.

They had also threatened me, through their undercover agents, that if I attempted to file my case with the Inter-American Commission of Human Rights, the European Court of Human Rights, or The Hague, they would stop me from working and turn me into a homeless person begging for food. In fact, they were already trying to do this to me.

Of course, they did not allow lawyers to sue them in Canada or worldwide. They even made threats, including death threats, if I attempted to tell a lawyer to sue them. They had also said to the public and everyone I knew that soon they would turn me into a homeless person begging for food. Even the bus drivers were aware and passed me messages, saying they would not let me on the bus without a ticket. They said that when I no longer had money for tickets, they would force me to go on foot and would not let me ride a bus at all.

They had also told my parents about what was going to happen, distressing them to the point where they would not live much longer, hastening their deaths.

On 9 November 2011, I applied for welfare, last resort financial assistance.

At the hospital, the doctors and nurses, conspiring with the police and taking orders from them, never let me talk about my case with the police. Every time I told them about it, they began threatening me, saying there was something wrong with me and that they would give me pills or even submit me to confinement in the hospital. They had also told my parents not to talk about it and to pretend that nothing was happening.

On 3 November 2011, at 2:30 p.m., I went to see psychiatrist Lepadatu at the Allan Memorial Institute for an appointment. When I told her about my case, she threatened that she would give me pills. I told her no. They never let me talk about my case with the police and the global governments.

Through all these odious offenses, the persecution, and the psychological warfare carried out daily, the police brought me to the point where I had no pleasure in my life, nor could I live as a normal human being. I lived in extreme fear and suffering, under the daily threat that at some point I would be turned into a homeless person.

On 18 November 2011, I received some translated documents from Anastasios Moussas (whose address was changed in 2012). I noticed that the police, conspiring with the place where I had faxed my documents and with him, had deliberately produced very poor-quality images of my documents, making them unreadable or barely readable. Beyond these deliberate mistakes, I had to send them back for correction and a clearer version.

The police and secret services of Canada had also told my friends, George and Theodore Tsoukalas, who participated in the conspiracy, whether or not to assemble with me, as a form of punishment. Sometimes, they even told them not to see me at all, which happened for about a month in 2010.

Since the beginning of November 2011, I had been experiencing health problems. My legs were constantly moving, even when I sat down, and I could not stay calm. Psychiatrist Lepadatu gave me pills called PMS-Clonazepam 1 mg for that purpose, and to help me sleep at night. However, they did not really help with the leg movement.

Since 9 November 2011, I had been receiving last resort welfare financial assistance, because they had tried to stop me from working. It had only been a matter of time before they did so. Now, they were threatening to stop giving me welfare, too, in order to turn me into a homeless person and torture me. At that time, I was only working a little bit, maybe two days a week, for about 3–4 hours.

Dr. Howard Margolese from the Allan Memorial Institute gave me some other pills, which reduced the movement of my legs, though I still suffered from different health problems.

If, as the doctors said, I suffered from schizophrenia just because I screamed at my father, telling him the truth about the police and secret services doing all these things to me, the psychological warfare and their effort to turn me into a homeless person, then it was clear they had caused me a serious health problem. As I described in this report, the police, with their psychological warfare, had created psychological and other health problems for me and caused me a nervous breakdown.

As for their claim that I had a delusional disorder, that was the mega fraud they committed, trying to show that I did not know what I was writing in this report, and that it was all my fantasy. But it was the truth and nothing but the truth—100%. Since they were unaware of the details of my case with the police, which also involved the government, they couldn't claim it was my imagination. That was why, when I told Dr. Howard Margolese to read my report, he said:

"No."

Since 2011, after the police told my family doctor, Jeffrey Revilis, that I had mentioned him in my report, he stopped accepting me as a patient. His secretary told me:

"Do not come here again."

They did not want me to have a family doctor.

On 10 January 2012, I shipped my documents to the European Court of Human Rights with track number

CC084414738CA (Canada Post). The undercover agents showed me that they had altered my documents so that my case would be struck from the court records, or that they had not sent anything at all. I realized I could not submit my case anywhere by post.

I also sent my petition by fax to the Inter-American Commission of Human Rights. Not all the pages might have been sent, because I saw that the fax machine had stalled. The same thing happened when I sent my documents by fax to the European Court of Human Rights on 6 January 2012, some pages were not transmitted. At the same time, I was receiving death threats from the police and secret services, telling me that I should not be sending documents to international courts.

What I understood was that, because the fax was not sent properly, they had either changed the documents I mailed to the European Court of Human Rights on 10 January 2012, sent something else, or sent nothing at all.

On 10 February 2012, my doctor, Jeffrey Revilis, refused to accept me as a patient, in conspiracy with the police. He had been my doctor for more than ten years, but they told him that I had mentioned him in my report.

In January 2012, I opened a trading account with the TD Waterhouse brokerage firm under my father's name, Christos Margelis, who had excellent credit. Under the conspiracy, they refused to open a margin account and instead opened only a cash account.

On 12 April 2012, at 2:00 p.m., I went to an appointment at the Allan Memorial Institute to get the injection they forced on me. Nurse Lowella Granflor created a scene when I told her the police were still applying psychological warfare against me, trying to show that I was aggressive. She called a psychiatrist to see me, and they gave me an injection to "calm down." Of course, there was absolutely no reason for them to do so. I was calm. They were trying to show that this was the kind of person I was, and also to discredit me because I had said that the police were still applying psychological warfare against me. They were committing fraud, trying to make it look like I had psychological problems by manipulating incidents.

Every time I told the doctors about my case with the police, they increased the dose of my medication. Of course, everyone in the hospital was participating in the conspiracy, along with the government.

The doctor who looked after me was psychiatrist Howard Margolese at the Allan Memorial Institute. On 17 April 2012, he tried to convince me that the police were not applying psychological warfare against me and that it was only my imagination. When I asked him, "What makes you believe that the police are not applying psychological warfare to me?" he said:

"The police wouldn't bother with you."

I told him there was a big case going on with the police, and if he wanted, I could give him my report to read. He refused to read it. (Of course, he knew what my report contained.)

On 6 January 2012, I had sent my case by fax to the European Court of Human Rights. On 10 January 2012, I sent my documents by mail, which the court received on 17 February 2012. Yet, on 15 February 2012, the court sent me a letter (which I received on 15 March 2012) urging me to send my documents by mail.

I responded with a registered letter on 23 March 2012 (track number RW637387301CA), telling them that I had already submitted my documents and, if they had them, to please use them. From the track number, I saw that the post office in France had not delivered my letter to the court. The conspiracy was international.

Most likely, the police and secret services had sent other documents, different from mine, to dismiss my case. The court sent me a letter on 9 June 2012, dated 29 May 2012, saying that my case was inadmissible, based on the fax they had received on 6 January 2012, and not on my mailed documents.

Also, on 10 January 2012, when I sent my documents by mail, the undercover agents showed me that they had either changed the content of my papers, not sent them at all, or sent something else. That was why the court only mentioned the fax of 6 January 2012 and not my mailed documents.

The same happened with the Inter-American Commission of Human Rights. I sent my case by fax, but they rejected it on 29 October 2012 (as they told me by email). I had faxed my case around 6 January 2012, but I noticed that my fax machine had stalled, and I was unsure if all the pages had been sent.

Because of the psychological warfare applied against me daily by the undercover agents, I had developed health problems. My legs continuously moved, and I had to take pills for that and other health issues. They still did not allow me to hire a lawyer to sue them.

On 2 August 2012, at 3:30 p.m., I went to my appointment with Dr. Howard Margolese at the Allan Memorial Institute of the Royal Victoria Hospital. He was working for the police. I told him the police were applying psychological warfare against me with their undercover agents and that they would turn me into a homeless person. Because I told him this, he said he could order my confinement in the hospital. He told me it was in my imagination and not in reality.

I told him, "It's facts and not my imagination. If it is my imagination, then why don't they let me sue them?"

He did not answer.

I also told him I did not want the injection of a medicine called Invega Sustenna, which they gave me once a month. He threatened me, saying that if I did not take it, he would order me confined in the hospital. He forced me to take the injection for no reason. They were trying to show that I was seeing things that did not exist, but they were caught red-handed lying.

On 27 September 2012, around 3:00 p.m., I went to see psychiatrist Margolese again. I told him the police were applying psychological warfare against me with their undercover agents. He gave me more pills. When I told him I did not want more pills and that it was not imagination but facts, he threatened me loudly, saying that if I did not take the pills, he would confine me in the psychiatric clinic.

He was forcing me to take pills whose potential health damage I could not even know. He also knew that justice did not exist for me. While he had once told me he would refer me to a general practitioner as my family doctor, he later said he could not find one for me. That was a lie. He wanted me to have no doctor at all.

On 11 October 2012, at 3:00 p.m., in order to stop Dr. Howard Margolese from giving me more pills, I lied to him, saying that the police were no longer bothering me. It was the only way to stop him from increasing my medication. He had already reached 11 pills a day and one injection a month, all while threatening to confine me in the psychiatric clinic.

The police and secret services continued putting death threats on me, saying they would torture me as a homeless person, not allow me to eat anywhere, make me die of starvation, and force me to sleep on the streets, especially if I submitted my case to The Hague International Criminal Court. They were constantly trying to find a way to make this happen.

On 22 November 2012, at 2:30 p.m., when I visited Dr. Howard Margolese at the Allan Memorial Institute, he asked me if I was being targeted by undercover agents using psychological warfare, as I had mentioned previously. Again, in order to stop him from giving me more pills, I told him no, I was not. He said to me, "I know you are seeing, but very little." I told him again, no, I was not seeing anything. He still insisted that I did see, but in lower volume.

When I asked him why, he said that I was seeing very few of them now. He told me, "Because this doesn't go away from patients completely. It remains in a very low volume."

The fact was that I told him I was not seeing them at all, but he did not want to accept it. He tried to make me look like a patient. He knew about undercover agents and wanted to show that it was just my imagination seeing them. The police, with their undercover agents, were applying psychological warfare all day long at the same volume, not "a little bit."

On 24 January 2013, I went to Mona Rassem's office to have my documents stamped for an actual copy, where she worked as a commissioner of oaths. Although I had previously visited, they had done a poor job, and I had to correct them on translations from French to English. This time, however, it seemed correct, as far as I understood, likely because they feared the court.

On 14 January 2013, Vi, the owner of Auto Vie car mechanics repair shop, suddenly stopped calling me for work twice a week, as he had been doing. I was doing electrical work on his vehicles, but now, in conspiracy, he would not call me for work. They did this to make me struggle financially so that I could not do anything in my life while I was trying to get a stable, full-time job to stop relying on welfare (last-resort financial assistance).

He had done this in the past as well, and also applied psychological warfare by saying he would not call me again for work during times when I was not collecting welfare. His wife, Min, also did this, as I mentioned in this report. Meanwhile, the police and secret services would not let me get a job anywhere else.

Psychiatrist Howard Margolese made me understand that he had a chart according to the pills he was giving me and how I was doing. In conspiracy with the police, they were manipulating this chart. At the beginning, when he started giving me pills, the secret services reduced the appearance of their secret agents applying psychological warfare to me so they could say the pills were working.

Later, around November 2012, when I decided to lie to him by saying I was not seeing anyone so that he would stop giving me more and more pills, he insisted otherwise. He wrote that I was seeing very few of the undercover agents, even though I had told him I was not seeing any. He refused to write down what I told him, preferring instead to portray me as a patient and manipulate the chart, claiming, "It never goes away totally."

The police and secret services made it clear to me that they would not allow me to find a job if I searched for one, as had happened in September 2010. The places I applied to told me that I would not get a job because they had already been spoken to. This forced me to live on welfare, last-resort financial assistance, where I could not develop in my life or do anything because of the very low amount of money I received. They also threatened that they would not provide me with welfare in the future if I applied again.

I tried to get a job at Auto Vie, which I mentioned in this report. However, since Vi was allegedly involved in a conspiracy with the secret services, as soon as he had the chance, he stopped calling me for work. It was unstable from the beginning, and he never wanted to put me on the payroll. I had no choice but to remain on welfare, since they had already destroyed my business and prevented me from starting a new one.

The police also threatened to put me in jail through their undercover agents in some fraudulent way, which I did not know. On 22 February 2013, I wrote in my report about how Vi had stopped calling me for work. As soon as I wrote this, the police gave him notice to start calling me twice a week again, in order to show that they had not stopped calling me, manipulating everything. The police and secret services would not let me find a job anywhere else, blocking me from the job market and forcing me to live on welfare in poverty. This was something I did not want, and they planned to stop even this welfare, turning me into a homeless person.

The police made me understand that I had embarrassed them in Greece at the Ministry of Public Security when I sent my complaint on 14 June 2010, which included my report and everything they had been doing to me. Because of that, they wanted to put me in jail for an unknown reason and turn me into a homeless person as punishment.

On 9 April 2013, I received my police reports from the authorities, but they did not include the false arrests that had followed. One was on 26 January 2008, when they arrested me and forced me to mention people involved in illegal activities I had seen at a workplace. They then triggered those people against me with the purpose of killing me. The second was on 7 April 2010, when they wanted to create an identity issue in order to prevent me from going to Greece, finding a lawyer there, and referring my case to the Hague International Criminal Court. I have mentioned both these arrests in this report.

By 29 January 2014, the police and secret agents reduced the amount of work they were sending me. For about a month, in conspiracy with Vi, the owner of Auto Vie, where I worked part-time as a car electrician, he reduced the amount of work he was calling me for. While I was trying to get a full-time job, the police would not allow it, threatening that they would stop calling me for work in order to make me struggle financially and suffer.

In June 2013, I learned from others that George Papaspirou, a member of the drug trafficking organization I mentioned earlier, had sold his car mechanics repair shop on St. Laurent in Montreal and moved to Fort Lauderdale, Florida. Also, Rajah, the owner of Auto Rajh, had moved to another place.

Since April 2013, the police and secret services had almost

stopped sending cars for electrical work at Garage Fujiaty, conspiring with the owner, Ty Fujiaty. As a result, I had virtually no work to do when I went once a week in a part-time arrangement. My income from there dropped to almost zero, only about one hour of work per week! This was a convenient excuse to eventually stop calling me for work altogether. Everything was orchestrated by the police and secret services, manipulating my income and preventing me from doing anything with my life.

On 20 October 2013, I noticed that people from the secret services had stolen $600 from my drawer in my room. My house had essentially become their house too. They had placed cameras everywhere and had also disappeared documents, as I mentioned earlier in my report.

Since 19 December 2013, psychiatrist Carl Chiniara looked at me a couple of times instead of Howard Margolese, pretending that I had psychological problems without knowing my case.

On 5 February 2014, Hoa from Garage Hoa, through his mechanic Ann, who had recommended me to him, told me that he had many cars in need of electrical repairs and remote starters, and that he would be calling me often. I installed a car starter for him and checked another vehicle, but he never called me again. The police and secret services had told him not to contact me for work, as their efforts were to turn me into a homeless person. There was absolutely no reason for him to stop calling me, as he needed me there.

On 27 February 2014, the police sent me a letter asking for a payment of $43.50 for some police reports they had sent me in March 2013, claiming that the check I had given them had bounced. With the penalty, the total came to $78.50. At first, they had already withdrawn the money from my new bank account, I had seen it. Now, to make me spend more money, they asked for the payment again. Scotia Bank, a participant in the conspiracy, did not disclose the March 2013 withdrawal in order to make me pay again. I sent them the new sum by check and explained that I had already paid for the reports last year. If I had not paid, they would have contacted me within a month, not after a year.

On 24 March 2014, I went to see lawyer Robert Brankin and told him about my case. He said he did not want to take it because there was no evidence of what I was saying. When I told him that the police had put me under secret, unofficial police protection, he replied, "There, they have put you under police protection," trying to make me feel I should be grateful for it, if such a thing were possible.

When I asked him why the police would not give me the report of my false arrest on 26 January 2008, he did not answer but kept repeating that I had no evidence for my claims. He also began misleading the conversation so that I could not explain further, as it would become clear what the police had been doing to me. He kept turning the discussion toward another case. This was one more lawyer they had spoken to, instructing him not to take my case. He continuously misled the conversation.

On 4 April 2014, Hoa from Garage Hoa called me again through his mechanic Ann to check a car. He had called me only twice about two months earlier, and ever since then, nothing, because he had been told not to. When they saw I was trying to find out through lawyer Robert Brankin who I could sue, Hoa wanted to create the impression that he had a relationship with me and that he called me for work. In reality, he called me only once.

Around September 2013, while I was at an appointment with psychiatrist Howard Margolese, I entered a room next to the appointment counter. I saw a doctor speaking to my parents, brainwashing them into believing I had psychological problems. My father was crying like a baby. From what I understood, he had come to think I had some kind of problem, even though nothing on my part suggested such a thing. They feared my report because it contained the truth, and they wanted to cancel it.

The Canadian secret services had also been putting, on a daily basis, couples kissing provocatively in front of me to pass me messages.

The police of Montreal, Canada, wanted to put me in jail for an unknown reason and turn me into a homeless person to punish me severely because I had embarrassed them at the Ministry of Public Security in Athens, Greece, when I sent my complaint on 14 June 2010. That complaint contained my report describing everything the police had been doing to me since 2008. They also wanted to punish me because I had tried to hire a lawyer in Greece to submit my case to the International Criminal Court in The Hague, a lawyer the police and government of Greece did not allow me to hire.

The police, with the secret services, committed fraud after fraud. At first, they falsely arrested me on 26 January 2008, claiming identity issues—that I was some illegal alien using my identity, and threatened to deport me. They had other methods to confirm someone's identity, but their plan, as I mentioned earlier in this book, was to send me to Romania. There, Stere Craciun (Gigi) would send someone to kill me. Since nobody had entered the country with my passport, why did they arrest me as an illegal alien? They intended to send me to Romania so that Gigi's people could kill me.

Afterwards, they refused to let me hire a lawyer to take my case. They blocked lawyers in Canada, Greece, and the United States. Then they instructed the Royal Victoria Hospital to declare that I had psychological problems in order to discredit my report.

They told my parents to say that the police were doing nothing to me and that it was all my imagination. I saw with my own eyes a doctor or nurse at the Allan Memorial Institute brainwashing my parents into believing I had psychological issues.

Later, when I reported to them about the criminal organization after they attempted to kill me on 8 May 2009, they put me under unofficial police protection. Also, in late 2009 and early 2010, they developed a mathematical method, counting "points of guilt" and converting signs of weakness into signs of guilt in order to charge me with murder. At the time, I had no idea about murders, yet their method was real, and they were preparing to accuse me of murder, an accusation that would, of course, lead to a charge.

Since April 2014, they had been undermining my job as a car electrician at Auto Vie, where I was working part-time. Customers whose cars I repaired often refused to pay for the work or wanted it done for free or at very low prices. This sometimes made it very difficult to profit from repairs and was a deliberate attempt to undermine my job.

On 3 August 2014, their agents from Apartment 4 blasted loud music with heavy bass from 8 p.m. until 10 p.m. to get on my nerves and apply psychological warfare against me.

On 9 November 2014, I noticed that €5,000 in an envelope was missing from my drawer. My father had given me the money in his room around 29 October 2014. I couldn't lie, it was caught on the hidden cameras the police had placed in my room. It was yet another effort by the police to drag me down financially. Their undercover agents had stolen the money.

On 11 November 2014 at 5:45 p.m., I went to Police Station 33 on Beaumont Street to report the theft. The police officer asked me who I thought had stolen the money. I said most likely their undercover agents, though I knew it was them. There were no signs of robbery in my house, no locks broken. They had simply opened the door and the drawer, taken the money, and left. They knew exactly how much was there and where I had placed it because of the hidden cameras.

The officer typed on his computer. When I asked him for a report form to write down what had happened, he gave me an incident report, most likely meant for car theft or insurance purposes. When I asked him if this was the correct report for my case, he said yes. When I told him it was for cars, he said, "It's universal." But since I was under police protection and my house was full of hidden cameras, the police knew perfectly well who had stolen the money: their undercover agents.

On 15 December 2014 at 6:55 p.m. in Rosemont Metro station, they placed a man who appeared homeless, pretending to sleep on the floor, to hint that they would make me end up like that.

It was not the only time, they had done this many times before.

On 18 December 2014 at 3:00 p.m. in the Allan Memorial Institute, the psychiatrist I saw was no longer Howard Margolese but Carl Chammas. Acting on orders from the police and secret services, and in conspiracy with Margolese, he behaved as if I were a psychiatric patient. Without knowing anything about my case with the police, he claimed I had psychological problems.

On 23 November 2014, I wrote an email to Giannis, my accountant in Greece, inquiring about taxation on stock market profits. When I mentioned to him what had happened in the summer of 2009 in Greece, when I started a business selling remote car starters but was prevented from continuing because the Greek police and government, in conspiracy with Canadian authorities, told all my partners not to deal with me, he stopped replying. Their goal had been to force me back to Canada and put me under police protection. Giannis was told by Greek authorities not to continue the conversation, as it would expose what they had been doing to me. He did not answer my two follow-up emails.

The Montreal police, in collusion with Vi, the owner of Auto Vie, drastically reduced my work hours on 13 February 2015. They were calling me for only about five hours a week, making it impossible for me to earn enough money. On 7 March 2015, they stopped calling me for work altogether, again to keep me financially struggling and force me to rely on welfare, which provided only a very low income and kept me living in poverty. The police had blocked me from the job market entirely, making sure I could not get work anywhere else.

At Garage Fujiaty, where I also worked, the owner, Ty Fujiaty, had almost stopped calling me for work since April 2013, allowing me only one hour per week. Around September 2014, I asked his wife, Hi Fujiaty, to bring a poster advertising remote car starters from their old address to the new one so we could advertise. She never brought it. When I asked why, she lied and said it was lost. It was a large poster, how did she even lose it? The truth was, they did not want to give me work and were preparing to phase me out, as instructed by the police.

On 20 February 2015, I asked Hi Fujiaty to call me for work any time during the week, but they still would not call me. I was only allowed to go on Fridays for one hour.

The police and government of Canada feared only two things: that my case might go to court, or that I might go to Iran to apply for asylum. Between 7 March and 26 April 2015, Auto Vie called me for work only about three times. When the police thought I might sue them or go to Iran for asylum, they allowed me some work. When they realized I would not, they cut me off again.

They also interfered with my bank accounts and credit cards. Around February 2015, my trading account at TD Waterhouse was suddenly placed "out of order," preventing me from using it and from making money in the stock market. It took two weeks at TD Bank on Jean Talon to straighten it out so I could use it again. They had mixed it up in such a way that it was almost impossible to fix. It was a margin account.

# Chapter 7

# Interference on My Credit Cards by the Police – Major Psychological Warfare 2015–2019)

In April 2015, the police and secret services began interfering with my credit cards to give me bad credit. They made one Scotia Bank Visa bill disappear, then called me, claiming I had not paid. When I received the second bill, I spent it and told them so. Around the same time, my National Bank Mastercard did not send me a new card. When I called, the teller said he would activate my old one. At the end of the call, he told me to "activate the card and remove the sticker." I replied, "Which sticker? It's an old card." He insisted it would work, but it didn't.

When I called again, they admitted they needed to send a new card. The first one they claimed to have sent never arrived, it was made to disappear. I had to request another. These tricks were deliberate. The government feared I might go to Iran to apply for asylum, so they wanted to drain my finances, block me from access to money, and eventually turn me into a homeless person.

By April 27, 2015, I had sent this report as part of my 8th complaint to the Montreal police (Police Service des Affaires Juridiques) and to the Ministry of Public Safety. Both letters were registered. The police complaint (track no. RN080434167CA) and the ministry complaint (track no. RN080434153CA) were both received on May 5, 2015, signed by Marc L. for the police and by M. Mahi for the ministry.

On May 6, 2015, around 6:00 p.m., my father, Christos Margelis, went to Auto Vie to ask why the owner wasn't calling me for work. Vie told him I spent too much time "looking at the computer." That was a lie, Vie had no internet, only the Mitchell program for wiring diagrams. He even admitted, "I have work," yet still refused to call me. On May 28, 2015, Vie stopped calling me altogether.

They had blocked me from the job market entirely. I could no longer run my own business. I was forced into poverty, surviving only on last-resort welfare assistance. In this way, I could not buy a car, find a girlfriend, or move forward in life. Their plan was likely to cut even that assistance and turn me into a homeless person.

Around May 1, 2015, I called President's Choice Financial Mastercard to ask about my card expiring in June. They told me a replacement had been sent on April 23, but I never received it. They promised another, yet it disappeared again. This was one more case of interference.

Despite my complaints to both the police and Minister Lise Thériault, nothing changed. They continued to act the same, if not worse. Thériault and police headquarters were clearly part of the conspiracy.

On June 2, 2015, I emailed the Commission des Droits de la Personne et des Droits de la Jeunesse (Quebec Human Rights Commission) to see if I could file my case. They replied that my situation did not meet their grounds of discrimination, so they could not consider it. I had no way to hire a lawyer. Justice was blocked.

The ministry and police never replied to my registered complaints. By not answering, they effectively admitted everything.

On June 18, 2015, around 4:30 p.m., at Rosemont Metro Station, I saw an older man in poor physical condition, dragging two travel bags, one of which was broken. They were hinting that this would be my fate. Scenes like this were staged daily.

On June 25, 2015, at 6:20 p.m., I called Sears Mastercard because I hadn't received my replacement card due in July. They said they had mailed it on June 3, but again, it never came. The police and secret services were repeatedly stealing my cards and tampering with my bank accounts.

On June 29, 2015, around 1:00 p.m., I used my Sears Mastercard at Provigo on Hutchison and Jean Talon. It was declined. At 1:35 p.m., I called Sears. First, the teller lied, saying the card had expired. I corrected her: "It expires next month." Then she claimed it was canceled because I never received the replacement card sent on June 3. I told her, "Canceling the new card has nothing to do with my old one." She then gave another lie: both cards had the same number. That was impossible. Finally, she admitted I would have no working card and must wait again for a replacement.

This was clear proof of interference, placing my cards out of order, making them disappear, and stealing money from my accounts. The police and government of Canada, knowing I might go to Iran for asylum, were determined to keep me financially broken, push me toward homelessness, and make me suffer daily.

By August 21, 2015, Vie from Auto Vie had completely stopped calling me for work. They had blocked me entirely from the job market. I also noticed that the police and secret services had forced my brother, George Margelis, onto welfare (last resort financial assistance) since 2011, draining all his savings. Their goal was to keep him dependent so that if I were ever turned into a homeless person, George would be unable to help me.

By early 2016, George told me his savings were almost gone and that he would soon be left only with welfare, about $640 per month. He warned the family that he would not have enough for rent and bills, even though he was already paying less by claiming low income. He did not go to work, as the police and secret services had ordered him not to, deliberately creating financial strain for me, my father, and my mother. Their goal was to make our entire family suffer financially.

Meanwhile, Vie at Auto Vie refused to call me for work, following their instructions to make me suffer. They also blocked me from hiring lawyers, warning them immediately not to take my case. The lawyers who took part in this conspiracy were already mentioned in my book and official reports. Their only fear was that I might go to Iran, apply for asylum, publish my book, and possibly make a movie about my case.

They even stole clothes from my home, trying to ensure that if I were forced onto the streets, I would have no clothes. They wanted me to spend more money replacing them. Under this constant pressure, George developed psychological problems and depression.

On July 26, 2016, I finally received an email from the Inter-American Commission of Human Rights—four years after I first submitted my case. It vaguely explained in which situations they could grant precautionary measures, but the overall clarity was unclear.

On January 21, 2017 (Saturday), a customer brought in a 2004 Acura TSX to Auto Vie for a remote starter. Around 2:00 p.m., Vie blasted me over the phone, accusing me of not having the starter. I explained that I had gone to the warehouse, but it was closed; I promised to have the starter by Monday at 6:00 p.m. He agreed.

However, on January 23, 2017, when I arrived, the customer,

who was a secret agent—already had his own starter and bypass unit from Canadian Tire. The bypass wasn't compatible: it had no wiring diagram and hadn't been flashed for that car. I told him, "Use my bypass; it costs $60. I can give it to you for $40 with a one-year warranty." He refused, insisting on the useless one. I then said, "Okay, $20 for the bypass so I can do the job." He replied, "Even if you give it to me for free, I don't want it. I want the Canadian Tire one."

He refused the job entirely. It was a scam designed to waste my time—2.5 hours on the road with no result. This proved he had planned it all along, since he admitted the starter had been purchased more than 40 days earlier. Usually, Vie would have been furious at such a wasted job, but this time he laughed, showing he was in on the setup.

When I left around 5:45 p.m. at Jean Talon Metro, heading toward Snowdon, I saw two police officers talking to a supposed homeless man lying on the floor asking for money. It was a staged message—showing me "who was behind it."

The police and secret agents continued their psychological warfare against me daily, using undercover operatives and involving nearly everyone around me in the conspiracy.

On 10 November 2016, I underwent a Holter test to monitor my heartbeats because I was experiencing irregular ones. On 12

January 2017, I went to get the results at Clinique Médicale de la Cité at 18:30. The doctor there told me, "It's normal." I did not think irregular heartbeats were normal; I believed he was trying to hide the problem they had caused me.

On 8 March 2017, I tested my blood pressure, and it was higher than usual, at 14 and 9, caused by the psychological warfare they carried out on me daily.

I was considering filing for asylum in Iran to publish my book, make a movie of my case, and leave something in history. At that time, my parents did not want me to leave Canada, but that could change.

On 5 July 2017, George Margelis told me that our parents might throw him out of the house. He said, "If this happens, I will go live at a shelter." This meant the police had banned him from working. They forced him to live off me, making me spend my money to support him. The police did not want it to look like he worked for them, but they were working together discreetly.

They sent secret agents to places like McDonald's, Tim Hortons, and other stores to hike prices when I went. In September 2017, at the Tim Hortons on Jean Talon and Hutchison, I bought a chocolate chill. The price was $2.30, but they charged me $3.30. When I pointed it out, the employee gave me the money back. It happened with McDonald's many times as well.

That same month, my father, Christos Margelis, went to Copie 2000 to make three color copies. They charged him $3. A few days later, when I asked the price, they told me 50 cents per copy. They had raised the price for my father as the police told them to.

Around 15 July 2017, the Government of Canada sent a letter to my parents, Christos and Evgenia Margelis, informing them they would discontinue the Guaranteed Income Supplement—about $550 per month for my father and $300 for my mother. They gave no reason. I was paying household expenses by cheque ($450 per month), and they tried to count that as income. When I told my mother out loud that my cheque payments were for rent and bills, the police and government reversed course. Later, when I called again, they said it had been a mistake in their files, and by September 2017, they restored the supplement. Still, they had tried to cause almost $12,000 in financial damage, which would have driven my parents into depression.

In September 2017, my mother went to Jean Coutu on Parc Avenue, Montreal, to develop five pictures. They charged her $13.50. On 9 November 2017, she went again for the same images, and they charged her $30. It was clear they had been told to raise prices to cause financial problems.

Also in July 2017, the police and government created new financial damage by reducing George Margelis' welfare cheque by

$100 per month, a disaster for him. Now he was asking me for more money, putting more strain on me. They claimed the Guaranteed Income Supplement of my parents was $26 less than the maximum, so they reduced his welfare. But George had been receiving the same amount for at least four years, with no change in our parents' income.

They also gave notice to buses on Bloomfield and Ball not to arrive on time. At the end of December 2017 and early January 2018, the bus that was supposed to come every 8 minutes came half an hour late. I waited outside in -25°C cold. It was the 80 bus south.

On 9 January 2018, I wrote in my official report that the 80 du Parc buses were coming half an hour late instead of every 7 minutes, leaving me in -25°C. The next day, 10 January 2018, John Vlahakis, who worked for the secret services, called my house and spoke to George Margelis. He told him, "When I go to work, the bus delays for over 20 minutes, and I wait outside in -20." He said this over the phone (which was tapped) to make it appear that bus delays were usual, not specifically targeted at me.

This was more proof that John Vlahakis worked for the police and secret services.

On 5 February 2018, while I was talking with my cousin Nikos on Facebook, I told him what had happened in Greece in the summer of 2010, when police, undercover, and secret agents were trying to turn me into a homeless person. He admitted that he knew what had happened and what was happening.

On 8 February 2018, Facebook deleted his account. My cousin Nikos told me that Facebook had removed it without explanation. He opened a new account under the same name, but our conversation had disappeared. The Greek and Canadian police, governments, and secret agents did not want any proof of what happened in the summer of 2010. Nikos knew very well what happened that summer; it was written in my report, and he was a witness.

On 11 March 2018, at 4:40 p.m. at Snowdon Metro station, they placed a person acting homeless who begged for money. They wanted to show me what they planned to turn me into. They continuously used either real or fake homeless people to send me messages that they would not allow me to rent a house, even when old, and would force me to live outside.

On 15 March 2018, I saw Ted Wright at McDonald's in Atwater. He asked, "How is it going with the police?"

I told him, "They are doing all kinds of things to me."

He said, "If you had a camera, you could take them on camera."

I replied, "The police and secret services have already admitted to their doings, along with my eight complaints. A camera is useless."

Ted stopped eating. When I asked if he remembered the emails we exchanged in the summer of 2010 in Greece, he said, "Yes, I remember." He also told me that he no longer worked at the Westmount Legal Clinic but was now an advisor.

On 1 April 2018, around 5:45 p.m., they placed one of their agents on bus 80 south, number 31816. A man entered and started talking to himself, again showing me what they wanted to turn me into. Later, on 8 April 2018, at 1:00 a.m., the police agents in apartment 5 next door played music with a bass subwoofer at low but noticeable volume. After 20 minutes, they stopped.

On 16 April 2018, my father went to CUSM/MUHC – Lachine Hospital for cataract surgery with Dr. Marino Discepola. Although my father had signed to pay $350 for the lens, the hospital charged him $450. While waiting with my mother, an older woman told her she had paid $350 for the same lens. It was a clear case of theft.

Meanwhile, drug traffickers and killers George Papaspirou, Sterie Craciun (Gigi), Peter Maltezos, Mike Plaras, John Koubarakos, and Theo Anastasopoulos were free and laughing at me because I took the legal path. They continued selling drugs, while the police tried to turn me into a homeless person because I sued them. Police officers themselves were involved with this criminal organization (I have their names in this report). They informed the traffickers that I had mentioned them after my arrest on 26 January 2008, when I was pressured to give information. After that, the traffickers tried to kill me twice. That was when I went to the police station on Parc Avenue, told them what was happening, and was placed in police protection after seeing someone in my back lane looking for suspects.

Since early April 2018, I noticed that Garage Fujiaty had no cars for electrical repairs. I received a few calls asking about remote starters, and although I gave low prices, the customers disappeared. This was the police and secret services regulating my work down to zero. Even when I worked for free to keep customers, it was useless. The police and their agents controlled the business entirely.

On the nights of 10 and 11 May 2018, around midnight, I noticed that the secret agents next door in apartment 5 had placed something that made a low-frequency vibration, like a subwoofer, to prevent me from sleeping. Around 1:00 a.m., I finally fell asleep.

On 2 June 2018, at 11:40 p.m., while riding the 80 Parc Avenue south bus, number 31820, a man boarded who appeared to be homeless, pushing a carriage with things inside. This was yet another message they sent to me, something they did very often.

From 10 July 2018 onward, airplanes began flying low over my neighborhood, making loud noise as a form of psychological warfare. This revealed that the government was also involved in the conspiracy. The airport flight controllers were instructing pilots to fly low until they reached my neighborhood, then rise, creating as much noise as possible. When the planes did this, I asked George Margelis if he heard the noise. He said yes.

On Friday, 13 July 2018, while waiting for bus 94 at Iberville at 12:45 p.m., the bus failed to arrive at 1:00 p.m. as scheduled. Even by 1:35 p.m., it still had not come. I called Ty Fujiaty to tell him, "The bus hasn't arrived yet; I'll be there in about 20 minutes." They had clearly ordered the driver not to show up, as they usually did. The bus finally arrived at 1:40 p.m.

Fujiaty, although supposed to have work for me with electrical problems, only let me come in on Fridays, usually for one hour, sometimes two, and rarely longer. The conspiracy was apparent, they did not want me to earn money and wanted me to suffer financially.

On 20 July 2018, at Iberville Metro South, I was at the bus stop by 12:50 p.m. The bus was supposed to arrive at 1:00 p.m., but it did not. At 1:15 p.m., I called Garage Fujiaty and informed them that the bus had not arrived, and I would be about 20 minutes late. Just three minutes after my call, the bus arrived. When leaving later, the 94 Iberville north bus, scheduled for 2:39 p.m., did not arrive until 3:10 p.m. Again, it was clear that the buses, police, and secret services were working together in conspiracy.

That same day, around 1:30 p.m., Carlos the painter at Garage Fujiaty said out loud that during the week, a vehicle had come in with an electrical problem. He said that their mechanic, Mohan, told Ty Fujiaty not to call me because I "did a lot of bypasses" on electrical issues. This was a lie. Sometimes bypasses were necessary, but only if there was no other way to fix the problem. What Carlos and Fujiaty tried to show was that it wasn't them in conspiracy with the police, but Mohan. In reality, Ty and his family were the bosses, not Mohan. He took responsibility to cover them, hiding that they were indeed conspiring with the police and secret services. They were in the conspiracy in a big way.

I also remembered back to 13 September 2011, when, after a court order, I was sent to the psychiatric hospital at McGill University Health Centre. As mentioned earlier in this book, my parents had called the police after I shouted at my father and brother, who kept insisting, as the police had told them to, that it wasn't the police doing these things to me. It had been a nervous breakdown caused by the psychological warfare of undercover agents showing me daily that they wanted to turn me into a homeless person.

At the hospital, Dr. Silvia Monti de Flores wrote in her motion that my parents told the police to send me. In reality, it was George Margelis, my brother, whom the police had instructed to push them to do it. She claimed I threatened my parents, which was a lie. I never threatened anyone. I was simply loud. She also claimed my parents feared for their safety, but they visited me almost every day. When I was released, they immediately brought me home. My father even said he would come to court, though when the hearing took place on 19 September 2011, he did not, because the police and secret services told him not to.

Dr. Monti de Flores also said I became "agitated" and "potentially aggressive." Another lie. All I told her was that there was a big case involving the police. As soon as I mentioned the word police, she called someone to inject my leg. If the hospital had surveillance cameras, they could confirm what really happened. By the time I told them there was a big case with the police, why didn't they investigate?

On 14 September 2011, Dr. Gerald Wiviott also wrote that I had delusions, claiming I thought the police stopped me from working and that I wanted to sue the government. He didn't even get it right, I tried to sue the police, not the government. He called me delusional without ever reading the answers the police themselves had sent me in response to the seven complaints I had filed.

He also claimed I believed my family wanted me hospitalized so that I couldn't sue the police. More lies. These doctors made reports without knowing anything about the real case, never even contacting the police to get the documents they had on me.

After that, I was sent to psychiatrist Howard Margolese, who did the same. He said I had delusions and prescribed me medication for schizophrenia—Invega Sustenna injections, Seroquel, Kemadrin (for leg movements he said were side effects), and Epival (for "aggressive behavior"). But I did not have schizophrenia, nor did I have aggressive behavior. At most, I sometimes shouted at my father or my brother George about the case. I understood I should have been quieter, but that didn't mean I needed pills.

When I asked Margolese to read my report, he refused. They only wanted to cancel my case by labeling me, but it was too late— the police had already admitted to their actions in response to the eight complaints I had submitted.

On 19 August 2018, around 9:00 p.m., they sent a fire truck almost in front of my house to terrorize me. They seemed to know I might not be able to go to Iran to apply for asylum. It was not the first time they did this. A few days later, on the 25th, around 11:30 a.m., on bus 80 south (Park Avenue, bus number 31-801), they sent a man who looked homeless. He wore no shirt, only shorts, and carried three bags full of cans—another hint that they wanted me to believe I would end up like that, surviving only by recycling cans. They did these things every day, constantly.

The police, through undercover and secret agents, kept showing me that when my parents died, the building owner would throw me out. Wherever I asked to rent an apartment, they would speak to the landlords not to rent to me, forcing me into shelters and homelessness. They always showed only me in this scenario, meaning my brother George Margelis would be given housing for himself.

As I mentioned earlier, ever since welfare gave me a raise, Garage Fujiaty had stopped bringing me cars for electrical work. By 8 September 2018, they hadn't brought me any cars since April. I still went there every Friday from 1:00 to 2:00 p.m., but with no work, Fujiaty just gave me $20 and sent me home.

Often, they even used real homeless people against me, applying psychological warfare by showing me "what I would become."

On 5 October 2018, I went to Fido to get a SIM card and put a $10 voucher for my father's new phone. At Galerie d'Anjou, I had previously not been charged for a SIM card, but this store charged me $10. When I checked my balance by calling 611, it showed "zero." On 6 October 2018, when I called 611 again, it still said zero, though my real balance was $9.80.

The representative told me, "That's how it is now—you can't know your balance unless you speak to a representative." Yet when I checked by dialing 225, it showed 45 cents left, not $9.80. The rep also claimed calls to Greece cost $1 per minute. Later that day, around 4:40 p.m., I went back to Mobiphone on Jean Talon, where I had bought the SIM and voucher. The teller repeated the same story: that balances could only be checked by calling Fido. When I asked about the Greece rate, he pretended he couldn't find it in his computer—impossible for someone who worked all day with phones.

I knew they had spoken to Fido to arrange these tricks. Two years earlier, when I used vouchers, I could easily check my balance via the automated system without speaking to a representative. On the Jean Talon receipt, it said about 65 cents per minute for international calls, not $1 as they claimed. They were overcharging me and trying to prevent me from monitoring my balance.

On 6 October 2018 at 6:30 p.m., I called Fido again at 611, and it still said 45 cents when it should have been $9.80. Sometimes, before visiting the store, it showed zero balance.

On 8 October 2018 at 7:40 p.m., when I called 611, the representative finally admitted that for a $10 voucher, they gave 50 minutes. Only after I repeatedly asked did he tell me I could check my balance by calling 611 and pressing option 2. Then it worked, showing me how many minutes remained.

Meanwhile, my father was not a very smart man, making it easier for the police and psychiatric doctors to brainwash him about my health condition. My mother, however, knew what was happening, and George also knew, since he worked for them.

The police and secret services had pressured George heavily to obey them (keeping him on welfare and controlling what he did). As a result, he showed early signs of psychosis, severe depression, and melancholia. He was "finished." He refused to see a psychiatrist because they had told him not to.

At the end of September 2018, I told him to call the government to ask why my parents' supplement had been cut by $27, which reduced his welfare check by about $100 per month. He said he would call, but by the end of October, he still hadn't. They told him not to call, creating further financial problems for my parents and me.

This section of the report was submitted as part of my 9th complaint to the Montreal Police Service, specifically the Police Service des Affaires Juridiques.

On 29 November 2018, I sent my 9th complaint to the police, track number RN355406454CA. It was delivered the next day and signed by Marc M.

On 12 December 2018 at 12:30 p.m., the police called me to Station 33 on Beaumont Street. They told me they would not turn me into a homeless person when I got old. Yet when I left, the police agents acted oppositely. I told them to leave me alone and let me work, but they didn't.

Around 1 February 2019 at 1:30 p.m. at Garage Ty Fujiaty, a police agent brought in a car with a faulty clock spring under the steering wheel. The ABS and horn didn't work. I told him to replace it. Mohan, the mechanic, interfered again and told Fujiaty not to do it. It was a straightforward one-hour job, as Carlos from the body shop pointed out while laughing. The customer left, and Carlos told me, "It's that guy Mohan who told Fujiaty not to change it." It was the second time Mohan interfered with cars that needed electrical work. He tried to make it seem like it was his decision, not Fujiaty's, so that once again I had work one time and none for months, as happened in 2018. Mohan was covering for Ty and Hi Fujiaty.

On 10 January 2019, my mother, Eugenia Gioni Margelis, was diagnosed with multiple myeloma, a cancer of the bone marrow. Part of this was due to the distress caused by my case with the police and secret services.

On 17 January 2019, I saw Dr. Margolese at the old Royal Victoria. Since my 9th complaint was clear that the pills, injections, and schizophrenia diagnosis had no basis, the police had no choice but to inform him. At first, he was cold and upset. I noticed, so I told him, "Sometimes I see things that don't exist." He immediately became happier and started writing in his chart. I said this because they were paying me welfare while not letting me work.

On 14 February 2019 at 12:00 p.m., I was at the Royal Victoria Glen site waiting for bus 77 with my mother. I waved, but the driver ignored us even when I knocked on the window several times. My mother witnessed it—clear proof that the buses took orders from police and secret services.

Later that same day, around 6:00 p.m., I went to Provigo at Jean Talon and Hutchison. My Visa Tim Hortons card was suddenly "out of order." Luckily, I had cash. Around 7:15 p.m., my parents waited at Jarry Metro for bus 193. It came one hour and fifteen minutes late. The driver blamed traffic, but earlier that day, there was none.

On 17 February 2019 at 3:30 p.m., my mother and I waited for bus 80 at Bloomfield and Ball. It was delayed 30 minutes, though it was supposed to pass every 10. George arrived 20 minutes later. I told my mother what was happening, but George, as always, sided with the police: "This is nonsense." My mother had witnessed these delays many times.

On 25 February 2019 at 3:38 p.m., at the same stop, we waited again for bus 80 south. It never came. After 28 minutes, my mother, frustrated, called my father and scolded him for not telling her the bus schedule so she wouldn't wait in the cold. But the bus was supposed to pass every 10 minutes. Again—proof.

They also harassed us by phone. On 20 March 2019 at 11:45 a.m., my mother picked up a call where no one spoke English, then they hung up. A week later, the same thing happened. On 28 March 2019, her friend Voula called twice. I picked up, but Voula pretended it was the wrong number, even though she knew my voice. She wanted to normalize "wrong calls." Voula also brainwashed my mother with whatever messages the police wished to pass.

I noticed the police and secret services watched my face expression 24 hours a day. Whenever they saw my thoughts (through agents or hidden cameras), sirens would suddenly go off— police or fire trucks. It was meant to intimidate me, fearing I might go to Iran for asylum.

Around November 2018, someone from Microsoft called, saying my computer had malware and spyware. Clearly, they were monitoring my every move.

I also caught stores raising prices on police orders. On 1 April 2019 at 5:55 p.m., I bought a medium coffee at McDonald's Jean Talon West. An assistant manager charged me $1.60, though the promotion was $1 for any size. At 6:06 p.m., I messaged my friend George Tsoukalas, who worked at McDonald's. By 6:08 p.m., he confirmed: "It's $1 any size." The next day, at the McGill Eaton Centre, I was correctly charged $1. I kept both receipts as proof.

On 4 April 2019 at 4:25 p.m., my mother and I went to McDonald's in Atwater. They charged $1.69 instead of $1. My mother noticed. When I complained, the manager refunded 70 cents, pretending he didn't know, a lie.

On 21 May 2019 at 5:35 p.m., I went to Provigo Jean Talon for toilet paper. My father had seen it at $5.49 that morning, but when I arrived, the tag said $8.99. I took it to the price machine, it read $5.49, as my father said. They had tried to trick me into paying more or leaving without it.

By then, 80% of the businesses and stores involved in the conspiracy had closed or relocated. Garage Fujiaty had almost no electrical work for me since January 2019. Lacité Walk-In Clinic, where I once tested my irregular heartbeat (40 irregular beats in 20 hours at CHUM Hôtel-Dieu), announced closure on 28 June 2019.

On 5 June 2019 at 6:00 p.m., my mother saw shoes she liked at Hudson's Bay downtown. She planned to buy them the next day, but they had "disappeared." They often did this to me, and now they are doing it to her.

On 1 July 2019, I tried two TD Bank ATMs. At noon on Jean Talon and Querbes, and at 6:00 p.m. on Bernard and Hutchison, both were out of order. The next day at TD Guy and Sainte-Catherine, the ATM worked, but I couldn't deposit cash, only withdraw. Same issue, multiple times. That evening at 7:30 p.m., I saw a supposed homeless man rummaging in a garbage bag for food and cans, hinting again at my "future."

Meanwhile, George Margelis, my so-called brother working for the police and secret services, always liked his own posts on Facebook from my account, but never mine.

Back in July 2010, my mother and I visited my Aunt Eleni. She told my mother to apply for welfare because of her kidney transplant. Eleni, in conspiracy with Greek authorities, pretended that maybe it was my imagination. But she knew the truth, that the authorities were working against us. That's why she wanted us trapped on welfare, unable to leave the country, fearing international courts and publicity.

On 12 July 2019, I reminded my mother about Eleni's advice. She said she didn't remember, but I did. I heard it myself. It was crystal clear proof of what was happening in Greece that summer of 2010: the police, undercover and secret agents, and the Ministry of Public Security working together in psychological warfare, planning to turn me into a homeless man, torturing me indefinitely, until I died.

Around 9 July 2010, I went to my so-called aunt Filio, a

person working for the Greek secret services. My mother called my other aunt, Maria, and told her that what she saw there she didn't like at all, saying she would not talk to them again. Maria and her daughters, Areti and Sofia, were communicating over their cell phones with the rest of the secret agents at that time.

On 19 July 2019, I discovered how police agents and secret services communicated with each other and with the police: through massive text messages. These messages came from agents watching my status and face expressions, or from hidden cameras aimed at me. They interpreted whether I was mad, scared, or nervous, and immediately sent agents to pass messages to me—threats that I was dead, that they would torture me, or make me suffer.

When I thought about suing them, within a minute, I would hear police sirens in the distance. This revealed that the text messages were also being sent directly to the police. The police listened to all my conversations daily with an electronic device. If I said something against them, the secret services sent people nearby, often pretending to be homeless, searching in garbage bins to hint that's how I would live in the future.

They had about 10–15 people around me at all times. If they heard me say something, they sent them to pass messages. For example, someone carried a big backpack to suggest I would have to survive like that; an empty backpack meant I wouldn't need one.

Colors of clothes or even cars passing by also carried interpretations. Red or green meant I couldn't do anything about my case, while grey suggested I might be able to sue them. Military pants implied "we are at war."

For about ten years, I saw this daily and could tell if it was them passing messages or just a coincidence. They feared I would go to Iran for asylum or talk to the media about my case. If they thought this, within a minute, I would again hear police sirens.

In early 2019, when they realized I wouldn't be able to sue them, I went to Burger King downtown across from Hudson Bay with my so-called brother, George Margelis (who worked for the police and secret services). At the counter, there was a paper saying no hamburgers, only chicken, hinting that stores would deny me food or hike prices once I was turned into a homeless person.

On 19 July 2019, I went again with George Tsoukalas and Lambros Xerakias from Laval. Same story: Burger King said they ran out of meat, only chicken was available.

On 21 July 2019, I asked my so-called friends to go to the Old Port at night. George Tsoukalas said we wouldn't go because his brother Theo was tired. At 9:40 p.m., George called again and told me to go for coffee at McDonald's in Laval on St. Martin. When we arrived, a sign on the door stated that it was closed for cleaning until morning. This was not a coincidence. They wanted to show me: NO FOOD.

On 1 August 2019 at 4:13 p.m., I went to McDonald's on Jean Talon West, Montreal, and ordered a medium regular iced coffee. The employee told me they had only caramel or vanilla. Usually, iced coffee came plain for $1, but with caramel or vanilla it was $1.70. Again, McDonald's was caught hiking prices on me. I kept the receipts as proof.

On 19 August 2019, in the afternoon, George Margelis argued with my father and then angrily called me, saying, "Go home, because I'm going to give a bad beating to your father."

On 29 August 2019, my father called Hermis Overseas Traffic about shipping a small container of olive oil from Greece. The person told him $80. My father said it cost $55 last year. The man quickly corrected himself, saying it was a mistake, and charged a final price of $50. They tried to hike the price but were caught red-handed.

On 1 September 2019 at 8:00 p.m. Greece time, TV station Antenna showed in the news a person in the background who looked exactly like my father, showing the Greek government was still participating in the conspiracy with Canada against me.

Meanwhile, in Montreal, people called my house asking for the "owner of the apartment," hinting that I didn't have a home and could easily be turned into a homeless person when my parents passed away.

On 2 September 2019 around 1:00 a.m., my mother, George Margelis, and I returned from the casino and went to McDonald's on Jean Talon West for ice cream. They told me they had none. I didn't believe this, it wasn't the first time.

Later that day at 5:45 p.m., outside Parc Metro, I noticed an African-Canadian man, often seen there, displaying books for sale (like the one I wanted to create about my case). I told George he was working for the police. George replied, "That's nonsense." Within three minutes, a police vehicle passed, and the officer waved at the man. I told George, "Look, he waved at him." George denied seeing it, saying again it was nonsense. Of course, he worked for them.

That same evening at 8:00 p.m. Greece time, Antenna TV news again showed a person resembling my father in the background. This confirmed that Greece was still conspiring with Canada since the summer of 2010.

As soon as I wrote this in my report, immediately on ERT1 news at 9:00 p.m. Greece time, they showed a taxi from Athens going toward another town colliding with a truck, though nobody died. I understood the message clearly: it was directed at me.

Back in 2010, when Greece conspired with Canada to turn me into a homeless man, I tried to hire a lawyer to appeal to the International Criminal Court. I even obtained a taxi license in

Athens. But the Ministry of Public Security ordered all taxi owners not to rent me a taxi. This was further evidence of how the Greek, Canadian, and American governments collaborated, exchanging threatening messages and carrying out their conspiracy.

On Sunday night, 1 September 2019, around 11:50 p.m., while George Margelis, my mother Eugenia Margelis, and I were returning home from the casino, I told George I would get an ice cream from McDonald's on Jean Talon West, Montreal. When I asked for one, they told me they didn't have ice cream. It was on purpose, they had it but refused to give it to me, following police orders.

I was 100% right. The next day, 3 September 2019 at 4:11 p.m., I went back for a small coffee, and they charged me 89 cents instead of $1.45. They did this to cover up the fact that they had denied me ice cream the previous day. I kept the bills as proof. This was one more time McDonald's took part in the conspiracy.

On 4 September 2019, I repurchased a coffee at McDonald's in Atwater, downtown. They charged the regular price of $1.45 for a small coffee. This showed clearly that they were acting against me through different stores, hiking prices, and creating trouble. Even my father complained that many places gave him higher prices.

On 11 September 2019, while I was talking with my father about the house increases Peter Strifas, the owner, imposed on us, my father said, "Because we have bed bugs lately, it's George Margelis bringing clothes over the net, mostly sports clothes." This was wrong—George bought only new clothes occasionally. (Our conversations were tapped; the police listened to everything.)

The next day, my father called Peter Strifas to arrange for a company to spray for bed bugs. Peter demanded half the money we typically paid and said he wouldn't cover it again. He also claimed that "a relative or someone else in the house brings stuff that causes the bed bugs."

Peter knew everything happening in the building. In apartment 5, next to us, there was an agent, just like when we lived in Côte-des-Neiges, where apartment 11 was full of agents. The police often placed agents in the apartment directly below ours, and sometimes even the one below that. Peter, the tenant at apartment 3, had previously lived in apartment 2. They moved there immediately after we arrived in apartment 6. This explained why their agents were always one or two floors directly beneath us.

On 12 September 2019 at 9:09 p.m. Greece time (2:09 p.m. Montreal), I saw news on Greek TV station ERT1 about a two-year-old baby killed in its home by a dangerous Rottweiler. On the left side of the picture, I noticed someone who looked exactly like my friend Mike from Greece. He had a cross-body bag, a white shirt with a red "3" on it (like the one Mike used to wear), and he once owned the same kind of dog.

We had been friends for years, but in the summer of 2010, during the big conspiracy in Greece with the Canadian and Greek governments, he worked for them for a while. This scene showed clearly that the Greek government was still in the conspiracy and still sending threats through TV. It was the third time in one month that I saw them do this. I even believed this story about the dog might have been fake news, created just to pass me messages.

The Minister of Public Security was still the same as in summer 2010: Mihalis Chrisochoidis.

On 2 October 2019, from 10:45 to 10:50 p.m., police agents aimed a humming, vibrating noise at my apartment to get on my nerves.

On 7 November 2019 at 9:00 a.m., I noticed my bus pass wasn't working. At Parc Metro, an African-Canadian worker checked it and told me, "I can't do anything." At 3:30 p.m., at Vendôme Metro, I asked another worker what was happening. He pretended to make a call, then told me the same thing. At 4:00 p.m., I went to Berri-UQAM, where they deal with cards. I had the receipt with me. They checked, and after a while, they gave me a new one. What the police tried to do was show that a second person was using my identity, something they had tried to do nine years ago. They also wanted me to pay for a new card to create financial damage, but since I had the receipt, I did not have to pay.

Now, either they copied my card from the machine when I entered the metro and placed it out of order, or, at night, when I was sleeping, George Margelis gave them my card (since he was working for them) and they placed it out of order. What I started doing at night was putting my keys and wallet under my pillow. I had noticed one day that George Margelis had removed papers from my purse and put them back in the wrong way. I realized he was giving the information to the police and secret services, so I also began keeping my bus pass under my pillow.

On 20 November 2019 at 2:00 p.m., I went to get an injection at the Allan Memorial Institute (McGill University Health Center, Pine Avenue Psychiatric Clinic). I went to see the nurse, Joey, who gave me injections once every three months, supposedly for schizophrenia. Doctor Howard Margolese was not there, which did not seem like a coincidence.

Joey told me he would introduce me to a girl named Elizabeth Jacob-Goldman, who helped people with psychological problems. She and her group gathered together and did all kinds of activities. I knew from the beginning that they were up to something. Elizabeth urged me to join them, and Joey also kept insisting that I join her for help. I told them that I did not have a problem that required assistance.

Despite this, Joey continued, even after the girl left, applying indescribable pressure for about twenty minutes, urging me to join her team. I knew this was a major trick and fraud. Back in December 2018, I had sent the police my 9th complaint, clearly stating why the doctors from the psychiatric clinic had not contacted the police to learn how the case looked. When I saw him, he seemed to be in panic mode, so I calmed him down. (They were paying me welfare.) I even told him that I heard my mother calling me in the hospital, even though she was not there.

Now, if I joined Elizabeth's group for so-called help, it would mean I admitted I was sick, which would make complaint #9 invalid. The question would be: why did you join them if you were fine? Joey, noticing the trick was not working, became frustrated. He pressured me further, demanding I look at him in the face whenever I turned away. I understood then that Joey knew everything happening, even if he did not reveal it openly. After he attempted to force me to go with that girl for activities, it became very clear who he was and what he had been doing.

Joey also refused to give me the next appointment for Doctor Howard Margolese and the injection I was supposed to receive every three months. He told me he would call me, and added that, whether I wanted it or not, I was going to meet Elizabeth again. They recorded the conversation.

On 21 November 2019 at 6:00 p.m., I had to call Capital One to request a refund for a charge of $82.46 that Kaspersky Antivirus had billed to my credit card (Capital One) without notice. It was set up automatically, since I had purchased the product the previous year, so they charged me again annually without my knowledge.

Kaspersky had sent documents to Capital One, claiming it was a legal transaction. Capital One told me to contact Kaspersky. I did so, and they said to me that Capital One needed to send me a "letter of dispute," which I would then forward to their email. Once they received it, they would issue the refund. This was not normal because Capital One could have sent it themselves without involving me.

I called Capital One again. The representative told me it was an old dispute and had been closed. I told her I never received any document from them. She said she would send it again. When I asked her to provide the "lift of dispute," she said those things had already been done by Kaspersky when they had sent the documents to Capital One to show the charge was legal. The representative refused to send me such a letter.

It was clear that either Capital One did not want to send it themselves to Kaspersky to process the refund, or Kaspersky did not want to talk directly to Capital One. This was not normal. I spent from 6:00 p.m. to 6:50 p.m. talking to them, but no one wanted to resolve the matter. This was a clear sign that the police and secret services were interfering with people's credit cards and other financial matters. Normally, this should have been a one-call solution.

I had been trying to get a refund since early October, but nobody had resolved it. The purpose was to force me to spend money. It was a straightforward case that should have been solved with one call.

On 3 December 2019 at 3:30 p.m., I went to TD Bank at Jean Talon, Montreal, to do a wire transfer to Greece. Although I had power of attorney for my father's account, the bank, participating in the conspiracy, refused to process it. The supervisor insisted my father had to be there.

The next day at 11:00 a.m., I went again with my father. While the banker did the transfer and asked the supervisor to check, she refused again, saying my father had to be present. So, my father showed her his medical card, and only then did she proceed with the transfer.

What happened here was that TD Bank, as part of the conspiracy, was still trying to show—stupidly—that someone else was walking around with my identity. This case had been closed years earlier, but they continued to raise the same theory.

When I lost my passport in 2007, I went to the passport office within three days and received a new one. At the police station, when they arrested me on 26 January 2008, I saw on their computer that somebody from Romania, named Pavel, had used my identity with a forged passport. My former lawyer, Sally Butler Grand, told me around April 2009 that the person who tried to enter Canada was deported immediately.

The police had admitted to my nine complaints. It was clear what was happening: while they had me under significant police protection, monitoring me every second, knowing exactly who I was, they were still telling the bank otherwise. TD Bank, despite knowing my identity, would not allow me to complete the wire transfer without my father's approval. They were blocking me financially, so I could not act without my father's presence, even on accounts for which I had full power of attorney.

Also, in January 2017, I did a wire transfer to Greece without my father being there. Why did they not say anything at that time? Now, while I was preparing to sue the police, they were trying every fraud possible to make my report invalid. At that time, no one was walking around with my identity. And now, all of a sudden, they claimed someone was using my identity?

Pavel, the person from Romania, as they showed me on their computer at the police station when they arrested me on 26 January 2008, how did they know his real name? This meant that they had already charged him and were familiar with his identity. Once they identified him, they shipped him back to Romania.

On 13 December 2019 at 5:00 p.m., I called Capital One and reported the disputed $82.46 charge from Kaspersky Antivirus. I explained that they never sent me an email warning that they would soon charge me again for the subscription. Instead, they charged me without notice. When I saw it on my Capital One credit card bill, I called them to dispute the transaction with Kaspersky.

Kaspersky sent Capital One documents showing that the charge was not fraud (even though they billed me without notice), and Capital One put the charge back onto my account. I called Kaspersky again, and for the fourth time, they told me that in order to refund me, Capital One had to send them (or me) a letter lifting the dispute.

I called Capital One back and told them this, but they refused, saying the dispute had already been lifted. They would not send me the letter under any circumstances. I called Kaspersky again, and they told me that on 12 October 2019, they had refunded the amount back to my Capital One credit card, but Capital One declined the refund.

I called Capital One again, and the same lady from the disputes department told me they had not declined the refund and that such a thing could not happen. She was lying, clearly trying to block my rebate. She also told me that around 3 October 2019, they gave back $60.48 USD to Kaspersky (an amount they had waived from my credit card on 17 August 2019). When I asked her why they gave the money back, she said it was because the charge was not fraud, so they returned it to Kaspersky.

I called Kaspersky again, and they informed me that they had refunded the amount to me. However, Capital One declined the refund on 12 October 2019. It was a trick by Capital One to stop me from getting my refund. I asked Capital One to send me a letter confirming the dispute was lifted so Kaspersky could process the refund. They told me this about five times, but they still refused to send it.

Kaspersky also told me that since 12 October 2019, when Capital One declined their refund, my status remained under dispute, so they could not refund me again while the disagreement was open. Capital One had been instructed to keep it this way so I would not receive a refund.

The person from Kaspersky also confirmed that there was no money coming into their account from Capital One for me. This meant that on 3 October 2019, it was Capital One itself that rebilled me. On my August statement, I noticed that Kaspersky Antivirus charged me $82.46 on 16 August 2019, and then it was waived the next day, on 17 August 2019. This proved the waiver came from

Capital One, not from Kaspersky.

Then, on 3 October 2019, after Kaspersky sent documents showing the charge was valid, I saw that Capital One had rebilled me $82.46. But this amount was never sent to Kaspersky, as Capital One falsely claimed. The person from Kaspersky also confirmed that they never received anything from Capital One.

My main question with Capital One was simple: Why wouldn't they send me the letter lifting the dispute? It was such an easy step that would resolve the issue. The answer was clear, because they were part of the conspiracy with the police to take my money. They continuously refused to give me the letter, ensuring that I could not get my refund from Kaspersky.

# Chapter 8

# Psychological Warfare Continues

On December 1, 2019, at 11:20 p.m., I went with George Margelis for coffee at Starbucks, St. Catherine West, Montreal. The employee told me they didn't accept cash, only cards, hinting that if the police and secret services turned me into a homeless person without bank cards, I wouldn't even be able to buy coffee. The same thing happened again on December 15, 2019, at the same time. But after they realized their participation in the conspiracy, on December 21, 2019, at 11:20 p.m., and on later visits, they accepted cash as if nothing had happened.

On January 10, 2020, at 11:20 p.m., I went again to the same Starbucks to get one more receipt as proof, but the store was already closed. Around 11:45 p.m., George Margelis texted me asking where I was. I replied that Starbucks was closed and told him to meet me at Second Cup on St. Catherine. It was clear to me what they were preparing, if I became homeless, I would be denied service.

On January 27, 2020, at 11:00 a.m., my father went to TD Bank on Jean Talon corner Querbes (already mentioned earlier) and asked for online banking access. The bank told him his son had to be present. When he came home and told me, I went with him, but then they refused to serve me, saying now my father had to go with me. They repeated the same game, refusing both of us service depending on the situation, clearly following instructions.

On January 25, 2020, at 11:55 p.m., I went with George Margelis for coffee at Second Cup, St. Catherine, Montreal. The employee again said they had closed cash and only accepted cards, so I paid with a debit card. They were trying to confuse things and cover for Starbucks' earlier actions.

On February 1, 2020, I went to Starbucks on Crescent Street around 11:15 p.m., but they were closed again. I found this suspicious.

On February 2, 2020, at 1:00 p.m., I went to the dépanneur at Bloomfield corner St. Roch to buy cigarettes. The price of Pall Mall had jumped from $11 to $12.40. It was clear they were hiking prices under police orders.

In summer 2010, when I returned to Canada with my mother (July 14, 2010), I called Theodore Anastasopoulos. He was now working for the criminal organization. Over the phone, he admitted giving information to drug traffickers but claimed he had been blackmailed. I understood he had been working with George Papaspirou, gathering information about where I lived or went at night to help the criminal organization find and kill me. At that time, however, I was under police protection. Theodore Anastasopoulos was part of that gang.

On March 7, 2020, at 11:20 p.m., George Margelis and I

were at Place des Arts metro station. The metro had just left, and we had to wait 10 minutes. On March 8, 2020, at 12:20 a.m., we went to catch bus 80 going north, but it had just left, so we waited another 20 minutes. We returned to the metro at Place des Arts, but again the train had just left, and we had to wait another 10 minutes. I found this suspicious—clearly, STM had been instructed to delay services to make me stay longer.

When I told George, he insisted, "It's just a coincidence. It happens to me too." He was covering for them again. But when we reached Jean Talon station, the metro arrived on time, about 3 minutes. At Parc metro around 12:30 a.m., the bus was waiting, and we boarded immediately. Suddenly, the STM service was back to normal, just because I had spoken about it.

Although George had read my report and knew what was happening, he always sided with the police. He also kept going to my Facebook account, liking his own posts. When I asked why, he said, "If someone likes a post, more people follow." I knew this was a lie. He wanted to make it look like I was trying to have a good relationship with him, even though I had named him in my report.

On March 8, 2020, around noon, George again tried to brainwash my parents. They told me, "You shouldn't be saying these things; it's just a coincidence." But I knew there was no coincidence when something happened over and over. It was done on purpose.

My parents kept saying nothing was happening. They believed that as long as I stayed away from the police, they wouldn't bother me. But the truth was, the only thing the police feared was my going to Iran to file for asylum. Fearing harm from the police, my parents always tried to stop me from writing my report.

On March 8, 2020, at 5:50 p.m., my mother and I went to McDonald's at Atwater Mall in Montreal. We ordered two Egg McMuffins. The employee, whom I had seen working there for more than a month, charged us $4 each. My mother noticed the mistake and told her it should be $3. The employee gave her back $2—again, McDonald's was hiking prices right in front of us. I kept the receipt, order number 314-1.

On March 20, 2020, Hi and Ty Fujiati, owners of Garage Fujiati, told me I could no longer come every Friday for 1–2 hours at 1:00 p.m. as before. Instead, they would call me only if they had a car for repair. Since business for electrical problems was regulated by the police in conspiracy with the Fujiatis, this meant they could call me just once a month, or not at all. They were clearly manipulating my work.

On April 8, 2020, my father went to Scotiabank on Parc Avenue, Montreal. Supervisor Catherine Tsihlis did not allow him to access his safety deposit box, using coronavirus as an excuse. On

April 15, she told him not to come again for the box. When my father later asked to remove my mother, Eugenia Margelis, from the box, Tsihlis claimed he had to empty it and start over, another lie.

On April 17, 2020, at 9:15 p.m., I called Scotiabank's head office and asked about the correct procedure. They told me that my parents only needed to go to the bank with IDs, fill out a form, and sign it, then Eugenia would be removed. Tsihlis's claims were complete lies.

One thing I noticed about my so-called brother, George Margelis, was how they used him against me and my parents. Since 2011, he had been living on welfare, unable to survive without family support. I often had to give him money for house expenses, as he contributed very little. This dependence caused him severe depression and psychological issues, but he refused to see a psychiatrist.

The police had told him not to work, so they could keep financial pressure on the family. If he tried to work, they wouldn't let him and might even punish him. The constant threat was that, if he didn't obey, they would make him homeless, just as they had been trying to do to me since 2010.

On June 11, 2020, at 11:00 a.m., my father, Christos Margelis, went to Western Union on Jean Talon West, Montreal, to send €50 to Dimitrios in Greece. They charged him $83, setting the exchange rate at 1.66, while the actual conversion rate was 1.536. They also charged a $15 fee, while the same transfer the year before had cost $6. This was more proof of businesses conspiring with the police to overcharge my family. I kept the receipt.

In May 2020, I noticed my father appearing around seven times downtown Montreal while I was with my mother. He would suddenly show up wherever we went for coffee. Once, at Édouard-Montpetit metro, while I was heading toward Parc station, I saw a man from behind who looked exactly like my father. He appeared to prepare to lie down on a bench, as if to sleep. The police and secret services wanted me to believe they would turn either me or my father into a homeless person, and my father was listening to them.

Since the end of March 2020, Garage Fujiati (owned by Ty and Hi Fujiati) had stopped calling me to work. By June 28, 2020, I still hadn't received a single call. It was impossible that not one car with electrical problems had come in during that time. The conspiracy with the police was clear as day. That garage had been my last source of occasional work, 1–3 hours per week, but now even that was gone. They were openly preparing to turn me into a homeless person when it suited them.

On July 8, 2020, around 11:00 a.m., I called the City of Montreal and asked who I should send a formal notice to about my case with the police. The person first gave me a police number. I told him, "Police do not let me hire a lawyer!" Then he gave me another number—Ville de Montréal, Access to Documents. I waited on hold for an hour and a half, giving the police plenty of time to tell him what to do.

This was how the police responded to the nine complaints I had filed since 2010, by deliberately mixing up information so I couldn't get the correct address or number. The letter should have been sent to the City of Montreal, not the police. They confused everything.

On July 4, 2020, at 10:15 p.m., I went downtown with George Margelis. We arrived at the bus stop at Bloomfield and St. Roch at 10:05 p.m. for the 80 bus, which was supposed to pass at 10:15. It never came. At 10:30, one bus passed marked 80 du Parc going south, but it had no passengers. When the driver saw me watching, he quickly changed the sign to "en transit." The next bus finally arrived at 10:50 p.m. They had clearly skipped one run to make me wait, a common tactic they used.

On July 24, 2020, at 6:14 p.m., Vie, the owner of Auto Vie, sent me a message saying I hadn't been there for a while and calling me for work. He had stopped calling me since mid-2015—five years earlier. Now, while the police knew I was preparing my case for court, he tried to make it look like he hadn't cut me off.

At 6:36 p.m. that same day, George Tsoukalas, a friend of mine, texted to cancel our dinner plans for that night. We had arranged earlier at 3:00 p.m. to go out after 8:30 p.m. The timing was suspicious, it came just after I ignored Vie's message. George was in conspiracy with the police. When I asked him why he cancelled, he said, "My brother, Theodore Tsoukalas, didn't want to go anywhere." The messages came one after another, very clearly connected.

On that same day, July 24, 2020, I also discovered that my official report about the police case—103 pages long—was missing from my house. They had removed it.

On July 25, 2020, at 12:27 p.m., I asked our friend Lambros Xerakias who had cancelled the plan. He told me it was George and Theodore Tsoukalas. But George had said the day before that it was only his brother Theodore. It was apparent he was covering himself. I had already discovered about eight months earlier that George Tsoukalas was in conspiracy with the police and secret services.

Later, on July 25 at 8:00 p.m., I started writing about what happened in my report. At 8:19 p.m., George Tsoukalas quickly sent me a message inviting me to go to the Old Port that night, clearly trying to cover up the previous day's incident.

On August 1, 2020, at 10:18 p.m., the 80 bus going south at Bloomfield and St. Roch once again never arrived. The next bus only came at 10:50 p.m. George Margelis was with me and saw everything.

I noticed a pattern: whenever I wrote something about someone in my report, their behavior changed immediately. That meant the police and secret services were instantly informing them of what I wrote.

The drug traffickers whose names and numbers I had included were Sterie Craciun, George Papaspirou, Peter Maltezos, Mike Plaras, John Koubarakos, and Theodore Anastasopoulos. In July or August 2010, I spoke with Anastasopoulos over the phone, and he admitted the traffickers had blackmailed him to give them information about me, where I lived, where I went at night, and other details. At that time, I was under police protection.

During the summer of 2010, all my phone conversations were being recorded while the police and the Greek government carried out psychological warfare against me. They even claimed there was a warrant for my arrest. They repeated the same trick about a month before, and again on August 21, 2020, at 12:20 p.m. That time, when I called back the number, it turned out to be from a bank in the U.S.—the Republic Bank of Chicago. It was the police trying to terrorize me because I was preparing to sue them on my own, since they would not let me hire a lawyer.

On August 30, 2020, at 4:30 p.m., I was at the bus stop at Bloomfield and Ball with my mother. The 80 bus, scheduled for 4:34, never arrived until 4:50. They had deliberately delayed it to make us wait. My parents, especially my mother—had also noticed that buses often came very late, very early, or skipped runs altogether. They had been told to operate this way so we would suffer long waits.

On the 2nd September 2020 at 11:30 a.m., somebody called us from Quebecor and asked about the owner of the house, hinting that I had no house and it would be easy for the police to turn me into a homeless person.

On the 3rd September 2020 at 11:00 a.m., I had a call where they told me that someone had used my Social Insurance Number and that I should speak to an officer. The phone then disconnected. It was one of the tricks the police played to show that someone was using my identity.

Back in 2007, a person tried to enter Canada with my stolen passport. At that time, I had a lawyer who told me that the person was deported. At my arrest on 26 January 2008, the police showed me on the computer, for about three seconds, the name of the person—Pavel, from Romania. The police were now trying to show that someone was using my identity to prove themselves right, but they were wrong. Nobody entered the country. My lawyer, Sally

Butler Grand, confirmed this to me in April 2009.

After three minutes, I called back the number I had received the call from, but it said "no longer in service."

On September 2, 2020, at 3:00 p.m., I went to deposit funds into my father's account at TD Bank, located at Jean Talon West, Montreal. The machine was out of order. I asked them about it, and the person there told me I could have both accounts (CAD and USD) on his other card. He claimed that the other card was only for USD and had no currency conversion when withdrawing funds. This was a significant lie. Why had they given me a USD card in the first place if it could not convert? Of course, currency conversion existed from USD to CAD. One reason they did this was to create problems if I needed to use my debit card.

On the 5th of September 2020, I sent a letter to Garage Fujiaty accusing them of conspiracy with the police to stop calling me for work, leaving me with zero income. The letter was received on the 8th of September 2020, but I got no answer.

On the 1st of October 2020 at 12:30 p.m., I went to Metro Parc to fill my bus pass using my Laurentian Bank debit card. It worked with no problem. At 12:45 p.m., I went to the pharmacy at Provigo (Dimitra Alevetsovitis), Jean Talon West, Montreal. One man at the cash was speaking Russian, pretending not to know English or French. He was a police agent delaying me from being served. I waited about 20 minutes. As I stood waiting, the man told me to move further down, even though I was already about two meters away, and he pushed me. I removed his hands and told him not to touch me. The police, watching through the secret services, did not like that, but they had no problem if someone forced me. Finally, he left, and I got my mother's medication.

At 1:05 p.m., I went to withdraw money from the bank machine at Jarry Corner Champagneur. A woman had just withdrawn funds before me, but when I tried, the machine said my card was invalid. They had placed my debit card on hold because I had not behaved as they wished at the pharmacy. Just half an hour earlier, I had used it at Metro Parc with no issue.

At 1:20 p.m., I called Laurentian Bank. The person told me either the machine was not working or my card was demagnetized. I told him I had just used it half an hour ago. He said he would send me a new card within a week. This showed how they made my life difficult daily.

Around this time (26th September 2020 onward), they also began harassing my mother on her cell phone, closing the call before she could answer, applying psychological warfare.

On the 4th October 2020, Alain, a mechanic at Fujiaty, called me, saying there was a car for a remote starter. I told him I had taken my toolbox from there at the end of August since they had stopped calling me for work. On the 5th September 2020, I had sent Fujiaty a letter accusing them of conspiracy with the police not to bring me electrical jobs. Alain's call was a way to cover themselves after the letter. Of course, I did not go.

On the 9th October 2020, around 2:30 p.m., after receiving my new Laurentian Bank debit card, I went to the ATM at Jarry, corner Champagneur. The machine was not working. I then went to the ATM at Parc Avenue, corner Laurier, but noticed they had moved to 1100 Mont Royal East. I did not go, it was too far.

On the 11th October 2020 at around 5:30 p.m., I went to the ATM in Eaton Center, St. Catherine Street West. That machine was also out of order. They were doing everything to make my life difficult. Now my only choice was to go to 1100 Mont Royal East. This also hinted at what would happen if they turned me into a homeless person. My mother, Eugenia Margelis, was a witness to this.

That same day, I went downtown with my mother. The 80 Du Parc South bus, scheduled for 4:11 p.m. at Bloomfield, corner Ball, never arrived. We were there at 4:05 p.m. The next bus came at 4:30 p.m., leaving us waiting in the cold for half an hour. My mother, who had cancer, was suffering. The police knew this.

On the 12th October 2020 at 1:15 p.m., I went to activate my new Laurentian Bank debit card at 1100 Mont Royal East. The banks were closed for the holiday. I tried the ATM, but it said "invalid card." Two days later, I returned to the teller, who activated it for me. The police and their agents had prevented me from activating my card earlier.

On the 15th October 2020, around 3:30 p.m., I was walking downtown Montreal on St. Catherine and noticed a church with a security guard at the door watching me. The hint was that, if they turned me homeless, the church would not help me.

On the 22nd October 2020, around 1:15 p.m., I went to see psychiatrist Howard Margolese at the psychiatric clinic of the old Royal Victoria. Another woman psychiatrist was also there, asking me different questions. From what I understood, she was trying to show me as capable of working, so I would be sent to work. I told her stories about hearing voices and psychological problems, so she would not be able to say I could work.

(Anything I said verbally was not valid. Everything written in this report and my exhibits was valid and the truth of what was really going on.)

If welfare stopped my payments and forced me to work, their next move would be to push me into homelessness. Most likely, even shelters would refuse me after police intervention.

I also noticed many times that wherever I went—stores, even toilets—they sent their agents ahead of me to delay me, making life difficult.

On the 6th November 2020 at 10:54 a.m., somebody called me, saying they were from the government and that there was an arrest order against me related to my Social Insurance Number. Suspicious, I gave them my address but did not give my SIN. I hung up. Two minutes later, I called back. It was a private number, unrelated to the call.

At 12:47 p.m., I got the same call. I hung up and called back, it was another private number, unrelated. At 1:20 p.m., a new number left me a voicemail with the same story. Again, when I called back, it was a private number.

The police and secret services were watching me prepare my case for the Superior Court. They were terrorizing me to stop me from suing them. From what I found, they had hacked these numbers to make the calls.

One more thing I noticed: the police and their agents were watching my face 24/7 from hidden cameras. Sometimes, when my facial expression showed anger, I heard sirens from police vehicles in the distance.

On the 11th November 2020, between 10:45 p.m. and 11:05 p.m., I noticed again the low-frequency humming noise in our apartment. I mentioned this to George Margelis, who quickly found an excuse to cover up for the police, saying the noise was coming from the fridge. I told him and my mother to come to the living room to listen. George went to his room (no evidence), but my mother stayed and said she heard it. They were trying to make me severely sick. The first health damage they caused was to my heart—I developed irregular heartbeats from fright and shock, a condition that could easily become fatal.

On the 15th November 2020 at 10:00 p.m., their agents again put the low-frequency humming noise on until 2:00 a.m., when I finally fell asleep. They did this often, to drive me crazy and cause severe health damage.

Since mid-October 2020, I have also noticed a Cadillac with its engine running in front of my home, acting as police protection. My mother noticed it too. The license plate read M74TTY. Translated into Greek: "M" stood for my name, Margelis; "74" for my year of birth; "TTY" as "what what why." The messages were clear, sometimes even noticeable from far away.

Around the 27th December 2020, at noon, I went to Place-des-Arts at the Complexe Desjardins to Winners to buy a shirt. At the entrance, the security guard asked where I was going. I said, "Winners." He told me Winners was closed and they didn't know when it would open, in other words, he refused me entry.

Later, I asked my father, who confirmed that Winners stores were open, the one at Atwater and the one at McGill. It was clear what the police and secret services were doing: making everybody mistreat me. Even in the washrooms, they sent someone in ahead of me so there would be no toilet available, forcing me to wait. In stores, they placed people ahead of me, so I waited a long time for service. Some stores refused me service altogether, for example, Ophone on Hutchison across from Metro Parc. When I told the worker to check my cell phone because Wi-Fi didn't work at hospitals or malls, he suggested I go to Fido and get a new phone. He didn't even try to sell me one, though he was running a cell phone shop.

At home, we had recently developed a cockroach problem, something we had never had in 10 years of living in the apartment. This was dangerous for infections. I believed the police agents had somehow planted them. The tenants downstairs in apartments 2 and 4 had been there more than a year and a half, so it could not have come from them.

On the 13th July 2020, I sent an email to the Barreau du Québec (lawyers' bar association) asking about my case with the police, whether I should sue the police or the city. They replied the same day, saying they could offer referral services by area of law to help me find a lawyer, and provided me with a number for the Montreal Island area. At the end of the email, they stated that JurisReference.ca was a web platform to search for resources. I did not reply, it was useless information. For over 10 years, police and secret services had prevented me from hiring a lawyer. Why would this suddenly change? I only wanted to know whom to sue. A lawyer would be useless, they would not do the job properly, as I had already seen in the past 10 years.

On the 8th February 2021, JurisReference sent me an email —eight months later—giving me a reference number (ZX041540) to hire a lawyer. This happened just as the police saw me preparing my case to submit to court by myself. They were trying to push me toward a lawyer who would make me lose the case. Why, after eight months, did they suddenly give me a referral? I replied, asking why they were giving me this number when I had not requested a lawyer. It was clear the police wanted me to hire one of their lawyers, lose money on fees, and lose the case. Then it would be easier to turn me into a homeless person. They never replied to my email.

On the 22nd March 2021, Greek TV station ERTflix, during the 9:00 p.m. news, showed a volcano eruption in Iceland. Large amounts of ash and lava were flying, but they filmed two people baking eggs on the lava. This was a joke. In reality, when such a volcano erupts, people run, it is hazardous. Showing people baking eggs was their way of downplaying the significance of the event.

On the 15th April 2010, just before I left Canada to go to Greece (as I mentioned above), they wanted the public to see it as funny. But it was not funny, it was dangerous. They even showed another volcano eruption in South America where people were baking pizza. Again, they were downplaying the event.

This showed that the 15th April 2010 volcano eruption in Iceland was manipulated. They wanted to downplay the event so I could not travel to Greece, hire a lawyer, and file with the International Criminal Court against Canada (police and government).

Later, realizing they had gone too far with the "baking eggs on lava," they tried to cover it up by saying there had been a public evacuation due to the eruption, which had moved people many kilometers away. The conspiracy between Canada and Iceland was major.

Before the April 15, 2010, volcano eruption in Iceland, there had been no eruptions for hundreds of years. After that date, there were two or three more, which I believed could have been manipulated to make it seem like eruptions were common and that the April 15 one was just a coincidence.

On April 23, 2021, at 11:00 a.m., I called the Parc Extension CLSC on Hutchison Street in Montreal to book an IV appointment for my mother, which she did every three months. They did not answer. After 5–10 minutes, they hung up. I called again, and a nurse responded, told me to hold on, then hung up after two minutes. I called once more; the phone rang for ten minutes before they hung up again.

I tried using an extension number (6860). A receptionist answered and said she would connect me to the nurses, but again, the phone rang for about ten minutes before they hung up. I kept calling; same result—hang-ups after a few minutes. At 1:10 p.m., I called 6860 again. The woman said she was in another building and could only transfer me. I told her out loud that they had hung up on me five times. At 1:45 p.m., I tried extension 6870. The phone rang from 1:45 to 2:25 p.m.—forty minutes—before I gave up. I tried again, this time directly, not through the extension, and the phone rang until 2:55 p.m.—thirty minutes—still with no answer.

This proved the police were interfering. They had told the CLSC not to answer my calls because they knew I was preparing a case to sue them. The last two calls rang for half an hour each, showing they wanted to make it appear they weren't hanging up, but still refused to help. In total, I tried from 11:00 a.m. to 3:00 p.m.— no answer.

On April 26, 2021, at 10:15 a.m., I called again. Same thing, no pickup, hang-ups. I kept trying until noon with no luck. On April 27, at 10:20 a.m., I called again, and again they would not pick up. I kept trying until 11:10 a.m. Finally, I took my voice recorder and went in person to the CLSC.

At the reception, the woman told me to take a number. I said,

"I've been trying for three days to book this appointment, and they don't answer the phone." She switched to Greek so that I couldn't record the conversation. Within four minutes, she booked the appointment. Why hadn't they answered the phone if it was only a four-minute job? It was crystal clear: the conspiracy was ongoing. They didn't want to book my mother's appointment because I was preparing my case against the police.

On May 16, 2021, Greek TV channel ERT1 showed, during the 9:00 p.m. news, people in Guatemala on top of a volcano baking pizza for the hungry. One man was even walking near the lava. I said, "This is impossible." Lava would melt shoes and feet in seconds. It was another attempt to downplay volcano eruptions, just like they had done with the manipulated April 15, 2010, eruption in Iceland.

Around 2018, I noticed the police had removed the time-and-temperature display from the wall at the station at 7035 Parc Avenue and placed another one on the ground. I believed they did this so that in photos it would seem I didn't know the police station's location.

On April 29, 2021, at 5:26 p.m., I visited the McDonald's on Atwater Avenue in Montreal, a location that had previously caused issues. I bought my mother a poutine. When she opened it, it had almost no sauce. I went back and told them to add sauce. A woman in a white shirt said, "That's how it comes."

I replied out loud, "I've been buying poutine at McDonald's for years and never got one almost dry."

She said, "You have to pay extra for sauce."

This was absurd. Sauce was supposed to be included. I refused to pay extra. They clearly spoke to stores too, using them to apply psychological warfare on me in any way possible.

They had already caused damage to my health, giving me irregular heartbeats, and I believed they would try to cause more. On April 27, 2021, around 11:10 p.m., the police noticed something unfavorable for me and turned on the low-frequency humming noise they sometimes used at night. This time, it came full blast from apartment 5 next door, proving the woman there was working for the police as an agent.

I also noticed that the police and secret services had terrorized George Margelis, their agent, by telling him that if he were left alone, he would end up living on the streets. Whenever I mentioned going to Greece, he cried and said he would be abandoned, which confirmed this threat was real.

From March 2021 to May, as I prepared my case for court, uniformed police terrorized me, showing me that they wouldn't let me reach court. One day, the 80 South bus on Avenue du Parc stopped at Mont Royal, and everyone had to get out, with the excuse that the road was blocked. I checked carefully, nothing was blocked.

I had to transfer buses just to reach downtown.

Other times, police cars blocked streets, pretending to stop me from reaching court. Sometimes, they spoke to African Canadians—agents meant to threaten me (black representing homelessness). Another time, they pretended to ticket a Honda Civic, the same model I once had, just to terrorize me. On another occasion, the 80 North bus driver detoured to St. Laurent, claiming that Parc Avenue was blocked, but when I later passed by Mont-Royal and Parc, the road was clear. It was apparent they were staging these scenes.

On May 11, 2021, at 11:40 a.m., Lee from Garage Fujiaty called me from an unknown number so I would pick up. He told me I had no supplier for remote starters, trying to back up Alain the mechanic's earlier claim, when I refused a job. This was false, I had three suppliers (GIT, Sobel Imports, and Automobility). Then Lee suddenly said he had another car needing a remote starter. This was a trick: they wanted me to work so they could later cut off jobs and lay me off again, as they had done before. I wasn't fooled.

From February to May 2021, I noticed George Papaspirou's mother repeatedly taking the 80 South bus at the same time as me and my mother. The purpose was to overhear my mother revealing where we lived in Greece, so George Papaspirou, a major criminal— could send someone to kill me there. Once I told my mother about this, the police must have heard, because she stopped appearing on the bus. This proved that the police and secret services were working with the criminal organization.

From mid-April to May 30, 2021, whenever I recorded fire trucks using sirens to terrorize me, they began diverting them onto other streets so I couldn't capture evidence. The woman downstairs also stopped letting her babies cry whenever she saw me preparing to record. Every time I added to my report or something negative happened, John Vlahakis called my home, pretending to talk to George Margelis. His calls always came with bad news, they were in close contact.

By late May 2021, the woman in apartment 5 increased the low-frequency humming, causing me more suffering. Meanwhile, known drug traffickers—Sterie Craciun (Gigi), George Papaspirou, Mike Plaras, Peter Maltezos, John Koubarakos, Theodore Anastasopoulos, and others—were free, enjoying their lives and illegal profits. The police never jailed them because they collected commissions from their trafficking. Yet they kept me under so-called police protection for more than ten years. It was clear: the police were a criminal organization after me.

On June 17, 18, and 23, 2021, I called the McGill Legal Information Clinic for help with my case, leaving four messages. They never returned my calls, they were told not to. On June 24, at

7:15 p.m., I bought two iced coffees on St. Catherine West. The regular price was $1, but I was charged $2.39 for a medium and $1.79 for a small. I confronted the cashier:

"You overcharged me."

He replied, "Because you bought more things, that's the price."

I said out loud, "You don't know what you're talking about."

The manager came, checked, and refunded me. They had been caught red-handed, raising prices to steal money from me.

On July 2, 2021, the McGill Legal Aid Clinic finally contacted me to inquire about my request. I told them I wanted to know who I should sue in my dispute with the police, I believed it was the city, and if aggravated damages were included under civil law. They delayed, saying they'd call me back in five business days for such a simple question. On July 13, at 11:30 a.m., they called again. The woman explained that aggravated damages applied only in common law systems, which I doubted, but she still refused to give me a clear answer on who to sue. She promised another call.

On July 21, 2021, they finally said I had to sue the City of Montreal, something I had already found out myself online. It was obvious that the police didn't want this information to be given.

Meanwhile, they continued to terrorize me, trying to start

fights. Twice, people swore at me, hoping I'd react, but I walked away. Fire trucks with sirens blasted past my home constantly, it was impossible that there were fires every other day in Parc Extension. Yet after months of this harassment, for five straight months, no fire trucks passed by my home at all.

Up to this point, I had sent my report to the City of Montreal on July 26, 2021, along with a formal notice. The post office clerk even refused to send it by registered mail with signature.

On July 26, 2021, around 2:30 p.m., I went to Canada Post on Avenue du Parc, Montreal, to ship my formal notice to the City of Montreal. The clerk told me they couldn't send it registered with a signature because the package was "a little bit big." I said, "It's just a package, I need to send it registered with a signature." He refused and sent it only by regular mail.

The next day, at 1:30 p.m., I called FedEx. They told me there was no problem shipping a package of any size with signature confirmation. On July 28, 2021, around 11:30 a.m., I called the City of Montreal to ask if they had received my formal notice. They said the department was closed and the correct address was 800 de Maisonneuve East. I waited a few days to see if they would forward my notice there.

On July 29, 2021, I emailed Access Montreal (Office Ville-Marie), asking which address to send a formal notice to. They replied that I should send it through the SPVM website. It was clear the police had told them to avoid giving me the correct address. I emailed the SPVM as well to test them. I asked directly: "What is the address of the City of Montreal to send a formal letter regarding a dispute I have with the SPVM?" They avoided answering and instead told me I could file a complaint with the SPVM—once again changing the subject.

On August 2, 2021, I went to my hairdresser, Salon de Barbier Carlo Albanese in Montreal. Although I told him not to cut the top where I was missing hair, he cut it deliberately, clearly following instructions. His name was Mohamad.

I also noticed that my court documents were being mixed up. Either they broke into my home and tampered with them, or they used George Margelis to do it. My home had become their house.

On August 13, 2021, at 11:15 a.m., I called 311 from home and asked for the address of the City of Montreal's legal affairs department. They told me, "There is no such department." They avoided giving me the address, fearing I would send the formal notice and then sue them. Later, I called the legal affairs department itself, as advised by the McGill Legal Aid Clinic. They confirmed the same address I had, but when I asked if the office was open, they said, "It's always closed. We pick up letters once a week."

On August 5, 2021, I texted my so-called friend George

Tsoukalas to meet for coffee. He didn't answer—police and secret services had told my "friends" to cut me off. By August 14, we still hadn't met, with different excuses. On August 8, I texted his brother, Theodore Tsoukalas, for coffee. He never replied. On August 6 and 8, I texted another so-called friend, Lambros Xerakias, who also ignored me.

On August 18, 2021, at 8:30 p.m., I texted George Tsoukalas: "The police told you guys not to come out for a coffee." He replied, "What b…l are you talking about? We have health issues with our father and mother."

This was a lie. His father was on hemodialysis, which required no special care. His mother had Parkinson's, but from what they told me, they always put her to bed by 9:45–10:00 p.m., and then one or both brothers would come out for coffee, sometimes with Lambros too.

On August 5, while I had texted George to meet, he didn't answer. But on August 10, when I had a 39°C fever from the COVID vaccine, he suddenly told me to go for coffee. I said, "I have a fever from the vaccine." At that moment, he had no health issues with his parents. How could he suddenly come out?

On August 12, at 5:54 p.m., I texted George again about coffee. He replied he didn't know because Lambros had his phone off. Again, no mention of health issues. On August 13, at 1:41 p.m.,

George texted me to meet at Harvey's around 8:00 p.m. I agreed, but at 7:56 p.m., he canceled, saying Lambros was busy. Clearly, George and Theodore's "health issues" excuse was false. Lambros was not busy either, he too was pressured not to come out.

Between August 5 and 18, I texted Lambros three times. He read the texts but never replied. On August 18, I accused him and the others of following police orders not to meet. Again, no reply.

On July 22, 2021, I went to Provigo on Jean Talon West, Montreal. They charged me tax on goods, including orange juice. I wasn't sure if that was correct. The following week, I went to the PA Supermarket on Parc Avenue, repurchased orange juice, and was also charged tax. Suspicious, on August 9, I tested it at Épicerie Mile End on Avenue du Parc. They did not charge tax. It was now clear, they were telling certain stores to overcharge me, treating me like a homeless person, raising my cost of living.

On August 18, 2021, I went to McDonald's on Ste. Catherine West. The medium iced coffee was advertised at $1 plus tax, but they charged me $2.39 plus tax. I bought it deliberately to get the receipt. When I told the cashier, "The price is $1," she said, "No, that's the price." I pointed to the display. She pretended not to know, then refunded me. They were caught.

On August 19, 2021, I finally managed to go for coffee with George and Theodore Tsoukalas, as well as Lambros Xerakias.

From early August 2021, while I was preparing my formal notice, I discovered the City of Montreal's legal affairs department was "closed for COVID reasons." This was only an excuse, every other department was open. They closed it deliberately to make sending the formal notice and later serving a court bailiff's letter more difficult.

On August 27, 2021, I went to Canada Post at Atwater (Place Alexis Nihon, Pharmaprix). They didn't send my package as registered, the receipt said "regular parcel", but in reality, it was treated as registered because it required a signature. I asked the clerk, "If the office is closed, do they leave a card so the office can pick it up?" She said, "Yes."

On August 28, 2021, at 10:47 p.m., I went to McDonald's on Ste. Catherine West. The iced coffee was $1, but they refused to serve me at the counter, saying I had to order from the display with a credit or debit card. They wanted to show that if I were homeless and had no card, I wouldn't be served. In 2019, Starbucks at Ste. Catherine and Crescent had done the same.

On September 1, 2021, in the morning, the City of Montreal's legal affairs department received my formal notice by registered letter. At 9:55 a.m., it was signed for. That night, at 10:30 p.m., as I saw the confirmation on the Canada Post website, a fire truck and an ambulance parked in front of my house, pretending to go to the house across the street, another attempt to terrorize me. They were at fault, not me.

On September 17, 2021, I talked with George Tsoukalas. He told me he had applied for the National Disability Credit Alliance (NDCA) for his parents, who had health problems and needed a caregiver. He and his brother were approved and received a monthly amount from the Government of Canada.

I told him I would apply for my mother too, since she had multiple myeloma, a cancer that left her very tired and sometimes exhausted. She couldn't wash dishes, cook, or clean the house. Often, we went to the hospital by taxi. She needed constant help at home, in other words, a caregiver.

I told my so-called brother, George Margelis, to apply for NDCA the next day. However, the secret services had already been in contact with him online, typically through chat rooms. He told me, "This is stories, b.s. I shouldn't apply, because they might stop giving me $650 welfare a month. If Mom passes away, I'd have to reapply for welfare, and they may tell me to work." These were cheap excuses.

I said, "So go to work." He replied he had health problems, though he had none. This proved what I had said before: the police would not let George Margelis work. That way, he could not help me if they turned me into a homeless person. In the meantime, they wanted my family to struggle financially. If this were not their goal, they would have let him get NDCA and help reduce the burden on me, since I was paying higher household costs. They would never allow him to have a higher income as long as I lived in Montreal at the same house, because they planned to make me suffer financially.

On September 18, 2021, I checked my old email conversations with Kostas, the man I rented cars from in Greece during the summers of 2008–2010. I wanted to review what the police and drug traffickers had done.

In May 2008, I sent an email and spoke on the phone with Kostas to reserve a car. The police, who had hacked my computer and phones, immediately told George Papaspirou and Sterie Craciun (Gigi) that I would be going to Greece for more than two months.

Between May 20–25, 2008, Papaspirou and later Craciun came to Café Cosmos, where I often went in the mornings. They likely got information about me from the owner or staff. Papaspirou shook my hand very angrily. The next day, Craciun came pretending to do paperwork with the owner (who was also an accountant), but really to threaten me. He came two or three times.

Around June 20, 2008, they even sent someone to kill me at Café Cosmos. The man sat in the chair right beside me, though the café was almost empty. I immediately changed seats and left within four minutes. He had likely planned to stab me with a knife. This proved the police were working closely with drug traffickers.

In 2009, the same thing happened. On April 10, I emailed Kostas again to rent a car for early May. The police saw it. On May 8, 2009, they sent an African Canadian man in a black Honda Accord (1992–1994) to trap me at a traffic light and shoot me. I realized what he was up to and forced him to go first. I followed him a couple of streets, then went to the Parc Avenue police station around 2:00 p.m. I spoke for 2.5 hours with Officer Juil Ammi, telling him everything I knew about the drug traffickers.

This incident again showed police collaboration with traffickers. Proof of it was that they secretly put me under unofficial police protection. If it weren't them, they would have done it formally with signed papers.

Another proof was when I told Ted Write, a police/secret services contact, that we now had enough evidence to sue the traffickers. He declined and changed the subject. The police never jailed any traffickers, even though we had names, addresses, phone numbers, and evidence. Instead, Papaspirou was now in Fort Lauderdale, Florida, where he owned Ferrari Autoparts on St. Laurent Street.

Another solid proof: in my nine complaints to the police, they never denied any of my accusations.

After I sent a letter to Garage Fujiaty accusing them of

conspiring with the police to make me homeless, they kept calling me nonstop to do work there. Alain called 100 times, trying to show we had a good relationship. I ignored him. Fujiaty was guilty.

The repair shops involved in the conspiracy included: SG Garage, Patel Garage, Auto Vie (main number listed), Auto Raja, Platine Garage (new name Garage Rosa), Auto Vince, Touan, Garage Fujiaty, Stephen Car Dealer, H.K. Auto Kouan & Van, Garage Hoa, and about 150 customers.

By October 13, 2021, my so-called friends still hadn't met me for coffee. George Tsoukalas kept giving excuses, Theodore didn't reply to texts, and Lambros ignored two of mine. The police and secret services had isolated me from society.

That same day, I called Amazon around 11:30 a.m. from home to ask why they hadn't shipped me Rogaine 5% Minoxidil for over a year. At first, they said the seller didn't ship to my area. I tried another seller—same thing. Then they told me the shippers wouldn't send it because of the chemicals. Another excuse. They said they'd send me the manufacturer's number.

I called the manufacturer, who told me, "We have nothing to do with shipping—it's Amazon." Of course. I called Amazon again two days later, around noon. They repeated that shippers wouldn't deliver to my area. I tested with another address—same issue. Even my address in Greece is the same. Clearly, they had been told not to ship it to me, forcing me to buy it at a pharmacy for double the price.

I lived in Parc Extension, in the middle of Montreal. They used to ship it to me before. Why not now? Meanwhile, eBay shipped it through Canada Post or UPS without problems.

In late August 2021, I saw my family doctor, Georgia Vriniotis, at the hospital. I told her about the pain in my lower back. Six years earlier, an X-ray had shown a crushed spine bone, and the doctor had offered surgery, which I refused. Now Vriniotis, influenced by police and secret services, told me it was just arthritis, so if I applied for disability, I wouldn't get it.

I also showed her hospital results from a Holter test: 40 irregular heartbeats in 20 hours. She looked and said, "Ah, it's only one irregular heartbeat." She downgraded the issue to hide the damage done to my heart by the police.

They had also ruined George Margelis, turning him into a man with mental problems. They kept him on welfare ($640/month), reducing it often to force me to give him money. I saw him crying constantly from depression and melancholia.

On October 21, 2021, I sent a letter to Amazon Canada, accusing them of conspiring with the police to block my Rogaine orders. The tracking number was RN 546 086 474 CA.

{This report, until this point, was sent on October 25, 2021, with a two-page letter (Complaint No. 10) to the Police Service, Des Affaires Juridiques, Saint Urbain, Montreal, Quebec.}

On the 26th October 2021, I went to Canada Post at Alexis Nihon, Av. Atwater, Montreal, to send my 10th complaint to the police. The employee told me that I could not send my package by registered mail because it was a package, and only letters could be sent that way. In other words, they refused to send my package as registered mail. She told me that she could send it by regular mail with the recipient's signature. I told her, "Okay, send it like this."

The police did not want to show that they had received my 10th complaint. I had sent my formal notice by registered mail two months before—how come there had been no problem then? Tracking number: 0343617001498624.

On 25th October 2021, Amazon Canada received my registered letter, signed by I. Haji. On 27th October 2021, my 10th complaint to the police was delivered and signed.

On 10th November 2021, while I was printing my documents for court, I noticed that the secret services had ruined my receipts from the Greek postal office (ELTA). These were receipts for my registered letters sent on 14th June 2010 to the Ministry of Public Security in Athens, to immigration lawyer Boyd Campbell, and to the taxi license office. The receipts were no longer readable!

However, the translation I completed in 2010 from Greek to

English was still precise and stamped "true copy" (document T). They were changing and ruining my documents! The police did not respond to my 10th complaint.

With this persecution, and all these odious offences and inhuman acts, the police and secret services were trying to make me sick and die. I already had heart problems. This was attempted murder and torture. They had tried to murder me in conspiracy with the drug traffickers at the beginning of the case, and now again, they were doing it differently.

On 27th October 2021, the police received my 10th complaint, and I noticed it said Marc Lapointe signed it. On 27th August 2021, I sent my formal notice to the Legal Affairs Department of the City of Montreal. Although I sent it by registered mail, the receipt said "regular parcel."

Around 10th November 2021, Amazon Canada returned to me, unopened and with no reason, the registered mail I had sent accusing them of conspiracy with the police for not shipping me the Rogaine for my hair thinning. They did not want to be charged with conspiracy with the police! I kept this document in my file. Why did they send it back unopened? They knew what it writes!

Meanwhile, after 11 years, I was still nowhere near being able to hire a lawyer. They had blocked my path to justice, so I had to do everything by myself.

# Christos Margelis

On December 10, 2021, at 12:00 a.m., the police placed their agent in the next apartment, number 5, and turned on a low-frequency humming noise until 3:00 a.m. The next day, around 2:30 a.m., I again woke up from the same humming noise.

On December 14, 2021, I called the McGill Legal Information Clinic to inquire about my lawsuit information. Strangely, the clinic was closed. The message said that if I needed information, I should go to their site at www.lscm.ca

.

I went, but the site was closed and did not exist.

On December 27, 2021, around 7:30 p.m., I was at Place Alexis Nihon in Atwater, downtown. An elderly woman approached me and asked for a cigarette. I told her I did not have one. She then asked if I were going to Ottawa to buy a house, saying it would cost 5 million dollars.

I did not hear her very clearly, so I replied, "I would better move to Iran, but tell me more clearly what you said about the house in Ottawa." She answered, "It's 5 million, dummy!" She swore at me as if she did not care. I did not respond, because I knew she was a secret agent. They already knew I had been looking online for a house in Ottawa at low prices, as one of the few options I had left to avoid becoming homeless.

On December 28, 2021, at 4:23 p.m., the 80 bus was supposed to pass downtown. It did not, and I was alone at the bus stop. At 4:35 p.m., my mother called me and asked where I was. I told her about the bus delay, something they often did when I was waiting at a stop. At the same time, my father also arrived at the bus stop, and finally, at 4:40 p.m., the bus came.

When I was returning from downtown, I again saw my father on the same bus. Later, around 7:30 p.m., my mother called me again, and I mentioned it to her: how come we saw him very often when we were coming back from downtown? I asked her, "How come this is happening?" The police and secret services were manipulating my father to appear on the same bus as me, applying psychological warfare to make me think something would happen if I sued them.

On December 30, 2021, around 5:00 p.m., I was again at the 80 bus stop. As the bus approached, I put my coffee down to take out my card. There was no garbage container nearby. A man, whom I recognized as a police agent, was sitting on the bench, occupying the entire seat so that my mother could not sit down.

He saw me put the coffee down and immediately began swearing at me. For eight minutes straight, he called me a piece of shit and a piece of garbage, continuously and aggressively. I told him, "You are the piece of garbage, not me." He kept repeating the same insults until he got off at Metro Parc. My mother, Eugenia Gioni Margelis, was a witness.

On January 20, 2022, I applied for a credit card, but my application was not approved. On my credit record, I had a fair rating, which should have been sufficient for approval. I had gone bankrupt on November 1, 2015, and by then seven years had already passed—the required time before credit could be granted again.

On January 25, 2022, at 11:40 a.m., I called TransUnion and spoke with a representative. I asked why the credit card company had not approved me. She told me it was up to the bank to decide, not dependent on my credit score or record. That was a lie.

I asked how long after bankruptcy I was eligible for credit again. She refused to answer at first, again repeating that it depended on the bank. When I pressed her, she finally said that in Quebec it was seven years after discharge. That too was false, I knew from other times it was six years after discharge, or seven years from the date of bankruptcy.

This clearly showed they were interfering with credit approvals in order to block me. It was a conspiracy between TransUnion, the credit bureau, and the government.

On March 16, 2022, at 2:10 p.m., I went with my mother, Eugenia Gioni Margelis, to the ophthalmologist on De Maisonneuve West to see Dr. Marino Discepola. He took in every patient who came after us and left my mother waiting until the very end, finally seeing her at 6:00 p.m., when the clinic was almost empty.

He did this deliberately as retaliation because, in my report, I had mentioned how, years earlier, he had performed cataract surgery on my father, Christos Margelis. Although he had told my father the lens would cost $350, at the cashier they charged him $450. They had robbed him, under orders from the police and secret services, who instructed Discepola to raise the price in order to cause financial damage to our family.

This retaliation was clear proof that the police and secret services were in close contact with everyone involved in the conspiracy against me and my family. As soon as I wrote about the overcharge in my report, Dr. Discepola retaliated by keeping my mother waiting until 6:00 p.m.

My mother confronted the other doctor there, asking why they had left her until the very end. He simply replied:

"We will see you now."

Very clearly, just like my family doctor, Dr. Revilis, Dr. Discepola had been informed by the police about what I had written in my report.

In late March 2022, George Margelis was diagnosed with red areas on his skin. Sometimes this comes from pressure, but mostly from psychological factors like extreme stress. This confirmed what I had mentioned earlier in this book: the Montreal police, together with the secret services, were applying indescribable pressure on George Margelis to force him to do whatever they told him. They pressured him to stay unemployed, live in poverty, do nothing in his life, and depend on his family to survive, expecting me, Christos Margelis, to live with him indefinitely to provide shelter and food. The amount of money he received from welfare was so little that it was barely enough for anything.

I was 100% correct when I previously described what the police and secret services had been doing to George Margelis and my family. George was in a constant state of panic, fearing that if left alone and without work, they might be put on the streets, just as they had tried to do with me.

On 3rd June 2022, I sent my 11th complaint to the Montreal police, signed by Marc Lapointe, but they didn't care; they continued their practices.

On December 10, 2021, my mother went to the CLSC Park Extension (7085 Rue Hutchison, Montreal) for a bone-strengthening intervention. During the visit, a nurse named Claude Valerie was present. She seemed to like me, and we spoke briefly. The police and their agents noticed this interaction.

At the next appointment, on March 9, 2022, she was absent.

It was clear that they had told her not to be present while I was there. They did not like that she had shown an interest in me and wanted to prevent me from having any kind of relationship with a woman who was not affiliated with the police.

On June 17, 2022, she was again absent during the morning hours. I walked around her office to check if she was there, but she was nowhere to be found. Later, around 2:45 p.m., when I went to pick up my mother, Eugenia Gioni Margelis, I finally saw Claude Valerie in her room. By then, it was evident that they had already instructed her.

She was wearing green clothing, which I interpreted as a coded message meaning, "Go for it, and you will be screwed." Her attitude had clearly changed, and I realized she had been briefed about me. The goal was to ensure that I only developed relationships with women controlled by secret agents, those who could drag me down financially and make me vulnerable to homelessness.

Since 2020, there's something else that has alarmed me and strengthened my belief. I have noticed that my Facebook account with my name, Christos Margelis, has lost nearly all my contacts. I had maybe two or three left. They didn't want me to post anything about my case or gain publicity because isolating me made it impossible for my messages to go viral. Facebook seemed complicit in this conspiracy; despite my complaints, they did nothing.

Meanwhile, my so-called friends would only occasionally meet me for coffee. This started around August 2021, when I began preparing my case against the Montreal police.

Coming back to the timelines of events, in early July 2022, I noticed a pair of short pants I had just bought had disappeared from my house. I told George Margelis, and he dismissed it, saying, "Oh, you are talking just about some shorts, that's not any big deal!" Instead of questioning how it had disappeared, he seemed complicit, following orders.

On 27th or 28th July 2022, John Vlahakis, a secret agent, called me at home and mentioned a police vehicle outside his house. He swore at the police over the phone, signaling that he was working for them like George Margelis. On 29th July 2022, around 3:15 p.m., John Vlahakis called again and reported that George had told him I smoked a lot and coughed. This was false—I smoke only eight cigarettes a day. He wanted to cover the police in case I had a lung condition. This confirms my previous claim that John Vlahakis passes messages to me over the phone for court purposes.

On 11th August 2022, at 4:00 a.m., I woke up with severe discomfort. I drank water, but felt faint, and my face was pale and sweating. I called my mother and told her I wasn't okay. George Margelis saw me and called an ambulance. In 10–15 minutes, the paramedics arrived. By then, I was conscious and no longer sweating. They checked my vital signs and performed an electrocardiogram (ECG). They said I was okay and left after advising me to call if it happened again. This episode was consistent with the irregular and negative heartbeats I had mentioned earlier in this report. A 10-second ECG is not sufficient; I need a stress test, ultrasound, and Holter monitoring. I plan to visit my family doctor for further testing.

During July and August 2022, although Borrowell, the credit rating company, had previously sent me updates every 10 days, they stopped sending updates for over a month. I believe the police and secret services instructed them to do so to prevent me from maintaining good credit.

On 30th August 2022, around 3:30 p.m., I was with my mother at the Royal Victoria Hospital, Glen Site. While she rested in the non-invasive cardiology room, a nurse asked if we had an ECG appointment. I told her she was resting before leaving. Later, while visiting the Jewish General Hospital emergency department around 3:00 p.m., they performed an ECG on me for no more than 10 seconds, although the standard ECG should last longer.

On 21st September 2022, around 3:00 p.m., I was waiting for bus 80 at the stop on Jean Talon and Hutchison. The driver pretended to look straight ahead and didn't pick up passengers, including me, despite us waving. This appeared intentional.

On 22nd September 2022, at 13:40, I went to my appointment at the Legal Aid Clinic at 201 Cremazie East, Montreal, H2M 1L2, Bureau 3.50, phone 514-864-2111, for my case with the police. Although I knew from the beginning that the lawyers were compromised, I wanted one to review my documents, including my originating application and summons, for my court submission.

At 15:30, the lawyer called me in. Her behavior was hostile. She said, "Tell me quickly, I don't have a lot of time. Briefly, what's your case?" I explained that the police had arrested me in 2008 over alleged identity issues after I lost my passport, which was later confirmed stolen. Someone had tried to enter the country with a forged passport, but that person was deported. I also told her I had identified the likely suspects—drug traffickers, and that the police had informed them I had reported them, after which they began threatening my life. I explained that because I was suing them, they had destroyed my business: I had 11 car repair shops and about 150 customers, all lost. I was forced onto welfare.

Before I could give more details, she interrupted me, ready to end the meeting. I requested that she at least review my originating application to see if changes were needed. She refused.

This was another instance where the police and secret services prevented a lawyer from reviewing my case and stopped me from hiring legal representation worldwide.

On 5 October 2022, I called the McGill Legal Aid Clinic at 13:30 from my cell. I requested that the City of Montreal's address be named as the defendant in my originating application. The woman repeatedly told me to file a complaint with the Montreal Police. I explained five times that my dispute was with the police and that I needed to sue the city for compensation. Eventually, she reluctantly gave me the legal affairs department's address, which I already had.

The police, along with their agent from Apartment 5 next to ours—supposed to provide protection—continued placing a low-frequency humming noise from 23:00 to late morning, preventing sleep. They did this on 20, 21, 22, and 23 October 2022. Their intention was clearly to drive me insane.

On 6 July 2022, I noticed on TV that the Icelandic volcano had erupted again. The police and the Canadian government, in conspiracy, tried to show these eruptions as frequent, though before 15 April 2010, when it first erupted, there had been no eruptions. This was propaganda to prevent me from traveling to Greece and seeking the International Criminal Court for crimes against humanity and genocide allegedly committed by the Montreal police and the government of Canada.

Around 20 November 2022, Madam Koula, who lived on the first floor of our building, returned from the hospital and, while climbing the stairs with her son and husband, felt discomfort and fell. She was taken to her apartment, suffered a heart attack, and died due to the long stairs and pre-existing health issues. Before we moved into Apartment 6, Madam Koula had lived in Apartment 2 but had moved upstairs to Apartment 3, because Apartments 2 and 4 were occupied by personnel under police protection. Had she not been forced, she would not have died. This was the first second-degree murder they committed, with more to follow.

On 1 December 2022, I saw on Greek TV station ERT1's 21:00 news that a package with explosives was sent to the Spanish Prime Minister, the American Embassy, and other locations, but was discovered in time and did not explode. The report showed someone walking with an orange toolbox, similar to one I had used for work. This was a message to me, signaling that they would continue preventing me from working.

This is connected to my complaint from 13 June 2010 to the Ministry of Public Security in Athens regarding persecution by the Montreal police and secret services during the summer of 2010, when they tried to make me homeless because I attempted to have a lawyer review my case and seek redress at the International Criminal Court. They never let me hire a lawyer for the ICC because they were deeply guilty.

On 13 December 2022 at 19:10, I went to catch the bus to

visit my mother at the Glen Site hospital, where she was in the emergency department. I waited at the Jarry and Bloomfield bus stop, but the 80 Parc Avenue bus didn't arrive. It was cold, and I had to wait another 17 minutes for the next one. I called my mother from my cell to update her.

When we reached Ogilvy, the bus scheduled for 19:20 passed the bus I was on and went to Metro Parc to pick up passengers. This felt deliberate.

On 12 December 2022, my mother, Eugenia Gioni, was brought to the Royal Victoria Glen Site emergency department at 1001 Decarie Boulevard, Montreal, Quebec H4A 3J1, with breathing problems and exhaustion. They conducted exams, including lung X-rays and scans for clots, as well as blood tests. By 18 December, they still hadn't found the problem.

On 18 December, I visited her in room 34 of the emergency department from 12:00 to 16:00. At 15:30, we repeatedly asked nurses to give her a puff device to help her breathe, but they ignored us for 45 minutes. An IV had finished, and they wouldn't even remove it. My mother was suffering and called my brother George Margelis at 18:30, telling him the nurses had abandoned her and that she feared she might die. George calmed her and promised to speak with the doctors the next morning. Their negligence directly endangered her life.

In December 2022, I discovered that the police and secret services had mostly instructed banks and credit card companies not to give me credit. I had applied for a President's Choice Financial card in October. In November, they claimed I was denied because I went bankrupt over seven years ago, which was false. National Bank approved me for a $3,000 credit card in October 2022. My mother, Eugenia Margelis, had gone bankrupt in 2008 but had excellent credit by 2018 with $34,000. There was no legitimate reason for credit denial.

On 30 January 2023 at 18:25, I went to catch the 80 bus south at Bloomfield Corner Ball. The bus skipped twice, and I boarded the third one around 19:15. This seemed intentional. Around two hours earlier, I had been unable to withdraw funds from a trading account. The temperature was -10°C.

Between mid-February and March 2023, items disappeared from my home, including my father's shoes and my mother's stockings (costing around $120) used for a clot issue.

On 8 March 2023, I searched online for information about Canadian government pensions for living abroad (Exhibit VVV). On 13 March, I received a letter from the Quebec government (dated 28 February, likely falsified) showing my monthly pension at 65 would be only $126. They were monitoring my actions closely.

On 17 March 2023, I arranged with George Tsoukalas to

meet for coffee after three months. At 19:15, George confirmed he would arrive at 22:20, but at 21:29, he canceled, citing Lambros Xerakias' mood. I noted in my exhibits that secret services were monitoring me and did not approve of my research on pensions. At 21:57, he finally confirmed the outing. They monitored my every move and influenced others accordingly.

Around 13 March 2023, I called Centre Dentaire Fairmount to make a dental appointment. The receptionist refused to accept me, claiming they didn't take patients on welfare. My brother, George Margelis, who was also on welfare, was accepted. This confirmed that police and secret services had interfered again. On 3 April, George had a tooth removed using welfare insurance.

Since 10 March 2023, the police and secret services, in conspiracy with the governments of Quebec and Canada, had maintained a low-frequency humming noise day and night, trying to drive me insane. Their agents worked around the clock, aiming to make me sick and possibly die.

# Chapter 9
# Court Case Legal Action

On 13 April 2023, I submitted my application to the Montreal Courthouse, located at 1 Notre-Dame East, which included my case originating application, summons, list of exhibits, affidavit, and notice of presentation.

When I attended the court for my notice of presentation on 26 April 2023, the judge told me I should not have been there. The court record incorrectly stated that I was not present. Additionally, my exhibits and the summons had disappeared from my court records. The court clerk was clearly part of the conspiracy, along with others in the Montreal Courthouse. I had to resubmit all the documents.

The City of Montreal did not respond to my summons either.

On 7 July 2023, for the third time, I noticed documents from my file were missing. The court had been disappearing my documents repeatedly, so I had to resubmit them. I also sent a letter pointing out the continuous disappearance of my papers.

On 25 May 2023, I submitted my application for setting down for trial and judgment upon default of the defendant. The court disappeared Exhibit 1, Exhibit 2, and proof of notification that I had sent the summons to the defendant. I consulted a lawyer for guidance, and she confirmed these documents were missing from my file. I had to resubmit them to the court.

Subsequently, the Government of Quebec passed a law requiring all court staff and clerks to conduct their work in French. They knew I could not speak French and intentionally prevented me from communicating with them. The court clerk failed to notify me whether my record was complete or, if incomplete, which documents were missing. By 12 August 2023, no notice had been sent.

When I called the court around 30 July 2023 to speak to the Superior Court clerk, they insisted I could only talk in French. This violated the United Nations International Covenant on Civil and Political Rights, Articles 2 and 23, regarding discrimination based on language. They ignored this and only enforced French, knowing I could not communicate.

On 16 August 2023, I called again, clarified that I was eligible to speak in English, and they finally talked to me in English. They promised to contact me to confirm if my record was complete. By the end of August, they had not called.

Meanwhile, my father, Christos Margelis, tried to get an appointment at the Jewish General Hospital, Montreal, with his family doctor, Georgia Vriniotis, for an MRI of his gallbladder stones. The hospital had refused him since March 2023. By mid-

September 2023, Dr. Vriniotis issued a requisition to go to D205 for the appointment. The office took the paper but gave no appointment, instructing him to call 514-340-8222 ext. 23777. When I called, the answering machine instructed that the requisition must be submitted in person.

This appears to be a systematic attempt by the hospital, likely under instructions from the police, secret services, and government, to prevent my father from getting an MRI, risking his health and life. This pattern seems aimed at destroying my family, especially as my mother is also sick, leaving us in severe poverty once they prevent me and George Margelis from working, a potentially explosive situation of suffering and deprivation.

This report was sent to the Prime Minister of Canada, Justin Trudeau, on 2 October 2023, via mail to 80 Wellington Street, Ottawa, K1A 0A2.

The report was received, signed by the Office of the Prime Minister, on 4 October 2023.

On 12 October 2023, I had an appointment with Doctor Georgia Vriniotis, my family doctor at the Jewish General Hospital, at 9:20 a.m. I arrived at 9:05 a.m., but the secretary informed me that the doctor was sick and had not yet arrived. I believed this was a prearranged trick by the police and secret services to prevent the doctor from seeing me and sending me for a blood test. I knew it was deliberate because they did not call or text me earlier. One email they sent me arrived at 9:25 a.m., after my appointment, supposedly giving notice. Notice after the appointment? This was absurd.

I had already reported that the Jewish General Hospital refused to give an appointment to my father, Christos Margelis, for an MRI to check stones in his stomach. I did not believe the doctor was actually sick; it seemed like a story invented to avoid seeing me.

On 20 November 2023, at McDonald's downtown, a lady sat beside my mother and me, sneezing excessively. I believed she was placed there intentionally to get my mother sick. The way she looked at me confirmed this suspicion.

On 22 November 2023, my mother called her so-called friend Voula (514-371-4245) about four times to get the phone number of her private family doctor. Voula did not answer any of the calls. I believed the police and secret services instructed her not to respond for sure.

On 21 November 2023, we went with my mother to her cancer doctor, Michael Sebag, at the Royal Victoria Hospital. He announced that he had no more treatments to offer, stating she had two to three months to live. He mentioned CAR T-cell therapy, with great potential for success, but he had not informed us about it early enough, he should have informed us at least eight months in advance. He had failed us like a 10-year-old. My brother, George

Margelis, found treatments online that the doctor had not mentioned. This suggested that the police and secret services had instructed him not to provide proper guidance, he didn't care.

In August 2023, I sent three emails to a notary in Greece, Fotini Danaka, to make a will. My mother wanted to transfer our parents' house to the names of me, Christos Margelis, and George Margelis after her death. The notary did not respond, likely following orders from the Greek government.

By the end of November 2023, I sent two emails to the Evangelismos Hospital in Athens, one to the administration and one to the commander, asking whether they performed stem cell transplantation for my mother's cancer. They did not respond, apparently following orders from the Greek government. I believed this was a deliberate attempt to prevent her treatment and ultimately cause her death.

My father mentioned that buses were often delayed unusually or did not arrive at all. In addition, shops frequently hiked prices or charged him arbitrarily. These actions seemed intended to make life extremely difficult for my father, who is 83, and to hasten his death.

I noticed that the CIA or Canadian secret services attempted to lure me into a relationship with an attractive girl pretending to be interested in me. This appeared to be a tactic to prevent me from seeking asylum in Russia or Iran. Similarly, secret agents tried to manipulate my personal relationships.

Beginning in December 2023, I was supposed to receive two USB flash drives from AliExpress for my laptop. The police and secret services intercepted and removed them. I documented all this information regarding my case.

On 19 December 2023, I saw on Greek news ERT1 that the Icelandic volcano had erupted several times recently. Previously, on 15 April 2010, I had planned to travel to Greece but could not due to the eruption. This time, the media appeared to downplay the danger, showing people baking eggs or pizza on lava. This was impossible; steel melts at 1,400°C, lava is around 1,200°C, and baking on lava would destroy a pan immediately.

This suggested a deliberate cover-up. I concluded that the 15 April 2010 eruption was intentionally timed in conspiracy with the Canadian and Icelandic governments to prevent me from reaching Greece and filing a case at the International Criminal Court for genocide and crimes against humanity allegedly committed against me by the Montreal police and the governments of Canada and Greece. The media misrepresentation of the lava confirmed that this event was staged.

On 17 December 2023, at 4:00 p.m., my mother instructed me to visit the Maxi supermarket at 375 Jean Talon West to check if the electric stairs were functioning. She had to go to the pharmacy there to check the amount of blood thinner she had. I went, and the stairs were working. I called her home (514-559-6190) and told her at 4:30 p.m.

I went back home to pick up my mother and take her to the pharmacy. When we arrived at 4:30 p.m., the elevator was not working. The secret services had told Maxi to stop them. My mother, who had mobility problems, could not walk long distances, so we left without checking her blood thinner. She was exhausted, and we did not know the level of her medication, warfarin.

They also pulled a molding from the front windshield of my car and broke it. The next day, 18 December, I returned to Maxi, and the stairs were working. It was clear that the previous day's malfunction was deliberate, to tire my mother and prevent her from checking her medication.

The Prime Minister of Canada, Justin Trudeau, did not respond to my complaint or request for action that I had sent by email and mail.

On 27 December 2023, my mother, Eugenia Gioni Margelis, was admitted to Royal Victoria Hospital in Montreal with breathing problems, a virus, and pneumonia. Her multiple myeloma had destroyed her immune system, leaving her unable to fight infections. After first going to the emergency room, she was moved to the ICU on 3 January 2024. The doctors appeared intent on letting her die to free up her bed. Her cancer doctor, Dr. Sebag, and kidney doctor, Dr. Lipman, both told us she was not a candidate for dialysis, effectively abandoning her care.

On 15 January 2024, my mother passed away. She suffered from untreated lung problems caused by multiple myeloma, which had been diagnosed in January 2019. I believe the police and government conspiracy to turn me into a homeless person contributed to her death. This was the second instance of what I consider second-degree murder, the first being Madam Soula a year earlier, who died after being forced to climb stairs unsuitable for her health.

On 18 January 2024, I suggested to my father and George Margelis that we sue Dr. Sebag for his negligence, which led to my mother's early death. George got angry and refused, claiming the doctor was not at fault. George, a secret agent, was protecting Sebag and showed no concern for my mother's death. When I confronted him, my father reacted as if my statements were delusions from ten years prior, showing the extent of the brainwashing he had received from the psychiatric clinic at Royal Victoria Hospital and the Montreal police.

On 23 January 2024, I discovered my two gold chains, worth $5,000, were missing from my drawer, stolen by the police and secret services.

On 27 January and 3 February 2024, when I returned home from coffee, the police and secret services had occupied all parking spaces in front of my house, forcing me to park far away. This happened repeatedly to make my life difficult.

In early January 2024, I ordered two USB flash drives from AliExpress to store my case documents. The tracking indicated delivery on 30 January, but I never received them. The secret services had intercepted them.

On 3 and 7 February 2024, I emailed lawyer Carol-Anne Gagnon (407 Saint Laurent Blvd, Office 410, Montreal, Quebec H2Y 2Y5), who helps people file lawsuits themselves. Although she had previously provided guidance, she gave incorrect advice when I asked what to say at the notice of presentation. I also asked who to sue for my mother's early death due to the doctor's negligence, and after a long delay, she finally replied.

On 12 February 2024, I watched Greek TV (ERT1, 9:00 p.m. news) report that someone had attempted to send a bomb in an envelope to a court in Salonika. This was related to my 2010 complaint to the Greek government, accusing them of conspiring with Canada to make me homeless. The news falsely presented it as a real bomb threat, showing that the Greek government under Kiriakos Mitsotakis continued its conspiracy with Canada and the

West, sending me hidden messages.

Beginning in January 2024, the police and secret services, noticing that I was going ahead with my case in court against them and that I might leave the country, put someone on WhatsApp to tell me that they had a job for me. It was the second time this had happened, which made it crystal clear who was behind it. They told me to communicate with one person who would tell me about the job. He said his name was Corann, and there was a simple task to do.

On 13 February 2024, the man offering me a "job" gave a short training session. Afterward, I performed some tasks on his site, Veeva, at veevasysbeta.com. The system involved clicking icons to earn commissions. Then it began asking for money—first 100 USDT, then about 170 USD, and on 17 February it demanded 300 USD to deposit before I could withdraw. After I sent that money, it immediately asked for 1,100 USD. I told the person what was happening, but he insisted I deposit the funds. When I told him this was fraud, he disappeared.

This showed clearly how the police and secret services collaborated with common criminals. They stole 500 USD from me. Luckily, I didn't send more. That was the "job" they were offering me.

On 26 February 2024, at 14:06, the City of Montreal issued

me a parking ticket while my car was in a space reserved for deliveries at PA Supermarket on Parc Avenue. In front of the supermarket, one door away, there was a copy store, Copie 2000. I went inside to make three copies. It took less than four minutes. Within that time, they had already issued a ticket. Since it takes about a minute and a half to place the ticket, this meant that after two and a half minutes they were already at my car.

This was crystal clear evidence they were following me everywhere. They could also have set a trap, since there was no parking space nearby except in front of the supermarket. I parked there, and as soon as I left my car, they came and put the ticket. Every minute, every second, their eyes were on me, watching what I was doing, where I was looking, and what I was thinking. Unbelievable.

On 7 March 2024, I took part in the case management room 16.61 of the Montreal court. The new lawyer for the police (City of Montreal), Hugo Filiatrault, said he would file a motion to reject my case. His email to me had no basis at all. On 23 April 2024, we went to the notice of presentation to apply to reject my case. The chief justice postponed the case for a later hearing. On 18 June 2024, we had another case management session with the Superior Court of Montreal. I knew the case was rigged.

Beginning in April 2024, I applied for and was approved for

a credit card from the Bank of Montreal. By 3 May 2024, for the second time, the credit card had not arrived. This was no coincidence, the police and secret services would not let the card reach my hands.

On 9 June 2024, I arrived in Greece with my father. The Greek secret services did not act for a while. Around 17 June 2024, I met a girl at the beach, and we talked for a while. On 22 June, when I went to that beach again, I noticed the girl was passing messages to me that the Greek secret services had already contacted her. This was the signal they received from the Canadian secret services to prevent me from finding a girlfriend in Greece.

On 5 July 2024, we returned to Montreal—me, George Margelis, and my father, Christos Margelis. At the Montreal airport, the security guards instructed us to proceed to immigration, despite our Canadian passports. We went to immigration again, not for the first time. From what I remembered, a person there told me they were looking for somebody from Romania. I asked, "Who, Pavel?" He looked at me for a while and said yes. They were trying to show that Pavel, the person who had attempted to enter the country in 2006 or 2007 with my stolen passport, was still being sought. By that time, he had never entered the country. These were cheap excuses.

Around September 2023, I noticed that our TV in the living

room, where I slept, was turning on by itself at night, waking me up. I believed the police and secret services were doing this to prevent me from sleeping. Around December 2023, I put a switch on the TV and turned it off. In February 2024, I stopped turning off the switch and noticed that the TV no longer turned on by itself at night. By August 2024, it was clear: the police and secret services had done this on purpose to wake me up at night.

By 30 August 2024, they were still applying psychological warfare, trying to turn me into a homeless person. They were using the so-called police protection in Apartment 5 next to us to emit a humming noise day and night, sometimes preventing me from sleeping. They were still trying to drive me crazy.

On 24 September 2024, I went to court to contest the motion that the City of Montreal had filed to reject my case, because their lawyer, Hugo Filiatrault, refused to speak in English. We had to postpone the hearing to 30 January 2025.

Meanwhile, from 20 September to 28 September 2024, the police and secret services emitted a humming, vibrating noise from Apartment 5, supposedly under police protection, day and night, in an attempt to drive me crazy. They were still trying to turn me into a homeless person. They continued to prevent me from conducting my business or working elsewhere. No lawyer was allowed, of course, and psychological warfare was applied every day. As soon as I left my home, they attempted to make me homeless.

On 10 October 2024, my father, Christos Margelis, went to the Canada Post at the Family Prix Pharmacy on Parc Avenue to send a registered letter to his sister in Greece. They charged him 28 USD, whereas last year it had cost 22 USD. He complained to the post office, and the manager reduced the price to 24 USD.

The previous day, my father had another issue. A cell phone company, Chatr, was asking for about 35 USD to give him a voucher of only 10 USD. Downtown Montreal, the Fido store told him to go to Chatr, claiming they didn't have vouchers of 10 or 15 USD. These actions were clearly designed to make my father pay more for goods and services. He had been telling me quite often that different stores were hiking prices on anything he bought. This was no coincidence, it was done intentionally by the police and secret services, who were constantly giving my father a hard time, trying to make him sick just as they were doing to me.

Finally, I found out that a one-month voucher with Chatr actually costs only 5 USD. They were trying to rob my father.

When my mother was alive, we used to go to a bar called Piranha at 680 Saint Catherine West. There were slot machines (casino machines) there, and my mother used to play and gamble. What they were doing was manipulating the machines: the ones that had previously given payouts, which already had low chances—

were left empty so my mother would be forced to play on them and almost always lose. On the other machines, they had placed their agents, leaving her no choice but to play on the empty ones. This resulted in constant losses. They didn't care that my mother had multiple myeloma cancer; they just wanted to create financial damage and distress, hoping to worsen her health.

After my mother died on 15 January 2024, while passing by that bar, I noticed that only a very few people were playing the slot machines, fewer than half were occupied. Was this a coincidence? No. It was intentional. The police and secret services had been manipulating the machines to ensure my mother would lose and die sooner.

The police and government secret services had committed two second-degree murders, as I mentioned above. They were also trying to kill my father with these malicious tactics.

Around March 2024, George Tsoukalas told me that his father had applied for and received a dental care card from the Government of Canada. The insurer was Sun Life. His father had received the application around February 2024, but my father did not receive any application—intentionally.

Around May 2024, I called the Government of Canada and explained what was happening. We applied again in late May 2024, but, again intentionally, they never sent the card to my father. By

October 2024, nothing had arrived. I called the government again regarding the dental plan, and they said they would resend it. This created an eight-month delay during which my father did not receive his dental care card, while everyone else had. This was done intentionally, as the Government of Canada was participating in the conspiracy with the police, targeting my father to make him suffer just as they had done with my mother.

In October 2024, George Margelis told me that if our father died, we should rent our house in Greece to pay the rent in Montreal. The police and secret services had intentionally put George on welfare; they did not let him work, as I explained earlier in this report. He didn't make enough money to pay rent, he earned 650 CAD a month, while the rent was 1,000 CAD. This was a malicious tactic in conspiracy with George Margelis. They wanted to rent the house we had in Greece and afterward make it impossible for me to remove the tenants. That way, if they managed to put me on the streets, I would have no home to return to and would end up homeless.

On 19 October 2024, around 6:30 p.m., I was downtown Montreal for a coffee. All of a sudden, I noticed a person appearing to be homeless, walking and screaming down Saint Catherine Street. This was something the police and secret services often did, showing me that from their torture, I would end up screaming and swearing on the streets.

The police and secret services had also been driving George Margelis crazy. They threatened him that if I left and went to live in Greece, he would be living alone and on the streets. At this point, George Margelis had psychological problems, depression, and was living in extreme fear and terror.

This report was sent to the Prime Minister of Canada's office as my second complaint to the Government of Canada, together with a two-page complaint letter (Complaint No. 2) up to the spot marked.

This report, up to the spot marked, was also sent to the Montreal Police as my 12th complaint, together with a two-page complaint letter (Complaint No. 12).

*2024/10/22*

In January–February 2023, on Viber, I noticed a club that invested in cryptocurrency. The person in charge told me his name was Robin (phone number +1 510-951-8059). He told me to put money into a platform called kcmbtc.com, and he would make money for me, while I would give him 10% of the profits. I agreed and invested around $4,000 on that platform. He supposedly made about $40,000 and demanded that I pay him commissions from my bank account via cryptocurrency (BTC), not from the platform.

Believing him, I sent around $4,500 USD to his BTC wallet. When I tried to withdraw, he refused and would not let me. He asked for more money, which I did not send. I realized he was a scammer who had stolen around $9,000 USD from me.

I suspected the police and secret services had sent this person, because whenever they realized I might leave Canada to go to Iran to file for asylum, they sent me "easy online job" offers from home. I initially followed them, but they turned out to be scammers. They had already stolen about $500 USD from me through their project at a company named Veeva Systems. If Robin was involved, he was another scammer in these fraudulent schemes. It seemed that the secret services and police were involved and had been stealing from me since 2010 to turn me into a homeless person.

On 17 October 2024, a girl named Isabella from New York (phone number +1 646-763-5352) sent me a message claiming it was a wrong number. We ended up chatting on WhatsApp. She showed me some pictures. On 29 October 2024, she told me the same thing Robin had told me: she could make me money over a crypto platform called TZONE. I checked the Play Store and saw the platform wasn't listed. Like Robin's kcmbtc.com, I realized it was a scam. She told me to put money in, but I refused. This woman was likely an agent, possibly from the U.S. (maybe CIA) or Canada's secret services. It was clear they were trying to steal my money by any means possible.

On 28 October 2024, around 11:00 a.m., they sent a virus to my laptop. It told me to call a number claiming it was Microsoft to fix the problem. I called the number. The person's name was Mike (phone number +1 240-466-4259). He guided me through removing the virus and told me the laptop was hacked. I already knew that, but he pretended to fix it. He then said that to prevent hackers from stealing usernames and passwords, another person from TD Bank would guide me through withdrawing $15,000 to avoid a charge from taking effect.

I listened. His name, as he told me, was Cooper. I went to TD Bank; they only allowed me to withdraw $5,000. Cooper, on the phone, told me to go to a money transfer place at 450 Jean Talon Street, Montreal, to use a Bitcoin machine where he would give me instructions. I went to the machine, but the instructions were to deposit the money in BTC and give it to him. I stopped and left the place, going back to TD Bank to check for pending transactions.

When I left the store, the owner called me back and told me they were scammers. I told him I had figured it out. The owner then told the scammer, Cooper, that he hoped his kids and parents would die slowly from cancer. I laughed; it was obviously a scam. At TD Bank, they told me there was no transaction pending. I changed my card and password, closed the Microsoft page at home, and my laptop worked fine.

The police and secret services were scammers. They were still trying to steal my money to turn me into a homeless person.

Another thing I noticed was that every time I drove home, the secret services and police, undercover, would occupy all parking spaces on the street in front of my home. I had to park on another street, forcing me to walk around searching for a space.

On 31 October 2024, my father told me he visited an eye store in downtown Montreal called New Look. They asked him 900 CAD to sell him eyeglasses, they were trying to rob him.

On 3 November 2024, I was at Plaza Alexis Nihon, downtown Montreal. There was a restaurant there called Roasters Sports Bar on Atwater Street. It had about seven slot machines from Loto-Québec. I noticed that all the machines were empty and nobody was playing, and this always happened. My mother, when we went to eat at McDonald's next to Roasters, would almost always go to Roasters to play slot machines. The secret services used to occupy all the machines and leave available only the one that was virtually impossible to pay out. My mother had no choice but to play that machine and very rarely won. It was rigged, just like at Bar Piranha downtown Montreal, as I mentioned above. They were trying to make my mother sicker and die faster.

On 3 May 2024, I sent my case to the United Nations Human Rights Council for the violation of my human rights by the police and secret services (Government of Canada).

Also, the undercover police from Apartment 5 next to us, supposedly under police protection, had been making a vibrating noise 24 hours a day for three days, not letting me sleep.

After my mother's death on 15 January 2024, I wanted to sue her oncology doctor, Dr. Michael Sebag. I had all the evidence of his negligence and indifference, which led to her early death. However, from what the secret services were showing me, they would not let me hire a lawyer to sue him (he was working for them). I had to file the lawsuit myself, knowing the case would be rigged, like my case with the police.

On 7 December 2024, at 11:30 a.m., Peter Strifas, the owner of the building we lived in, called me at home and informed me that the tenant of Apartment 5, next to us, had reported that I had knocked on the wall the previous night around 12:30 a.m. At that time, the secret services and police protection were occupying that apartment, and the vibrating humming noise was loud enough that I could not sleep. This was proof of what they had been doing. I mentioned above that from around 25 November 2024, they had the humming noise non-stop (it was now 11 December 2024). They were trying to drive me crazy. Peter Strifas told me to record the noise, it was not very loud, just a vibrating humming noise.

Upon sending my complaints on 22 October 2024 to the

Government of Canada (Complaint Number Two, Office of the Prime Minister) and the 12th complaint to the Montreal Police (SPVM), I received no response.

One thing I noticed on Facebook since December 2024 was that when I sent friend requests to girls from different places, I got replies, and they were interested. However, when I sent friend requests or messages to women from Athens, Greece, they did not reply. I concluded that Facebook had received messages from the secret services of Canada and Greece to prevent women from Greece from chatting with me. They feared I might go to Greece to live and plan to go to Russia or Iran to file for asylum, since my home was there and it was much closer to these countries.

On 30 January 2025, at 9:00 a.m., in Room 15.03 at the Montreal Courthouse, we had a court case in which the City of Montreal applied to reject my case as frivolous and abusive. Before I went to court, one car in front of me had a license plate that read "EMBARGO." I understood the message.

I went to court with a French-to-English interpreter named Norman because the lawyer for the City of Montreal wanted to speak in French. I explained what was happening to the judge and asked him to read my evidence, but he refused. I told him that the police and secret services would not let me hire a lawyer. The judge did not offer to appoint one for me but pretended everything was fine. I briefly explained my case. The judge had read my originating application, so he was familiar with my case, which was supported by all the evidence regarding my accusations against the police and secret services.

The lawyer for the City of Montreal stated that he had nothing to add beyond what his documents indicated, claiming that my case was abusive and frivolous. The judge said he would give a verdict in half an hour. When he returned, he brought examples of other cases, which was impossible, as a case like mine had never occurred in the history of the world, and dismissed my case as abusive and frivolous.

I knew they would never allow my case to proceed, but I did not expect it to be dismissed in such a blatantly absurd way. Anyone reading my file could clearly see what was happening, as there was solid evidence supporting my claims.

By the time I told the judge that they would not allow me to hire a lawyer, the court was obliged to appoint me one. They had already refused to do this in the summer of 2023. While I had submitted my case to the court, the court repeatedly removed my documents from the record (plumitif) and caused unusual delays. They were clearly searching for a way to dismiss my case, and they did so in a rigged manner on 30 January 2025.

It was obvious that the police and secret services were blocking my access to the judicial system, with the courts doing whatever they wanted and judges being influenced to dismiss my case. It was a rigged case from the start.

On 14 February 2025, I checked the website of the Société québécoise d'information juridique (SOQUIJ), which displays all court decisions, including what the plaintiff said about the case and the final verdict. I noticed that the Superior Court, where my case should have been listed, did not display it. I sent an email to SOQUIJ asking why my case was missing. They replied that because the judge gave the verdict "in the minutes," the court did not send the case to them. The judge knew this and deliberately gave the verdict "in the minutes" so that my case would never be published. The case was rigged.

Until 22 April 2025, the secret services in Montreal continued to apply psychological warfare, trying to turn me into a homeless person. On 15 April 2025, my father fell and broke his arm. He was taken by ambulance to the Montreal General Hospital. They put a holder on his hand, gave him pills for only three days, and sent him home. On 19 April, the pills ran out. I went to the pharmacy for a refill, but they told me there was no refill and that we would have to go back to the hospital emergency room to get a prescription.

We went to the Montreal General Hospital and waited from 2:00 p.m. to 8:30 p.m. without being served, even though everyone who arrived after us saw a doctor. This was clearly an order received from the Canadian secret services to make us wait indefinitely in the emergency room.

Around mid-May 2025, a so-called friend of mine, Theodore Tsoukalas, was about to move from his current apartment in Park Extension to another apartment in the same area. Although rents in this area for a 4½ apartment were about $1,200, he told me they were asking $1,650. A few days later, he said the price had gone up to $1,900, which was impossible. He was clearly acting under orders from the Canadian secret services to make me understand that if they forced me out of my current apartment (where the rent was $850), my welfare payments would not be enough to pay for another apartment. In other words, I would end up sleeping on the streets. This was crystal clear evidence of what they had been trying to do for the last 15 years, they were still waiting.

In November 2024, my father sent a letter to EFKA (the public insurance fund in Greece) to confirm that he was alive so that they would continue paying his pension of about €300 a month. Beginning in 2025, they put his pension on hold, claiming they had not received the letter from an office in Montreal called Asklipios, where the commissioner of oaths, Helen Stavroulaki, was supposed to send it to EFKA in Greece. She either failed to send it or conspired with the office in Greece and the Canadian government to discontinue the pension in order to upset my father. Helen Stavroulaki later told me she sent it again, and we waited about two months for a response.

Coincidentally, I sent an email to EFKA in Greece, and they explained what had happened. I sent them the letter stamped by the Greek consulate confirming that my father was alive to makris@efka.gov.gr or exot.ika@efka.gov.gr

In April 2024, we sent a stamped letter from the Greek consulate to the National Bank of Greece to cancel our home insurance. They discontinued the insurance in May 2025, but I noticed again in June 2025 that they had reapplied it, effectively doubling the coverage (including May) to cause us maximum financial damage. This revealed that the Greek government was actively participating in the conspiracy. They had also put my father's pension on hold since the beginning of 2025 to create financial damage and upset him; he was 85 years old and dependent on that pension. On 10 June 2025, I sent the letter confirming my father was alive, stamped by the Greek consulate in Montreal—to restore his pension.

On 25 June 2025, I bought some shoes from a downtown Montreal store. They were unused, and I wanted to return them. I planned to ask the store to exchange them or refund me. It was 5:45 p.m., and the store closed at 6:00 p.m. The secret services of Canada were following me and trying to prevent me from making any money.

Lately, I also noticed that planes were flying low over my neighborhood to apply psychological warfare against me.

On 25 June 2025, a notary from Greece sent me a document to sign at the Greek consulate. It was in PDF format. The consulate told me that I had to send it to them in Word format so that they could fill in the empty spaces. I went to Copie 2000, a store located on Park Avenue in Montreal that specializes in this kind of work. This store had previously taken orders from the secret services and continued to do so.

I asked them to convert the pages to Word format. They tried and told me that it could not be done—no way. So, I went home, opened Microsoft Word, and downloaded the file. I transferred it to Word format, and it saved perfectly in my documents. I opened the document, and it was perfect; I could write on it. What was that store telling me? It was obvious nonsense. It was clear they had already spoken to the "losers" before I arrived.

Since 20 June 2025, the Canadian secret services had been signaling airplanes near my home to fly low and terrorize me with loud, disturbing noise. This continued until 20 July 2025. At the same time, there was a major lawsuit pending against my mother's oncologist for mistakes he had made, which I could not file because the Canadian secret services were blocking me from accessing justice.

# Epilogue

In this book, I have mentioned many things that have happened, but there are still many things I have not mentioned. Every day, all day long, the police, secret services, and global Western governments apply psychological warfare. They have isolated me from many activities, destroying my business and my entire life. While they have me in global isolation, I could not send my case to another court or settlement, either local or international, because the conspirators had already made the documents disappear whenever I tried to submit them to the European Court of Human Rights against Greece, the Inter-American Commission of Human Rights, or the United Nations. I had sent my case by email in 2012, and they basically told me that I had to become homeless.

Since 2021, I have been reading Quebec laws to refer to the Montreal court, initially targeting those mainly responsible, the SPVM Montreal police—to court. There was a lot of legal reading involved; the laws and court processes were complicated. In 2022–23, I planned to file my case in Montreal once the police and governments were preventing me from hiring a lawyer to sue them, something they had blocked since 2009.

Truly, why wouldn't they let me hire a lawyer all over the world to refer my case to the International Criminal Court? Doesn't this clearly show that they committed crimes against me, crimes against humanity, genocide, persecution, odious offenses, and inhuman acts? They are guilty beyond doubt.

In my next book, I plan to discuss other issues regarding terrorism and terrorist groups (including who really Bin Laden was!), which were not what they appeared to be. Other hidden activities were happening. As an experienced investor and trader on the US stock exchanges, NYSE and NASDAQ, I also intend to reveal to the public what has been happening with the stock markets, who controls them, and much more.

Regarding my current book, I hoped that one day this case would become a movie that would shake the world. There are still countries not involved in this grand conspiracy, probably about three. I would love to go to Iran or Russia to make my movie and publish my book. I had shared a big part of my case, but writing everything that happened would require 10,000 pages or more!

I hope that the public who read my book would understand what was happening, how the police and Western governments are corrupted to the bone, and how so-called democratic countries are essentially fascist and criminal. Be aware, because if this could happen to me, what would stop it from happening to you?

To the citizens of Western countries: be united, speak loudly, and find a way to make it known to the public. If something similar happens to you, please inform me, and I will denounce it to the rest of the world. It would be my pleasure to do so.

Truly,

Christos Margelis

# About The Author

Christos Margelis was born in Montreal, Canada, in 1974, which he often described as being "born in his bad luck." He first attended school in Montreal, but when he was about six years old, his family moved to Greece. There, he completed his schooling and later graduated from college with a degree in electronics.

At the age of nineteen, he was called to serve in the Greek army, where he worked as a radar operator for ships on the island of Kos, located on Greece's eastern border with Turkey. He served for fifteen months before completing his military duty.

In 1995, at the age of twenty-one, he returned to Montreal, where his family was already living. He worked as a car stereo installer for several companies until 2003, after which he became self-employed. He specialized in remote car starter installations, alarm and audio systems, and car electrical work.

Alongside this, he developed a strong interest in the stock markets. Since 1999, when the markets were overinflated, he began investing actively, experiencing both the boom and the crash of 2000. Over time, he continued refining his skills and eventually became a successful investor.

On January 26, however, his life took a dramatic turn. The Montreal police arrested him under the claim of "identity issues"—

an arrest that was false and carried out on purpose, as an attempt to find a way to kill him. According to him, drug traffickers had pressured the Montreal police to act, wrongly believing that he had been involved in events that led to the arrest of one of their associates in the United States. Christos maintained that he had no connection whatsoever to such matters.

From that point forward, a global conspiracy began, involving the corrupted Montreal police, the Canadian government, and, as he later came to believe, networks across much of the world. By 2010, their goal became clear: to destroy his stability and turn him into a homeless person because he had dared to take legal action against the Montreal police, whom he described as "corrupted to the bone."

www.ingramcontent.com/pod-product-compliance
Lightning Source LLC
Chambersburg PA
CBHW051131120626
46547CB00012B/754